# Death & Trust

L. E. MacDonald

For information contact
L. E. MacDonald, PO Box 2307, Brighton, MI 48116
lopezzilinda@gmail.com

Cover design by: L. E. MacDonald

Library of Congress Control Number: 2011919771
ISBN 978-0-9847732-0-6

I dedicate this memoir, with love, to my son.

### *Introduction*

My name is Beth. My very Italian father, Nick Lopezzi, raised me and my three siblings in Detroit, Michigan. We were dark-haired, beautiful Italian children.

My mother, Jeanette, divorced my father in 1961. She was 23-years-old and the mother of four young children, eighteen months apart in age: Marie, 6, David, 4, me, 2, and Patty, 6 months. My father was a good Catholic man and he loved my mother, and if she had not left him, they would, most likely, have had more children. Perhaps that is one of the reasons she left. I can't imagine taking care of four young children so close in age.

Back then, it was unheard of for a mother to leave her children to be raised by their father. My father, six years older than my mother, suggested she leave us with him in Detroit, in the only home we'd ever known.

My mother was beautiful. In her youth, she looked like Elizabeth Taylor. My father, in his youth, looked like Eddie Fisher. When my parents met, my mother was in nursing school. She quit when she married my father, to focus on their family. My father worked for one of the auto companies in the paint department; when he was laid off, my mother went to work. She found a job doing in-home party sales, and she helped my father get a job working in the warehouse. Shortly thereafter, she filed for divorce. My mother moved out, quit her job, and continued her nursing education.

My mother's parents lived in Woodridge Park, Michigan. Grand-pap owned a gas station in Detroit. His business allowed for luxuries other families didn't have.

Grandma had grown up next to a coal mine in Pennsylvania and suffered from emphysema most of her life due to the coal dust she had breathed in. Grandma's father had been the superintendent of that coal mine.

My grandmother's illness caused her to be weak and very thin. She didn't have the strength to help raise her four grandchildren. She was also wise to the activity of a young single woman, so when her daughter Jeanette got a divorce, Grandma told her she could move back home and attend school, but agreed that leaving her four children with their father was the best solution for everyone.

The home my mother grew up in was a beautiful, three-story, craftsman-style house. Even though I was very young, I have wonderful memories of being in my grandparents' home. I also have wonderful memories of the stories my grandmother told. She was a great storyteller.

One evening after work, while standing in one of the many bedrooms, my grand-pap took out his gun, put it to his temple, and pulled the trigger. He died instantly. My mother's younger sister, Louise, who was 16-years-old at that time, found him. I was 3-years-old. No one discussed what had happened to Grand-pap with the grandchildren.

On the morning of the funeral, I remember my grandmother asking my mother to drive her to the cemetery, as it had rained all night. My mother told the four of us, her children, to get into the back seat.

We drove to the cemetery. Grandma got out of the car and walked across the water-soaked lawn to the grave. With the toe of her shoe, she pushed aside the large piece of plywood that covered the burial hole. Grandma walked back to the car, got in, and said, "It filled with water." She looked disgusted. Grand-pap was buried that day. The grandchildren did not attend any of the services.

Shortly after Grand-pap's funeral, my grandmother sold the house and moved to a small home in Edgecliff, Michigan. My mother moved one block away from my grandmother, and Aunt Louise moved two blocks. Their older brother John and his family lived less than a mile away from Grandma's. They all stayed close to her.

When my father drove the four of us to visit my grandmother in her new home for the first time, I asked, "Will Grand-pap be there, too?"

"No," Dad said.

"Does he know Grandma moved?" I asked with much concern. "How will he find her?"

"We gave the people who live in Grandma's old house her new address and phone number. If Grand-pap comes back, they'll give him the information so he'll know where to go," Dad explained. My dad could always give me an answer to keep me from worrying.

"Okay. I don't want Grand-pap to be afraid because she left without him," I said.

My siblings and I attended Catholic school and were raised by my father and an elderly housekeeper, Nola Hampton. Nola was like a second mother to us and a great southern cook. She loved us and, along with my dad, raised us from Monday through Friday. My mother picked us up every weekend to visit her at her parents and, years later, in her own home with her new husband.

Nola lived with and took care of us for many years. She had a sister, Lena, whose home was down the street from ours. On the weekends, Nola stayed with her sister, while we visited our mother. At one time, Nola's grandson, 2-year-old Larry Joe, came to live with us for a couple of months while his mother Wilma was ill. This allowed his father, Laurence, to continue working and help Wilma however he could. Nola was grateful to my father for letting her grandson become a member of our family for a while.

This new, temporary addition to our lives was very shy. I remember singing to him to make him laugh. Never being blessed with the ability to sing, my vocal outbursts tend to make most people laugh. "Little, little Larry, little, little Larry, little, little Larry Joe. Cutest baby in the world, at least that's what I'm told." The words were usually the same, but the melody always changed.

It's painful to think about Nola. We all loved her very much, but my sister Patty, being the youngest, felt this woman was her mother. Patty married in 1979, just after she graduated from high school. Unfortunately, Nola passed away in November of 1976 and would never see Patty married. It's sad to say we don't have one picture of this wonderful woman. But her memory will live with us forever.

My father's mother will be forever remembered as someone who loved and respected the opinions of her grandchildren. She taught me to sew, crochet, and cook the old-fashioned Italian way.

My mother's mother will be forever remembered as a kind woman who never raised her voice or her hand to her grandchildren. She was a great teacher and a beautiful woman, with large, romantic eyes, like those of actress Maggie Smith. She told wonderful stories of her childhood and used to call me "Althea," her favorite niece's name, because that is who I reminded her of. It was an honor to have her in my life, and I miss her every day.

When I was a child, I was surrounded by people who loved me: Nola, my parents, grandparents, aunts, and uncles, too. So how is it I married into a family that doesn't seem to know what love is? Was I blind, manipulated, or mentally ill? You decide…

## *I'm Engaged*

It was **1985**. I was engaged to a handsome, muscular, 27-year-old man. He had curly blond hair and beautiful green eyes. He looked like a young version of actor Ed Harris. When he put his arms around me, I felt small and safe. We were introduced at our five-year class reunion. Our graduating class was about 420 students. He had been somewhat of a jock, and I had hung out with the burnouts, so our paths had never crossed in high school. We dated for three years before he proposed marriage to me.

It was a Friday morning, and I arrived at work early. I was a teller at First Bank and Savings of Michigan. The bank manager was a delight to work for. She had the best sense of humor, but could also say things in jest to really make me think.

This particular morning, I told my boss, Ella, that Max had arrived early at my home and proposed to me.

"Where's the ring?" Ella asked.

"He didn't give me one. Max said he didn't want to bring me a ring I might not like," I said.

"Oh, Beth," she said, "he'll never marry you. His mother would NEVER allow that!"

"But he asked me this morning!" I said. "His parents were out of the country, in Scotland for two weeks. Max asked them if he could marry me when they came home. Max said his parents said he could do whatever he liked and...why wouldn't she allow that?"

“First of all, Irene telling Max he can do whatever he’d like is far from having her blessing. And I don’t think she’d allow it because you’ve been married before and you have a young child. Nothing against you, Beth, but Irene Edwards is not the sort of woman who would allow a divorcée with a kid to marry her son.”

“We’ll see about that!” I said.

Shortly after the bank opened that morning, I received half a dozen pink roses. Angered by my recent conversation with Ella and the fact that there were only six pink roses instead of a dozen red ones, I tossed them with great force across the bank lobby.

“Whoa! What did you do that for?” Ella asked.

“There are only six roses, and they’re PINK! And now I’m questioning this. What if you’re right?” I asked. “Doesn’t he realize that pink roses are a sign of gratitude and red roses mean love? One red rose speaks louder than six pink ones! This is a man who is surrounded by flowers daily—I would’ve thought he’d know this.”

That evening when I went home, I pulled out my high school yearbook and looked at Max’s picture. I had done the same thing the first night I met him. I started thinking about the past three years with Max...

### *Love at First Sight*

I was so nervous. It was **June 1982** and the night of my five-year class reunion from Willow High School, in Willow, Michigan. I hadn't planned to attend it because I was in the middle of a divorce, but I had changed my mind.

One of the reasons I got married was so I'd never be alone, but I'd spent most of my marriage alone. My husband didn't take our marriage vows seriously and continued dating throughout our three-year marriage. We had a baby boy together and named him Zack. I'd hoped that our son would change things. But after Zack's first birthday in May of 1982, I could see that nothing had changed, and I filed for divorce.

I arrived at the reunion alone and was afraid to get out of my car and walk in by myself. I also feared that no one would talk to me once inside.

"Oh, just suck it up! If no one talks to you, leave. Better yet, pretend to be someone else, someone outgoing and wonderful," I said out loud as I looked at myself in the rearview mirror to apply more lipstick. "Good Lord, girl, you're losing your mind!"

Always the punctual guest, I'd arrived on time. Fortunately for me, not many classmates were there yet. I went directly to the cash bar and got a glass of wine, picked out a place to sit, and sat down. Deciding I might be better off sitting closer to the bar, I got up and moved.

My plan worked well: as people arrived, they went directly to the bar and stopped to ask who I was. I knew only two people attending the reunion; one of them, Kathy, arrived shortly after I did and sat down next to me.

"Hi, Beth," Kathy said. "Are you still working at First Bank and Savings of Michigan?"

"Yes, I've been there three years now. Where are you working?" I asked.

"I work for Willow Country Florist in town," she replied.

Making conversation, I said, "My sister Patty's boyfriend sent her a dozen red roses one year for her birthday, which is at the end of May. I had never been given flowers, so I didn't know what to do with them. Whenever I saw flowers, they were being refrigerated at the florist. It was really hot that day, and for some reason I was afraid they would die without refrigeration before my sister got home. When I opened our refrigerator, it was too small for the large box. Even if I'd taken the shelves out, the box was too big to fit. I expected Patty home in one hour, so I put the flowers in the deep freeze for a few minutes to keep them chilled. It was the only cold place the box would fit. Unfortunately, I forgot about the flowers until Patty came in the door. I pulled the box out and handed it to her.

"'Why did you put them in the freezer?' she asked with anger.

"I explained, 'They had to be kept cold. I only meant to put them in for a few minutes, but I forgot to take them out. I'm so sorry!'

"My mother arrived home within minutes of Patty and, watching the tears steam down Patty's cheeks, she asked what had happened. I explained, and my mother told Patty to open the box. The flowers were beautiful, but as soon as she picked one up it went limp, like it had a little broken neck. Mom called the florist.

"'Yes, hello, someone delivered a dozen red roses to my home today. My daughter's boyfriend sent them for her 17th birthday. Well, we've just opened the box and the roses are beautiful. Unfortunately, when my daughter picked up one of the roses, the bud collapsed over to the side. She's afraid to pick up another one for fear they may all be this way.'

"Mom winked at Patty and me.

"'Yes,' Mom continued, 'I can pick one up. It appears to have the same problem. My daughter is a little nervous; her boyfriend will be here in an hour to take her to dinner. I'm certain he'll want to see the lovely flowers he's purchased from you. I just don't know what to do.' She paused and listened.

"'Well,' she said, 'instead of troubling your delivery man, I'm on my way into town now. I would be happy to bring the flowers in and get another batch if you think you have a fresh dozen available. Yes, you do? Oh, wonderful! I'm on my way.' She hung up the phone.

"'Okay, Beth, you owe me one,' Mom said."

Kathy said, "You'd be surprised. People bring back dead flowers all the time, mostly because they died within a week's time and, realistically, flowers should last a minimum of one full week. Of course, you have to factor in sunlight, fresh water, and temperature."

Kathy and I had had one glass of wine and were onto our second. We were feeling happy.

"Does your mom still live on the lake?" Kathy asked. "I remember when you moved here from Detroit and you'd never seen a Sandhill Crane before." She laughed out loud.

"I can't believe you still remember that story, Kathy."

A very cute classmate, Max Edwards, was waiting in line for a beer. His family owned the local funeral home. He knew Kathy not only from school, but also from the florist. Max asked, "What story? I'd like to hear a good story. I'm Max, by the way."

Kathy said, "I'm sorry, Max. My guess was that we all knew each other here, being from the same graduating class and all. Beth, this is Max."

"Hi, Max!" I said with great expectation. "It's so very nice to meet you."

"The pleasure is all mine," he said. "Now, about that story."

I said, "I must request you please be kind when I tell my story, okay?" I took a few gulps of wine and, feeling a little tipsy, I proceeded.

"My parents have been divorced since the dawn of man, so my father raised me along with my three siblings. We lived in Detroit. Dad took care of us Monday through Friday, and we visited my mother every weekend. When my sister Patty and I became teenagers, we decided to move in with our mother and attend high school here, for fear we would be killed at the high school we were scheduled to attend. The news media continually reported shootings or stabbings that took place there." The wine had just made its way to my head, and I was feeling silly.

"My older sister Marie was attending a private, all-girls school. She'd been going there for a couple of years—it's Up North somewhere—and my brother had moved in with my grandmother. That's my mom's mother, in case you were taking notes. Not that any of that really matters to my story. So, I moved here to live on a lake and attend your lovely high school. My dad was a busy guy, and my mom was a busy gal. Needless to say, I didn't get out much. Well, I didn't get out to the lake much. N-o-o, that's not true. I had been to several lakes, but they weren't quiet ones, they were noisy ones. That's the difference. In order to be amazed you must be on a quiet lake."

I finished off my wine and proceeded.

"So, here's my story. I moved into a house on a lake with my mom. One sunny, spring, Saturday morning, I got up around 6:00 a.m. I guess I couldn't sleep. Anyway, I stood looking out at the lake. The water was smooth as glass. And then, out of nowhere, I noticed this gigantic bird. It was the biggest bird I ever saw in my entire life! I swear it had to be at least 4- or 6-feet tall! It was huge! I stood there in awe. This gigantic bird was on our raft, floating in the lake! My adrenaline started pumping, and my heart started beating so fast! I didn't know what to do. Just then, the huge beast bird spread its wings and went screaming into flight! Screaming, screaming, screaming, and screaming some more! I thought, *Oh my God, I just saw a dinosaur bird, a PTERODACTYL, and no one was awake to witness this historic moment with me!*"

Kathy and Max laughed. "Pterodactyl, that's funny," Max said.

Even though the people I associated with in high school and really wanted to see hadn't shown up at the reunion, I was glad I went. Couldn't they afford it? Were they afraid like I was? Were they stoned? It was disappointing, but it allowed me to meet new and interesting people I might not have met otherwise. The classmates who came were mostly popular cheerleaders or jocks. No one there really knew who I was, but by the end of the evening, it seemed we'd all been friends for years. It's funny how people change with age.

Looking back on my high school years, I was kind of a cute girl, and five years later I was still thin and attractive. A couple guys from the reunion wanted to take me out. This was surprising because they'd never given me a second look in school. The only one who caught my eye that evening was Max Edwards. He was so handsome I could hardly stand it! He asked for my number and I gave it to him. No one could believe how much Max had changed in the past five years.

Towards the end of the evening, I noticed Max talking to a cute blond who was cleaning up the party mess. She must have been an employee of the hall. I didn't give it much thought. Max walked me to my car, kissed me on the cheek, and said he was going home, but he would call me sometime.

I couldn't drive home fast enough. I was eager to look for Max's picture in my yearbook.

*Crap! It's at my mom's*, I thought. *It's too late to wake her; I'll stop by to see her in the morning.*

I set my alarm for 9:00 a.m.

### *He Asked Me Out*

When the alarm rang the next morning, I dragged myself out of bed, shading my eyes with sunglasses. The daylight was blinding.

"Well, you're here bright and early," Mom said. "What gives us the privilege of your presence this fine day?"

"I need my yearbook," I said, yawning. I found it on my mother's bookshelf loaded with old magazines and miscellaneous self-help and diet books. I'd only been out of school for five years, but already my yearbook smelled old and its pages appeared out of date.

"Oh my God, I can't believe this is the same person!" I said. "Wow, he's really changed!"

"Who are you looking at?" my mother asked.

"Max Edwards. He's so handsome now—it's hard to believe this picture is the same person," I said. "Everyone at the class reunion said they couldn't believe how different Max looked. Now I understand why. The guy I met last night looks like a body builder. He's got gorgeous, blond, curly hair and beautiful, sexy, green eyes. This yearbook picture looks like a boy! He looks really skinny, and his haircut looks like someone put a bowl on his head. It looks like his mother cut it. Remember when you hacked up my hair and gave me those awful bangs? They were four inches above my eyebrows! It was so embarrassing. Does every mother do that to her child? I'd swear this is his fifth grade picture. He doesn't look old enough to have graduated, judging by this photo...I just can't believe it's him!"

My mom said, "Let me look, this could be my future son-in-law."

"That's jumping the gun a bit, but wouldn't it be funny if it turned out that way?" I said.

Prior to the class reunion, I had moved into town, not far from the Edwards's Funeral Home. I rented a two-bedroom house that couldn't have been more than 800 square feet. The house reminded me of a dollhouse. It was small and cozy. The owner had paneled the living room with old barn wood, and the bathroom had a small clawfoot tub instead of a shower. When I took a bath, I had to pull my knees into my chest in order to fit, and I'm only 5' 3." The bathroom was so small; I had to watch my head to avoid banging it into the slanted ceiling that hung over the tub.

Several weeks had passed since the reunion, and I hadn't received a phone call from Max. At that point, I never expected to hear from him.

Then one day, I pulled into my driveway after work and jumped out to get the mail, like I always did, and, to my surprise, Max happened to drive by in his sports car. He slammed on the brakes when he saw me at my mailbox.

"I'm sorry I haven't called. I didn't know where you lived. Your phone number blew out of my hand the night of the reunion, when I pulled my car keys out of my pocket. It was too dark to find, and I couldn't see which way it went. I had no way of getting a hold of you," Max explained.

"Oh, that's okay, I understand," I said. "Don't worry about it."

"Listen, I'm on my way somewhere. Can I get your number? I promise not to let it blow away this time," Max said.

"Sure, here's my number. Call anytime," I said.

A week went by before I heard a knock at my front door. It was Max.

"I have tickets for a concert this Friday, would you like to go?" Max asked.

"Yes," I said, "I'd love to go!"

Max gave me the details and left. I picked up my appointment book, flipped to the date, grabbed a pen, and jotted down: "Friday, August 13th, concert with Max, be ready 5:30 p.m."

*FRIDAY THE 13th? Please let this be a good sign*! I thought.

I picked up the phone and called Nora. She and I had been friends since high school, except Nora transferred to another school in eleventh grade, so we didn't graduate together.

"Hi, Nora. I have my first date this Friday. I'm so nervous."

"So, give me the details. Who's your date with?" Nora asked.

I told her about the class reunion, the loss of my phone number, and how Max Edwards drove by and later asked me out.

"Sounds like destiny to me, Beth," Nora said.

"Well, given the fact that he lost my phone number, accidentally drove by my house while I happened to be at the mailbox, and asked for a date on Friday the 13th, it really doesn't sound promising," I said. "I'll call and let you know how it goes".

### *The Date*

Max was on time, and I was a nervous wreck. He pulled into my driveway in a beautiful silver sports car that was polished to perfection. The car was clean and very cool; it really suited him. I talked non-stop all the way to the concert, asking 101 questions about dead people. I was curious and wanted to know everything. In Max's car, I sat on an angle to face him. In between breaths, I looked at Max and checked out every detail of his face, hair, and muscular body.

At first glance he was perfect. The more I looked at him, the less perfect looking he got. The tip of his nose was gently turned up, and his top teeth were slightly pushed inward. My eyes continued on this fascinating realization. Max had beautiful, curly, blond hair on the top of his head, but underneath it was a different color and texture—brown and sort of kinky curly. Regardless of his minimal flaws, he was still very handsome.

We arrived at the concert and sat next to Max's cousin Gary and a friend of his. Apparently, this was who Max acquired the tickets from. I wondered if the two guys were in college and might have planned to bring dates. Perhaps they couldn't find one and asked Max if he wanted the tickets. They were cute enough, so maybe that wasn't the case. Max's cousin was young and adorable, with dark brown hair and a boyish smile. He sat on one side of Max, and I sat on the other. It was a good concert, and I was in good company.

When Max dropped me off, he asked for my phone number for the third time.

"I'm sorry, Beth, I don't know what I did with your number. I'm sure I put it where I wouldn't lose it, but I couldn't find it anywhere. That's why I drove over to ask you to the concert. Once I got here, I was embarrassed to ask for it again," Max said.

"Well," I said, "this is the last time I'm giving it to you, so you better put it in your wallet so you'll know where it is next time."

"I promise I won't lose it. I'm putting it in my wallet now," Max said, and then kissed me on the cheek.

"Promises, promises," I said, before walking into the house.

"Hey, Max," I yelled, "thanks for the great evening!"

He smiled and waved goodbye as he drove off.

The next morning, the phone rang.

I answered, "Hello."

"Hello, Miss Beth?" the voice on the other end said.

"Ye-e-s," I said with hesitation.

"This is your friendly neighborhood funeral director calling to see if you'd like to go out again sometime," Max asked.

I giggled, "Well Mr. Funeral Director, I'd love to. And it's nice you haven't lost my phone number yet."

"It's in my wallet and that's where I plan to leave it," Max said.

Max and I started dating on a regular basis. We saw each other at least twice a week. It was hard to see him any more than that because I had a 1-year-old son to take care of.

After one month in my new relationship, I had to ask.

"Max, are you seeing anyone else? It's okay if you are. I just need to know. I'm not seeing anyone else, but if you're still going to date others, I feel I have that right as well, if the opportunity presents itself," I said.

"No, I'm not seeing anyone else. I really like you," Max said.

"I have to tell you," I said, "I'm breathing a sigh of relief. Dating is new for me, and I realize, given the fact that I've been married before and have a child, you might not want a committed relationship with me."

"Don't be ridiculous," Max said. "I think you're great!"

It had been six weeks since Max and I started dating officially. Max stopped by to inform me that he and his cousin Derrick, Gary's older brother, were going on a trip to see a buddy stationed at a naval base in California.

"California!" I said. "One of these days I'd like to go there. When are you leaving?"

Max said, "I leave in two weeks and I'll be gone for ten days. I have lots to do before I go so I may not be spending as much time with you, but I'll do my best."

"Don't stress about it," I said. "Do whatever you have to do. I have my son Zack to keep me busy. Don't worry, I'll be here when you get back. I love you."

There was no response from Max.

I didn't care. That was how I felt. But it had only been six weeks, and I didn't expect him to have those feelings just because I did. I once heard someone say, you can't love someone into loving you. How true that is. Besides, we had plenty of time to date and to get to know each other better.

The following week, after work, someone rang my doorbell. When I went to the door, no one was there. I thought it was a prank, but then saw a large vase with a big, beautiful bouquet of red roses with baby's breath tucked in. I had never received such a gift. There was no card. Within minutes, my phone rang.

"Beth?" Max said.

"Hi, Max. I got your beautiful flowers."

"Yeah, about the flowers...I have to come and pick them up. I can't believe this happened," Max said with embarrassment. "We had a funeral today, and the family decided which flowers they wanted to take home and which flowers were going to the cemetery. They told me to throw the rest of them away. When I saw the vase of red roses, it seemed a shame to throw away such a large bouquet of flowers, so I brought them to you instead," Max said. "Apparently, after the family luncheon, someone went back to the gravesite and noticed their flowers—the roses—weren't there. Lucky for them, I gave them to you and didn't throw them away." Max continued, "That's what I should have told them! I should have said I threw them away instead of bothering you with this. I'm so sorry."

"Max, please come over and get the flowers. It's no big deal," I said.

*How could he bring me a dead woman's flowers? Who does that? I thought he really liked me, and I was hoping for love. Never in a million years would I have ever believed this one. Flowers belonging to a dead woman, given to me, how romantic! He seems like a good guy, I'll just have to get over it,* I thought.

I only saw Max twice before he left for California—once when he came to pick up the flowers, and again when he took me shopping the day before he left.

*I sure will miss him while he's gone!*

### *The Airport Surprise*

I hadn't talked to Nora since my relationship with Max started. I had some extra time and thought I should call and bring her up to date.

"Hello, Nora. How the heck are you?" I asked.

"I've been doing great," Nora said. "I took a part-time job at Radicchio's Grocery Store."

"Really, how do you like it?" I asked.

"I like it," Nora said. "It'll give us some extra money for Christmas. Hey, now that I have you on the phone, are you still seeing Max?"

"As a matter of fact, I am," I said.

"Beth," Nora said, "I have to tell you something. There's a girl I work with, Carrie. She talks about Max all the time and said they're dating. She said she's been to the funeral home and met his mother."

"What? How could that be? Max has been dating me," I said. "Does this girl seem like a nut? Is she cute? When was the last time she said this?"

"Yesterday evening, when I was in the lunchroom at work," Nora said.

"Do you have her phone number? I want to talk to her," I said.

"How about I call Carrie and explain that I've talked to you. I'll tell her you let me know that you and Max are dating and as far as you knew, were exclusive. I'll ask if it's okay that I give you her phone number. How does that sound?" Nora asked.

"Yes, sounds good," I said. "If she is hesitant for you to give me her phone number, it's okay for you to give her mine. I really want to talk to her!"

"I'll call her now," Nora said.

Within ten minutes, my phone rang.

"Hello, is this Beth?" the voice on the other end asked.

"Yes, is this Carrie?"

"Yes," she said. "I can't believe what a snake Max is! If you don't mind, I'd like to compare notes with you on this. Is that okay with you?"

"Absolutely. Ask me anything you like," I said.

"Has Max told you he loves you?" Carrie asked.

"No. Did he say that to you?" I asked.

"No, he never said I love you, but I've slept with him a few times. Have you slept with him, too?" she asked. "Was it at the funeral home?"

"I slept with Max twice, not at the funeral home, at my house. I rent a small house a few blocks from the funeral home. I've never been to the funeral home, but I understand from Nora that you have," I said.

"Yes, and I've met his mother," Carrie said. "Max looks exactly like his mom. It's kind of freaky when you first meet her. It's like Max in drag."

"Well then, I hope to meet her soon. That freaky image sounds like something I'd rather think about, instead of carrying his face around in my head all day while he's breaking my heart," I said with sadness.

"Beth, I really have to cut this short. I've got to get to work. I would love to talk to you more. You sound like a nice person," Carrie said.

"What time do you get off work?" I asked.

"Eight. But my roommate can't pick me up until 9:00 p.m. or a little after. That's what time she gets off, and then she picks me up on her way," Carrie said. "I don't have a car."

"Would it be weird if I came to pick you up?" I asked. "My son is with his father for the weekend, so I don't have anything to do. We can stop and grab a bite to eat before I take you home, if you want."

"If you really don't mind, that would be great! I hate waiting for my roommate to pick me up. I usually end up spending money I don't have, or working for free until she gets there," Carrie said. "We can grab some drive-thru food and take it back to my apartment. I have a 2-year-old daughter and I hate to leave her longer than I have to. I'll come out of the store at 8:02 p.m. and stand by the bike rack so you'll know it's me. I'll be the short blond smoking a cigarette."

"Okay," I said. I have a cream-colored car with a brown leather roof. It's as big as a boat! You can't miss it. I'm really looking forward to meeting you. I promise to be on time."

I was anxious to meet Carrie. I spent a good hour putting on my make-up. As a female, I've always felt the need to out-beauty other women, especially if they were interested in the same man as I was.

I pulled into the parking lot, and had hoped she wasn't very cute. I was wrong. There she was, leaning against the bike rack, smoking. Carrie was adorable! She was petite, with a short haircut that framed her face perfectly. Her teeth were slightly crooked, but it added to her cuteness instead of taking away from it. I pulled up and beeped my horn. She got into the car with a big smile.

"Hi, Beth. I'm Carrie!"

"It's nice to meet you. I can't believe how cute you are," I said.

"Isn't that funny?" Carrie replied. "I was just thinking the same about you."

"Well," I said, "one thing's for certain: Max has great taste in women!"

We stopped for cigarettes. I hadn't smoked in years, but Carrie smoked daily, and she asked if we could pull into Stop-N-Gas and pick up a pack. We were both looking forward to our question-and-answer session. We grabbed some food and drove approximately ten miles to Carrie's place. Her daughter had just gone to bed, so I didn't get to meet her. I did, however, meet Carrie's sister Marianne.

"Marianne, this is Beth," Carrie said. "She's been dating Max."

I waved and said, "Nice to meet you."

"What? Has he been dating both of you?" Marianne askcd.

"Yep!  It would seem that he has been dating the both of us," Carrie replied.

"I understand why Max is seeing Carrie," I said. "She's really cute, and nice, too!"

"Yes, Carrie is extremely cute, and you are stunningly beautiful!" Marianne said.

"Thank you! What a nice thing to say," I said.

Carrie and I took a few bites of our burgers and started to compare our memories about when we were with Max. Max would tell me he was working when he was out with Carrie. Max would tell Carrie he was shopping with his mom or out with his cousin Derrick when he was with me.

Carrie was dating Derrick first, but when he introduced Max to Carrie, Max started flirting with her, and she with him. As soon as Derrick went to the restroom, Carrie handed Max her phone number. She really didn't want to hurt Derrick's feelings and was afraid he'd find out she was seeing Max. She went out with Derrick a couple more times before she stopped seeing him altogether.

This all took place around the same time as the class reunion. Carrie picked up a little extra money by cleaning the hall after events. It was pure coincidence that Carrie was there that night. After the reunion was over and the mess was cleaned up, she and Max went to an after party held at a classmate's house. I, of course, went home.

"I remember Max getting out his keys that night to open the car door and a piece of paper blew out from his pocket. He started running all over for it. He must have felt silly chasing the paper and gave up," Carrie said.

"That little square of paper had my phone number on it," I told her. "And if I have my dates correct, my guess is that it was your place Max was on his way to the day he saw me at my mailbox."

"Yes," she said. "Max was taking me to dinner and a movie. As a matter of fact, I slept with him that night for the first time."

"This is intense," I said. "I'm so angry I could scream!"

"If you want him, you can have him!" Carrie said.

"I don't think it's that easy," I said. "We both have feelings for him. Even if I do want him, who's to say he wants me and not you?"

Carrie stood up like a bolt of lightning. With great drama, she took a cigarette from her pack, lit it, took a long, deep drag of smoke, and then blew it out hard.

"I have a great idea!" she said. "Max and Derrick are in California right now. I'll call Derrick's house and ask his mom when Derrick is expected home. I'm sure I can get her to give me the flight number and time of arrival. I'll tell her I want to surprise him when he comes home or something like that. Then, on the day they arrive, you and I will be waiting at the gate when they get off the airplane. Max has no idea we've met. We live in different towns—what are the chances? Right! Max will crap his pants when he sees the both of us!"

"You're funny," I said. "But what about Derrick—isn't he going to question why you're there to see Max?"

"No, that's the best part of the plan," Carrie said. "Derrick has no idea I've been seeing Max. You, Max, and I are the only ones who know the truth about what has really been going on. I can't wait to see Max's face when he gets off the plane from his little vacation."

"I'm so excited!" I said. "This is going to be so much fun! I feel like I'm in an episode of *Mission Impossible*. It's getting late, so I'm going home. Call me as soon as you get the details."

All the way home, I giggled like a 12-year-old schoolgirl. I was looking forward to seeing Max when he got off the plane. *What will he do?* I thought. *What will good old Max do?*

I had a restless sleep that night, excited about my new friend and our plan. The next day, I did laundry to keep myself busy until my son came home. Around four o'clock, my phone rang. It was Max.

"Hi, Beth. It's Max."

"Hi, Max. Where are you?" I was afraid he might be home already and ruin the plan.

"I'm in California. The weather here is fantastic," he said.

"It's great to hear your voice. I'm sure you're having a great time. You've been behaving yourself I hope? But what am I saying—you'd never do anything like that. Great guys like you never do," I said with a hint of sarcasm.

"Well, I just wanted to call and say hi. I'll be home soon," he said.

When I hung up the phone, I growled like a lioness. The phone rang again; it was Carrie.

“Here is your mission, should you choose to accept it,” she said laughing. “Max and Derrick are coming in around 6:00 a.m. a week from today. I have all the information. Derrick’s mom gave it to me without question. I told her it was a surprise, and asked her not to tell Derrick if he called. She promised she wouldn’t, so we are all set.”

The following week dragged. The airport day was never going to get here. I set my alarm for 3:00 a.m. to give myself plenty of time to put on my make-up and do my hair. By 4:00 a.m., I was out the door. My mom agreed to keep Zack overnight as long as I was back by 9:00 a.m. so she could go to work. Carrie’s place was on the way to the airport, and it took just five minutes to pick her up and get back on the road.

“Damn, you’re quick! You flew out of your apartment and into my car. It was like magic—poof, you’re here!” I said laughing.

“As a matter of fact, I did,” she said. “I sprouted wings and flew around a bit before you got here. I’m so exhausted I need a cigarette to regain my energy. Got one?”

“Sure do,” I said, throwing the pack at her. We smoked our cigarettes, turned up the radio, and sang. We laughed all the way to the airport. I parked the car and we walked to the gate. We were thirty minutes early.

“Hey, did Max call you while he was gone?” I asked Carrie.

“No. Why, did he call you?” she asked.

"Yes, he did, but he really didn't have much to say." I quoted the conversation word for word to her.

"It's possible he called me and no one was home," Carrie said with hesitation. "I've been thinking. I don't want to date Max anymore. You know, I saw Max two days before he left. The last thing he said to me was he had a lot to think about while he was gone and hoped to make some changes when he got back. I don't know why I didn't remember that until now." She paused for a minute. "You and I could have become best friends if we met under different circumstances. I can see why Max is attracted to you. Hey, it looks like the passengers are exiting the plane now. Are you ready?"

"Ready, as I'll ever be."

We stood at the end of the gate to have a clear view. Here they come! The guys were walking side by side, each of them with a carry-on bag slung over his shoulder. Max looked at me and smiled, then looked at Carrie. His head went back as he rolled his eyes. He mouthed the words, "Oh shit."

Derrick looked at Max and said, "What's the matter Max? You look like someone just kicked you in the balls."

At this point Derrick could see Carrie and me at the end of the gate. Within seconds, we were facing one another. Max walked up to me, gave me a hug, and kissed me on the cheek. He totally ignored Carrie, as though she were invisible. I felt really bad for her. Had Max come to some realization that I was the one for him, or was he trying to save face in front of his cousin? Carrie and I hadn't given much thought to what we would do after the initial shock.

"Hey, what are you doing here?" Derrick asked. "I didn't know you two knew each other."

"We didn't," Carrie said. "We met while you were away."

"Hey," Derrick said, "small world!"

"No, more like two small towns right next to each other," I said with a hint of sarcasm.

"Are you two meeting someone here?" Derrick asked.

"Yes," Carrie piped up. "We're here to meet you and Max. We wanted to surprise you, and we *really* wanted to surprise Max!"

"Well, I'm pleasantly surprised. How about you Max?" Derrick asked.

"Yep, I'm surprised all right. Very surprised," Max said, totally embarrassed.

Carrie said, "I think I should ride back with Derrick, and Beth should take Max home."

"No!" Max blurted out. "The two of you ride back together. Derrick and I still have to get our bags, and it's going to be a while, so go home. We can talk later."

"Okay, if you're sure that's what you want," Carrie said.

She and I got into my car and headed home. Both of us had little to say, but wished we'd planned beyond the surprise greeting. We both felt heartache when we saw Max. Regardless of what was done, we were both left with the pain of being cheated on.

I pulled into her apartment complex. "Carrie," I said, "it's no wonder Max tried to date us both. Look how much fun we had together plotting his demise. I almost feel bad for him. How do you choose between the two of us when we are so much alike?"

"If you hear from Max, will you call and let me know?" Carrie asked.

"Of course," I said. "And you do the same for me." Carrie got out of my car, smiled, and waved goodbye.

I reminisced about the past few months during my drive home alone. It was depressing.

Suddenly, I remembered Kathy, the woman I'd been having a conversation with at the reunion when Max overheard and walked up. Kathy works at the local florist. I had an idea. I picked up my son from my mom's and went home and called the florist.

"Hello, is Kathy there?" I asked.

"Yes, this is she," Kathy replied.

"Kathy, this is Beth. Do you, by chance, have any dead flowers, preferably roses?" I asked.

"As a matter of fact, I do," Kathy said. "What would you like me to do with them?"

"I would like you to pretend they are alive and beautiful. Put them in a lovely box with a big, red bow on it. Include one of the "With deepest sympathy" cards, and sign it, "From the both of us." Please deliver it to Max at Edwards's Funeral Home today. He'll know who they're from."

Kathy laughed. “Okay, Beth. I can hardly wait to hear the story behind this one.”

“What’s the charge for this?” I asked.

“Normally we would charge you for the box, bow, and delivery, but it’s going to a local funeral home and we’re making a delivery this afternoon, so I won’t charge you for delivery. And as long as we can have lunch or dinner this week, I won’t charge you at all. What’s your schedule? I can hardly wait to hear what happened,” Kathy said.

“Sounds good,” I said. “How about today? Call me when you get off work, and we can meet for a quick bite.”

“Okay,” Kathy said. “I’ll call you later.”

I hung up the phone and called my boss to tell her I’d be late. I then called Carrie.

“Hello, Miss Carrie, did I catch you at a bad time?” I asked.

“No, of course not. Did Max call you?” she asked.

“No, he didn’t. I wanted to let you know what I did.” I explained what had transpired since I dropped her off.

“I LOVE IT!” Carrie said. “Man, we are the best team. Let me know if you hear anything.”

“Okey-dokey, Smokey!” I said before hanging up.

Kathy and I met for a quick bite at Alex’s Restaurant when she got off of work. I gave her all the details.

“Max doesn’t seem like the kind of guy who’d cheat,” Kathy said.

"I know!" I said. "Guys, and girls for that matter, who are too heavy, too thin, not attractive, etc., in high school and blossom afterward can get really full of themselves. I could not believe my eyes when I looked Max up in the yearbook to see who he was. I would never have recognized him, even if I had known him before. He's gone through a total transformation, from skinny weird-looking kid to body-building handsome hunk! But that doesn't give him a free pass to be dishonest. I asked him if he were seeing anyone else and he said no."

"Have you heard anything from him today? I had the flowers delivered shortly after noon, so I'm sure he's gotten them by now," Kathy said.

"No, I haven't heard a word, and I most likely won't. Before I forget, I really want to thank you for sending the flowers to him. What timing, that you actually had a dozen dead roses." I got up to leave. "I'll call you soon and catch you up on the latest."

When I got home, I decided to call Max. I couldn't wait for him to call me, because he was *never* going to call me. I picked up the phone and dialed.

Max's mom answered the phone, "Edwards's Funeral Home."

"Is Max there?" I asked.

"Who's calling, please?" she responded.

"It's Beth."

"One moment please," she said, putting me on hold.

Upon her return, she said, "I'm sorry, Max isn't available right now. Can I take a message?"

"Just let him know Beth called, please."

Several hours went by, and I put Zack to bed. My insides were all stirred up. I tried to lie down, but between my racing thoughts and my upset stomach, I couldn't sleep. I hoped that if I got up and watched a little TV, I might get sleepy. It was 2:00 a.m. I picked up the phone and called Max.

"Edwards's Funeral Home, this is Max."

"Hi, Max. Please don't hang up, it's Beth."

"Beth, I'm really tired. It's been a long day. Can I call you tomorrow?" he asked.

"Can you come over after work tomorrow? I'd really like to talk to you face to face, even if it's late. I feel it's important we talk."

"Sure," Max said. "I can be there by 8:00 p.m."

"Thanks for taking my call. I'll see you tomorrow. Goodnight," I said.

"Goodnight, Beth," Max said. I went to bed and slept the rest of the night.

The next evening, Max showed up at 8:00 p.m. sharp. He looked and smelled really good. I didn't know what to do, so I hugged him, and he hugged me back. I asked him to sit down.

"I'm not sure where to start," I said. "Did you get the flowers?"

"Yes," Max said. "When the flowers came, I took them into the kitchen and opened them. I knew when I opened the card and it said, "With deepest sympathy, from the both of us," that it wasn't going to be a good day. I was pissed and immediately threw the flowers in the trash!"

"You know you deserved that, don't you?" I asked. "I don't understand why you lied to me when I asked if you were seeing anyone else. That was your cue to say, 'Yes, I am.' That wasn't fair to me at all. I have feelings for you; now what am I supposed to do?"

Max pulled a card out from the inside of his coat pocket and gave it to me. He said, "The reason I didn't tell you is because I was trying to get out of the relationship with Carrie. I don't know if Carrie told you, but she dated Derrick and dumped him to come after me. I told her when I left for California that I had thinking to do and changes would be made when I got home. My plan was never to call her again."

"And you couldn't have dumped her as soon as you and I had our first couple of dates?" I asked.

"I could have, but I really hate confrontation. You might have guessed that at the airport," Max said.

I opened the card Max had given me and read it. It said he missed me and loved me. "Love...It says you love me?" I said, confused.

Max put his arms around me and pulled me next to him. "I realized something before I left for California. I realized that I love you. I'm sorry you found out about Carrie. I never meant to hurt you," Max said. "I want you to know that if she called, I was going to tell her it was over between us. My heart belongs to you."

“Okay, because you said all that, I guess I should be sorry for sending you the dead flowers. But, really, I’m not sorry for sending them,” I said.

“My dad laughed when I opened the box,” Max said. “My dad said ‘I warned you about dating two women at the same time.’ He felt I deserved it.”

“Yes, I’d have to say I agree with him!”

Max and I were starting over. There was nothing to hide, and I hoped for the best.

I had rented my little house for only six months when my ex-husband left town without a word or forwarding address. Without child support, I couldn’t afford to pay the rent. I didn’t make enough money at the bank to live on my own. I moved out of my little rental and in with my mom and her husband. Moving home meant following Mom’s rules. I didn’t gripe about it because she wasn’t charging me rent. In exchange, I cooked and cleaned and did the laundry for my mom and her husband. It would have been more than difficult to work and send my son to daycare on my small bank teller’s salary. Mom’s help allowed me to provide for Zack, so that he never had to go without.

I was able to see Max once during the week and every Saturday and Sunday if he wasn’t working. My mom insisted I put Zack to bed and that he be asleep before I left, except on Saturdays. That was the only day I could see Max and not have to put Zack to bed before I left. Those were my mom’s rules, and I abided by them.

### *Max Makes the Local Paper*

Max and I dated exclusively for over one year. One day in **1983**, while I was sitting in my boss's office, she opened the local county paper and threw a section from it at me.

"Read this!" she said.

I couldn't believe it. There was Max, right before my eyes, listed in a full-page ad with the headline, "County's Most Eligible Bachelors." There were about a dozen successful, handsome, single men pictured. Under each perfectly posed picture, the bachelor's name, age, career, goals, hobbies, height, weight, and eye color were given.

"Gee, they forgot to mention, THAT HE'S BEEN DATING SOMEONE FOR OVER A YEAR NOW! Someone hand me the wastebasket, I need to throw-up!" I said with pure disgust.

"How can Max be considered a bachelor when he and I have been dating for a while?" I asked. "Is it just me, or shouldn't I be upset about this?" I picked up the phone; I wanted to hear what Max had to say.

"Hi, Max. I got the paper today. Any guesses about what I saw in it?" I asked.

"No, what did you see, Beth?" he replied.

"Well, let me see here. Hmm, it looks like a picture of you and several handsome men posing and trying your best to look and sound available to the entire county. Gee Max, don't I keep you busy enough? Or are you looking for dates to replace me? What am I to think Max? Are you looking for someone else?" I asked.

"No, Beth," Max said. "It was a surprise for you. Didn't you think it was funny? My parents thought it was funny." He sounded like he was lying. "They thought it was good free advertising. I told them you wouldn't be happy about this, but they said it'd be fun and not to worry about it."

"Well, Max, for someone who has been dating you for over a year, I feel like this is a slap in my face, and that's all I have to say right now. Goodbye Max."

That evening when I got home from work, Max called.

"Hey, Beth, I wanted to let you know I talked to a couple of the other guys who did the most eligible bachelor thing. They have girlfriends, and one of them has a fiancée, and she was really mad about it! So I wanted you to know that you aren't the only one who got angry about this."

I explained, "What you don't seem to realize is the message you're sending. While you were having fun playing millionaire model, this article claims you are single, available, and one of the most desired men in the county. I find that hurtful."

"I'm sorry. I didn't mean to hurt you," Max said. "Do you still want to go out this weekend?"

"Yes, and you need to be extra nice to me to make up for that stupid article."

### *Dating a Funeral Director*

When Max and I met and started dating, he wanted to do what other men his age did: play golf, go out with the guys for a few beers, go out to dinner with a date, work from 8:00 a.m.–6:00 p.m., go home and not have to worry about work anymore for the evening.

But it seemed he worked all the time. His parents were hard on him and, in return, Max would get angry with them.

Max lived above the funeral home while we dated. He had lived above the funeral home since he was 16-years-old. Before him, Max's grandparents had lived there. It was where they raised their three sons, one of whom was Max's father, Lewis.

Sometimes while waiting for Max to finish work at the funeral home, I'd wait upstairs. The décor in this area made me feel like I'd travelled back in time. There were three bedrooms, each done with a Victorian theme. All had antique bedroom suites. The first room had a white bedspread on a dark cherry bed frame, white lace drapery over the windows, and a vanity topped with a lace runner and two small glass lamps. Displayed on the runner were a fancy crystal brush, mirror, and comb set, and an antique perfume bottle. A tall lingerie chest sat along the wall opposite the bed, with an oversized antique rocker beside it. The trim in all the rooms was heavy oak, painted white. It was clear this room had been decorated for a woman. At first glance, it appeared to be original to the building, but I later found out that Max's mother, Irene, had decorated every room.

The second bedroom had a patchwork quilt on an oversized, blond sleigh bed. It looked like something Paul Bunyan would have slept in.

There was a collection of old cameras displayed on an aged blackened bookshelf, with glass doors that hinged across the top of it. There were some old photos in a picture viewer and metal toys from Lewis's childhood. There were books on the other shelves. On top of the dresser was a gentleman's antique grooming set. All items were displayed as though they were in a museum. This was obviously decorated for a man. Across the room was a small antique organ.

The third bedroom had a simple, white cotton bedspread on a dark brown sleigh bed. There was a light blue Queen Anne velvet chair in the room, and an old torchiere reading lamp. An antique trunk with a plant growing from it sat against one wall, and a dresser that matched the bed sat against the other. Next to this room were a full bathroom done in blue and gold, with an old cast iron clawfoot tub, a second office, and a collection room filled with beautiful, old torchiere lamps. Several appeared to be from the 1920s era. They don't make lamps like that anymore. I couldn't wait to have a closer look at them.

The living room was directly across the large hall from the first bedroom. It had a 1970s theme to it: a gold velvet half-rounded sofa, two orange swivel chairs, and a blond bookcase filled with old mortuary schoolbooks from Max and his father's college years.

Periodically, out of boredom, I'd pick up a book and thumb through it. More often than not, I'd slam the book shut and put it back on the shelf as quickly as I could. Within the pages of those books were grotesque pictures that made me want to run screaming out of the building.

The pictures were for educational purposes. There were before and after photos of someone with his head blown halfway off; brain matter spilled out over the table from one side of the head, and on the other side, one eye, a half of a nose, and a full mouth remained. The after photo was remarkable—someone had put the disfigured half back together.

In time, I made an effort to become familiar with the ways of a funeral director. I learned that funeral directors have their own lingo. If there were a family function, Funeral Directors Association meeting, or anything that took the Edwardses away from the business, Max would ask if I'd *tend* the phone for the evening. Eagerly, I'd say, "Yes." Whatever he needed, I was there. I wanted to help Max get time off, no matter what it took. I'd take Zack with me, and we'd sit at the funeral home, just the two of us, and watch television. While we were there, I answered the phone and gave visitation hours, as well as funeral times. Periodically, I'd receive a *death call* and have to page Max to make the *removal.*

Naively, in the beginning, I did this service for free. I was too shy to ask about money for my time. Once in a while, as an afterthought, Max's mother Irene would think to pay me, but more often than not, she didn't. I could have used the extra money, but it was not in my nature to ask. Regardless of the pay, I was happy to do it for Max.

One evening, I went to the funeral home. It was *quiet,* so Max and I made plans to go out. In Max's small living room upstairs, I sat and waited for him while he got ready for our date. As he dressed, the phone rang. It was his father.

"Max, Mrs. Bloom just passed away. She's at the University Hospital. You'll have to make the removal and meet with the family."

Max slammed the phone down. "Son of a bitch!" he yelled. I went to his bedroom door to ask what the yelling was about.

"Why can't he leave me alone? I work every fucking day and they can't give me one evening off!" Max punched the top of his stereo and pieces flew. "I hate him!" Max said.

"No, you don't," I said. "You're just mad because you thought you were getting the night off."

Max glared at me. "What the hell do you know? You don't have to work every day of your life, morning to night, with no time off!" Max sat on the floor and began to cry. I bent over and hugged him.

"We'll go out another time," I said. "I'll go get you some dinner and bring it back for you."

Max asked, "Would you like to go on the removal with me?"

"Sure," I said. "What do I need to do?"

"Nothing, just ride with me and wait in the hearse," Max said.

This was a first for me, traveling in a hearse. *How weird, how creepy, how cool is this!*

I had never imagined that a hearse would be so luxurious inside. The sound system was incredible. Had I not turned around to look through the window between the hearse and the bed that holds the casket, I would have felt like I was in an expensive luxury sedan. Max and I talked all the way to the hospital. I asked all sorts of questions.

“Do bodies really move after they’re dead? Do they sit up?” I asked.

“Of course not, but that’s the most often asked question,” Max said. “The only time I ever saw movement from a dead body was while doing an embalming. It must have been from the transformation of fluids. When embalming takes place, the blood comes out and the fluid goes in simultaneously. The fluid coagulates. Once, I swear I saw the fingers move. They almost appeared to relax. That was it. No one sits up, nothing more happens, just that tiny bit of movement in the fingers, and that’s rare.”

I said, “I’ve never touched a dead person, and the thought of it grosses me out.”

“That’s understandable,” Max said. “They feel cold to the touch. The embalming fluid turns into a thick jell, for lack of a better word, once it hits a dead person’s system. That’s why people feel hard and cold.”

Max and I were having fun on this strange little road trip.

“My dad has a story he likes to tell,” Max said. “I’ve heard it a hundred times.

When Dad was a teenager, his parents had an ambulance service along with the funeral business.

Before that, they had a furniture store. That's how a lot of funeral homes got started—as furniture makers. Furniture makers crafted coffins. Years ago, families held the viewing in their homes—usually in a room called the 'parlor.' My grandparents would bring the coffin and the equipment to the home and prepare the body for viewing."

"So that must be where the phrase 'funeral parlor' came from? I didn't know that," I said.

Max continued, "My father was going on one of his first removals. It was night and very dark out. The hearse back then was fairly large, more like the size of a van today. My dad drove to the hospital and put the deceased into the back of the vehicle. He was driving back to the funeral home and heard groaning. He thought he must have been hearing things. More groaning went on and it was coming from the back. He was getting really nervous. He was downright scared! The groaning continued."

"No way!" I said.

Max said, "He pulled the hearse into the driveway and ran into the funeral home. 'DAD! THAT BODY I PICKED UP IS GROANING!'

"'I don't think so,' his father said. 'Come with me. Let's get that body out of the hearse and see if he's got anything to say.'

"When they opened the door, their dog jumped out. Apparently, he wanted to go for a ride and got in before Lewis left for the removal."

This was a silly old story, but Max had a good time telling it, and I had a good time listening to it.

### *Pictures Tell the Truth*

It was the spring of **1985**. Max was working in the prep room, embalming someone. He heard me come in and said he'd be up as soon as he'd finished with his work.

The funeral home was a large, old colonial building. It had been a family home at one time, built in the early 1900s.

The prep room was located on the main floor, and later moved to the basement, where the casket room was. I avoided the casket room. Max locked me in there one evening and shut off the lights. I screamed and begged him to open the door, while he laughed on the other side. By the time he opened the door, I was in tears. He hugged me and said he was sorry and would never do it again, but I didn't believe him.

The main floor had a full kitchen. It was last updated in the 1970s, and it showed. Gold Formica lined the counters under the oak cabinets. The formal dining room had flocked gold wallpaper, heavy oak doors and trim, base molding with corner pegs, and a plate rail that went around the entire room. It all appeared original to the old building before any renovations had been made. The living room and parlor were orange and gold and also screamed 1970s.

Another small parlor was used for making funeral arrangements. It had a fireplace that was once surrounded in bronze detail, but now was painted white to keep the theme flowing. An old painting of a farm scene, given to Max's grandfather many years ago as payment for a funeral service, hung over the fireplace.

There were two large viewing rooms that could be divided in half, both lined with golden orange carpet and antique furniture. The office was dark and gloomy, with brown paneled walls and green, red, and blue scotch plaid carpet. Just looking at it depressed me. The hallway was filled with antiques. The walls in the hall were papered in gold and, of course, that lovely orange carpet was on the floors. I'm sure it was lovely in the early '70s, but it was time for a much-needed update.

When I entered the upstairs living room, I usually sat in one of the orange chairs. They were very comfortable to sit in while I watched TV and waited for Max. One evening while waiting, I could see Max had pulled pictures out. There were hundreds of them spread all over the coffee table and floor. *Maybe he'd been looking for something?*

Instead of turning on the television, I decided to look at the pictures. There were many of Max from his college years, with dozens of women. Some of the same women appeared in several of the photos with him, and some were holding a beer or cigarette while smiling. Many of these were taken at parties. There were even pictures taken at the after party from the class reunion, the evening I met Max. There was one of Carrie.

As I picked up piles of photos to examine them, I soon realized there were no pictures of me. It was like I never existed. I found this sadly interesting, but Max had never taken a picture of me.

I picked up a very curious pile of pictures. They had been taken a few months before. Max and his cousin Derrick were in one photo, and Max appeared in another photo with a girl. I remember the girl from high school; she was in my younger sister Patty's class. There was another picture of Max, Derrick, and that girl again.

*But who's taking the picture? What's this? Max is lying on top of this girl, pinning her hands over her head. They were both laughing. I should have never forgiven him after I found out about Carrie. I'm such an idiot!*

I put on my coat and shoes and left without saying goodbye.

A few days went by before I took one of Max's calls.

"Hi, Beth. I've been trying to call you. How come you left the other night? Was I taking too long at work? Is everything okay?"

"I left upset. While you were working I looked at the pictures you had scattered all over your living room. I found an interesting one of you on a bed with another girl. You had her pinned to the bed and you were both laughing," I said with anger.

"Oh, that was taken a long time ago," Max said.

"No, it wasn't. It was bad enough to find it and bring it to your attention—now you're going to lie to me about it? There is a date on the back of the picture and on the photo envelope it came out of. Do you think I'm stupid?" I asked.

"Of course not," Max replied. "Why don't I pick you up, so we can talk?"

"Okay," I said. "I'll be ready when you get here."

Max picked me up and took me to dinner. While at dinner, the same girl Max was with in the picture came over to our table to ask if she could speak to Max for a minute. Max got up and they both walked to the side of the restaurant to talk. Apparently, he had left his wallet at her place. Max came back to the table.

"I know this doesn't look good. She was having some problems with her boyfriend and asked if I could come over to talk with her about it. I was trying to be a friend. I think she had the wrong idea, and she started putting the moves on me. That must have been when my wallet fell out. I want you to know, I just told her you and I are together and that isn't going to change. I love you, Beth," Max claimed, trying to convince me.

"I don't know what to think," I said. "I'm going to visit my dad this weekend. I need a day or so to think about this. I'll call you when I get back."

The visit with my dad gave me much to think about. He asked me about Max. "Have you and Max discussed getting married? How long have the two of you been together now?"

"We've been dating almost three years, and even though there's not been a discussion of marriage, there have been hints," I said.

"Do you love him?"

"Yes, I love him. I can't imagine my life without him."

"There is an old saying, 'Why buy the cow when the milk is free.' Are you familiar with this?" Dad asked. "I'm asking you this because I love you. You are a mother with a small son who you still need to raise. You have given Max three years of your life. That is long enough for him to know if his intentions are honorable or not."

"What should I do?" I asked.

"It's time you give him an ultimatum," Dad suggested.

"You need to ask what his intentions are, and if he plans to marry you, tell him you'd like to pick a date, *now*. But I need to let you know, he may not be ready, and you'll have to leave him and move on with your life if he's not. You must move on in order to raise your son. Do you understand? Dating for this length of time is not fair to your son or you."

"Yes, Dad, I understand. I'll go see him tomorrow," I said.

Driving home from my dad's that evening, I had a lot to think about. I prayed I'd have the strength to do what my dad had suggested. When I got home, I put my son to bed and went directly to bed myself, hoping I'd sleep.

The next day, I called Max and asked if I could stop by. He said, "Yes."

I walked into the funeral home, stopped in the office, and asked where I could find Max. "He's in the main chapel," his mother said.

I walked quietly into the room and peeked around the corner. I never knew what to expect. Max was in the distance, applying makeup to someone in a casket. This was uncomfortable for me to witness. I'd learned to hold my hand at the side of my face, creating my own private wall. This allowed me to slowly introduce myself to death. Every now and then, I gained enough courage to peek out from behind my hand.

"Max," I said. "I'm here."

"You can come over here and see what I'm doing if you want," hc said.

"No, I'm still not ready to watch. Is it okay if I meet you in the living room when you're finished?"

"Of course. I'll be right there," he said.

I was nervous. I went into the living room on the main floor, sat down, and waited. Within minutes, Max washed his hands in the kitchen, walked into the living room, and sat down next to me.

"Are you okay?" Max asked. "You don't look like yourself."

"I went to see my dad," I said. "My family is concerned I'm wasting my time with you. Dad said we've spent three years together and you've had plenty of time to recognize if you want to marry me or not."

Max started clenching his teeth. "So now I'm supposed to propose to you?" Max asked.

"Yes, and if you do, we need to set a date immediately," I said.

"Well, that's not going to happen! No one is going to tell me when I'm getting married, let alone force me to pick the date within minutes of becoming engaged!"

"I'm sorry to hear that," I said. "I can see you're not interested in a life with me. I'm sorry I spent so much time with you. I'm sorry I fell in love with you. And I'm actually sorry I ever met you. Goodbye, Max!"

I got up and headed for the door. Tears were streaming down my face and I didn't want to give Max the satisfaction of knowing he'd broken me.

"Beth!" Max yelled. "Beth, come back here!"

I kept walking. When I heard him behind me, I sped up. "You've said everything I need to know. There is nothing more to say," I said as I walked out the door.

"Beth, get back here and talk to me," Max demanded.

I refused to turn back. He wasn't going to suck me in again. I got into my car, and as I drove off, in my rearview mirror I could see Max standing in the street. I kept driving and went home.

Max never called.

I was doing great for the first three days, and then it hit: I was lovesick. I couldn't eat, sleep, or do anything except cry. Heartache had set in. I wanted to die. Looking forward to a brighter future felt impossible.

### *I Need a Date*

I called my sister Marie to see if I could visit her. She and her husband Steve lived in Cadbury Hills, about thirty minutes from me. Marie was the oldest sibling, and we all looked to her for advice. She had been more of an inspiration and parental figure than our own parents. The downside of Marie's advice was that if you didn't do what she suggested, she thought you were an idiot.

After I arrived at Marie's, she and Steve sat at their kitchen table with me while I explained my visit with Dad and with Max.

"You need to get back on the horse," Marie said. "Steve, do you have any single friends you can fix Beth up with?"

"Yes, what about Keith? He's an accountant. He's been dating someone, but their relationship has been on and off for years. I'm sure if he met the right person he'd drop her and move on. Who knows, you could be that right person," Steve said. "It couldn't hurt to try."

"I'm up for it, if you want to arrange it for me," I said.

"We'll take care of it and call you when everything is set to go," Marie said.

Driving home, I felt a sense of relief. I now had something to look forward to, even if it was a mystery man.

Two days later, I received a card in the mail from Marie. It was a funny card with two old ladies on the front, testifying to how men are worthless, and we really don't need them. On the inside, it said, "Keep your chin up, Beth. It'll get better, I promise. Love, Marie."

When I came home that evening, Marie called to tell me she wanted me to come to the Cadbury Hills Festival. "We can eat, drink, and socialize," she said. "We'll have a lot of fun! Steve and Keith play on the same baseball team. This is the perfect opportunity for you to meet him, without being obligated to go out with him if there isn't an attraction."

"When is the festival?" I asked.

"It's in two weeks," Marie replied.

"Sounds like a good plan. I'm looking forward to this," I said. "Thanks for your help, and thanks for sending the hilarious card. It made my day."

"You're welcome, Beth. I know this is a really tough time for you. Anything I can do to help, I will. I love you."

"I love you, too," I said. "Call me with the details when you get them. Goodbye."

For the next two weeks, every day in the mail I received a funny card from Marie. It helped to keep my spirits up.

It was now the Friday of the festival. My boss, Ella, told me to leave early so that I'd have plenty of time to get ready. I went home and packed a bag. Dad had suggested Zack and I stay the weekend with him and his wife. They also lived in Cadbury Hills, and that way they could spend time with Zack while I went out with Marie and Steve.

We were packed and ready to go. I put Zack in the car. He was 4-years-old and cute as a puppy. "Mama, are we going to see Max?" Zack asked.

"No, sweetie, Max didn't want to marry me, so we won't see him anymore," I explained as gently as I could.

"Well, I guess he doesn't want to be my dad," Zack said sadly.

"Zack, that's not true. You are a wonderful little boy, the best little boy ever! This is a loss for Max. He doesn't understand that you and I are really great people. We should feel sorry for Max because we had to leave him behind. Do you understand?"

"Mama and me are great people," Zack replied. "Poor Max. He will be sad without us, but that's okay, he didn't know we are great people."

"Yes, that's right sweetie," I said. "This weekend, we are going to stay with Grandpa and Grandma Lopezzi. You and Grandpa can swim in the pool. Mama is going with Aunt Marie and Uncle Steve to meet some new friends. How does that sound?"

"Fun, Mama," Zack said. "After you meet new friends, can you swim with me and Grandpa?"

"Yes, I will make time to swim with you," I said. "You're my little boy. I love you."

Zack and I pulled into my dad's driveway. Marie and Steve were already there. I dropped Zack and our bags in the house, kissed Zack goodbye, and got into the car with my sister and her husband.

"So how are you feeling?" Marie asked.

"I'm a nervous wreck, but I'm also really looking forward to this," I said.

The festival was close. We arrived within ten minutes. Steve parked the car and we all got out. There were people everywhere.

"Stay here. Let me get you both some wine to drink and I'll see if I can find Keith," Steve said as he disappeared into the crowd.

"Do I look okay?" I asked Marie.

"You look beautiful!" she responded. "Look, here come Steve and Keith."

"Hey, look at who I found," Steve said. "Beth, here is your wine, and I'd like you to meet my friend Keith."

Keith and I shook hands. Our eyes met. We looked one another over. He was tall and skinny. His blue shirt was untucked from his jeans. His hair was black, as were the rims of his glasses. He had a studious look about him. *I bet he was a nerd in school.* Keith and I knew immediately that there was no attraction on either end. We both said, "It was nice to meet you," and within minutes he was gone.

"What just happened?" Steve asked.

"Don't worry about it," I said. "The attraction just wasn't there. It's okay. I'll meet someone eventually."

"We're playing ball tomorrow," Steve said. "Why don't you stop by and watch. We're actually playing on a ballfield directly behind your dad's house. You might see someone there who piques your interest. It could be fun, right?"

"Right," I said.

"This is a tournament," Steve said. "So there will be several games being played. You can watch us play, or walk around and watch other teams. Marie will be there, so she can walk around with you."

"You guys are the best!" I said. "You've helped me so much since my break-up. I can't imagine what I'd have done without you. Thank you."

It was getting late, so my sister drove me back to Dad's, and then she went back to get Steve. She said she'd pick me up at 9:00 a.m. so we could go together to watch the ballgame.

Marie was on time and looked cute in her denim dress. I had on a pair of linen pants and a white cotton sleeveless top. I hoped my lightweight clothing would keep me looking fresh and cool on this hot, humid day.

We sat on the bleachers. I looked at every player. Marie leaned over and said in a whisper, "Don't look now, but there is the girl that Keith dates on and off. She's sitting behind you, but over to the far right. She's the tall blond wearing a short-sleeved khaki dress."

"Where is the restroom?" I asked. "I'll check her out when I get up."

Marie pointed, and I got up, looked at the blond, and left the bleachers. I couldn't imagine what Keith was thinking. The blond was stunning. She looked like a runway model. His looks were far beneath hers, so what was the problem?

When I returned, I noticed a nice-looking guy running the bases.

"Marie, what do you know about him?" I asked.

"He's going through a divorce, and he's got two little girls. Do you think he's cute?" she asked.

"Yes, I do sort of think he's cute," I said. "But right now, I'm burning up and want to go back to Dad's and go swimming with Zack. This has got to be the hottest day of the year. I can't take this heat anymore."

"Do you want me to drive you?" Marie asked.

"No," I said. "It's close, I can walk."

When I got to my dad's, his stepson Peter was there. Peter had brought his friend Mark over to go swimming. Mark was extremely handsome—sculpted jawline, big, beautiful smile with pearly white teeth, black, curly hair, big blue eyes. He looked like a model. Oh so handsome!

"Peter, aren't you going to introduce me to your friend?" I asked.

"I'm sorry, Beth, this is Mark," Peter said.

"Hi, Mark, it's nice to meet you," I replied.

"I live in the house across the street," Mark said.

"Mark is a friend and neighbor," Peter said. "We were playing ball in the tournament and lost. We decided to drown our sorrows in Mom's pool. I see Zack out there swimming with your dad. Mark, are you ready to go for a swim?" Peter asked.

"Sure am. Are you swimming too, Beth?" Mark asked.

"As a matter of fact, I am," I replied.

We all went for a swim. The water felt so good and cool on my skin. I played with Zack, dragging him around with his water wings, while Peter and Mark dove for quarters in the bottom of the pool. About an hour later, Marie and Steve came over to swim. Steve brought the guy I had asked Marie about earlier. *Oh crap!* I thought.

I got out of the pool, and Steve introduced me to his friend before they both jumped into the pool. I sat down to dry off, and Marie sat down beside me. "So what do you think?" Marie said. "Do you think he's cute close up?"

"I'd really like a date with Mark," I said.

"Who the hell is Mark?" Marie asked.

"He's the cute guy in the pool. He's a friend of Peter's."

"The neighbor guy?"

"Yes."

"Okay, I'll let Steve know that you've found a date," Marie said.

Dad turned on the grill to make hotdogs and hamburgers for everyone. Marie and I went into the kitchen to help make a tossed salad and fry up some potatoes. Later, we all sat around the pool in cushioned chairs to eat. Mark sat next to me, and we talked for hours.

"Are you going to be here long?" Mark asked. "I'd really like to see you again."

"My son and I are spending the night, and we're leaving tomorrow," I said.

"Do you live far from here?" Mark asked.

"No," I said. "It's about thirty minutes west of here."

"Would you mind if I followed you home tomorrow?" Mark asked. "That way I'll know where you live, and I can come and see you next week."

"I think that's a great idea," I said. "I'm terrible with directions, so if you're up to the drive, I'm all for it."

Mark followed me home the next afternoon and asked what evening during the week would be good for him to come back. "I don't usually like to date during the week because of my son. I'd like to get to know you, though," I said. "Why don't you come over on Saturday and we can go out then?" We said goodnight and looked forward to our date.

When I arrived at work on Monday, I told Ella about my weekend and asked to take a week's vacation starting next week. She told me the calendar was free, so she would schedule me off.

Mark came to pick me up at six o'clock, Saturday evening.

"Beth, you look so beautiful, would it be okay to drive you around and show you off before we go to dinner?" Mark asked. "I'd love to see the area you live in."

"Okay," I said. "Let's go for a drive through the downtown area. Willow is smaller than downtown Cadbury, but equally as charming."

As Mark and I drove into town, we had to stop at a light. As I looked at the car next to me, I noticed Craig, one of Max's closest friends, and he saw me.

Craig stretched his neck to see who I was with. I was certain he'd go running to Max to tell him what he'd seen. Craig was a gossip that way.

Mark drove me around a little more and then took me to dinner at a nice restaurant in Cadbury Hills. We had a wonderful evening.

Mark told me all about himself. He worked as the maintenance specialist for a pool store. He received calls 24/7 because he not only worked for homeowners, but also for hotels and motels. Mark also informed me that he was a recovering alcoholic and a cancer survivor. This was a lot of information to take in during dinner.

"I had Hodgkin's disease," Mark explained, "but I've been free and clear for six years now. It's a disease of the lymph nodes. I had been playing ball and was in the outfield. Someone hit the ball, and I ran backwards to catch it. The ball was hit with such force that it hit me in the cup and knocked me to the ground. I was in so much pain, I was rushed to the hospital. That's when they found I had the disease."

"Were you dating anyone at the time?" I asked.

"Yes, her name was Dawn," Mark said. "As soon as I was done with my treatments, I got engaged to her. Going through a life-threatening experience makes you realize how short life is; I don't take anything for granted anymore. Dawn and I moved in together and life was good. I was an engineer for a large corporation related to the auto industry. I went away for a business seminar, and when I returned home earlier than planned, Dawn was in bed with another man. I was devastated. That's when the drinking started."

"That's quite a story," I said. "Did you go to rehab?"

"Yes, I spent thirty days in rehab and went to AA every day for a year," he said. "The drinking took over my life. I lost my job, my apartment, and my car. I had to move back in with my parents—they live across the street from your dad. Every day is a challenge, but I keep pushing forward."

"It sounds like you've been through a lot, but it also sounds like you've learned a lot along the way," I said. "You should be proud of yourself. It will take time to completely recover the loss of your career and your credit, but, eventually, you'll be back on top. You didn't lose it overnight, so you can't expect to get it back overnight. You have a job at the pool store, and you've managed to buy a really nice used car. Clearly, you're on your way to making something good out of your life again."

I let Mark know I was on a one-week vacation from work and that Zack and I would be staying with my dad and his wife for the week.

Mark and I had been dating for six weeks. We saw each other three times each week: Friday, Saturday, and Sunday. We fell in love quickly. Mark talked about marrying me, but wanted to spend one holiday together with our families first. This would allow our families a little time to meet both of us before we made any big announcement. Mark hadn't actually proposed; he just talked about it. He seemed like a good man.

After work one afternoon, I got the mail and found an envelope addressed to me, from Max. It was a card. On the outside it read, "I keep wondering whatever happened to us." Inside it read, "and wondering, and wondering, and wondering, Love, Max."

I was certain Craig told Max he'd seen me with another guy and this is what inspired Max to send the card.

But why now? I'd moved on. I sat down with a pen and paper.

*Dear Max,*

*No need to wonder what happened to us, I will tell you what happened. I spent three years of my life with you. I was in love with you and thought you loved me too. I hoped that you would want to marry me. I was wrong for thinking this way; you're still waiting for someone, and it's not me.*

*I've been dating a really nice guy for the past six weeks. In this short time we've spent together, he is more committed to me than you were during the three years we were together.*

*I hope you find what you're looking for, but it's not me.*

*Beth*

I put my letter in the mail that same day.

That evening, I told Mark about the card. He seemed a little upset by it, questioning me over and over about it. This was a side of him I'd never seen before. I assured him he had nothing to worry about. Max didn't want me, and that's all there is to it. After Mark left that evening, I couldn't help but wonder what other personality traits he would reveal to me.

More than a week went by, and I didn't hear anything from Mark. Then he finally called.

"Hi, Beth, how are you?" he said. "I've been away at a resort hotel, taking care of their pool, but now I'm home and would like to come over to see you tonight."

"Okay," I said hesitantly. I hadn't heard from him—were there no phones to let me know he'd be away? Something didn't feel right. Mark came over that evening, and though he seemed fine, I could detect alcohol on his breath. The next night we went out to dinner again, and again I smelled alcohol. I didn't say anything at the time. But I grieved the following week, knowing that things were about to change. I hoped for the best and planned to go out with Mark one more time.

When he arrived and kissed me hello, I could smell alcohol. "Mark, have you been drinking?" I asked.

"No," he said.

"I'm sorry, Mark. I've been doing a lot of thinking this week. I can't see you anymore. Right now, my priority has to be my son. Forgive me for bringing you into a relationship, when realistically, I'm just not ready. All I can say is that I wish you nothing but the best."

I said goodnight to Mark, and he left. I had to do this; I didn't want an alcoholic around Zack. This was hard for me to do. It almost felt like I was being mean and unsympathetic. My son is the most important person in my life, so, mean or not, it had to be done.

Like always, when I need some words of wisdom, I called Marie. "Hi, Marie, it's Beth. Do you have a minute to talk?"

"Yes, what's up?" Marie asked.

"I just wanted to let you know, I stopped seeing Mark. He's an alcoholic. He claimed he was recovering, but the last few times I saw him, it was obvious he'd been drinking."

"I'm sorry," she said. "I know you were hoping this was going to be Mr. Right, instead of Mr. Right-Now. Not to change the subject, but I wanted to tell you that Keith and the on-again, off-again girlfriend eloped to Las Vegas last week."

"Happy to hear someone found true love," I said. "I'm not going to keep you on the line any longer. I just wanted to let you know what's going on with me. That would be a big *nothing*! I'll talk to you later."

### *A Year of Misery*

Max and I had been apart for almost three months. It was hard not to think of him and what could have been, but I had chosen to move on. I was hopeful that I'd find someone wonderful in my lifetime. The recent dating experience with Mark had taught me to be very careful before giving my heart away so quickly.

One Monday morning, I was pouring myself a cup of coffee before I headed out to work, and Zack came running into the kitchen with a red rose in his hand.

"Here, Mama," Zack handed me the rose.

"Thank you. Where did you get this?" I asked.

"From Max."

"Where is Max, sweetie?" I asked.

"He's at the door. He told me to give you the flower and tell you he is here. He wants to talk to you."

I put my cup down and went to the door. "Max, what are you doing here?"

"Hi, Beth. I know I might be too late. Craig told me you were seeing someone else, and I decided that I couldn't lose you! I wanted to come to you sooner, but my parents have been in Scotland with my sister Gladys," Max said, shaking. "I had to wait for them to return home so I could ask if it would be okay to marry you. I didn't buy you a ring because what if you said no, or what if I got you something you didn't like? My mom said I could do whatever I want. So, what do you think?"

"So what do I think about what?" I said. "You're not making any sense."

"Beth, I'm asking you to marry me."

I was stunned.

My heart said NO, but my head (and my mouth) said YES!

"YES, I'LL MARRY YOU!" I said.

We hugged and kissed. The kiss felt weird. I had forgotten Max's kisses. I hoped we could repair the damage of the past and make a fresh start and new life together.

Once Max proposed to me, he had nothing more to say about the marriage. I tried multiple times to get him to go ring shopping with me, but he wouldn't. I finally started looking for a ring on my own. Each time I found something I liked, Max said it was too expensive and refused to go look at it.

One Sunday, before the mall closed, Max agreed to go window-shopping for a ring with me. We stopped by several jewelry store window displays. Max didn't like anything he saw because they were all over $1,000, and he had set a limit.

There was still one more jewelry store to stop at on our way out of the mall. I grabbed Max by the arm and said, "Look at that one." It was a gold band with five small diamonds across the top of it. The wedding band was advertised as half a carat for $1,200. It was more than Max wanted to spend, but I put my foot down. The ring shopping had gone beyond embarrassing into cheapskate.

"Max," I said, "that is the ring I'd like to have. I have searched for months for something you felt was affordable. I'm not looking anymore. If you can't afford the additional $200, then I'll pay it!"

"No, you don't need to pay it," Max said. "If that's the ring you want, I'll give you some money to put a down payment on it. I'll buy it for you."

"Thank you," I said. "You have no idea what a relief this is."

In the following months, it was difficult to get money from Max to make the payment on the ring. This made no sense to me at all. Max had more money than he knew what to do with. He had a drawer at the funeral home filled with his paychecks; he tossed them in there, instead of taking them to the bank. His mother would get after him to take them to the bank and deposit them so she could balance the checking account.

Whenever I brought up the subject of the wedding, reception, or honeymoon, it left Max silent. If he didn't want to marry me, then why did he ask?

"Max, we have to make an appointment with the minister at your church, if that's where you'd like us to be married," I said. "This needs to be done now, in order to plan the reception."

Max was Presbyterian and had attended the same church since he was born. I was Catholic, but had no church to call my own since I moved from Detroit. I believe there should be a feeling, a connection to one's church. I attended several, but couldn't find one that fit my needs.

Max said, "Okay."

A week went by, and Max hadn't called his church for an appointment. I had to take control of everything. Max was useless.

"Max, I have a suggestion. Because you are very busy, I'm going to call the church and set up the appointment to meet with your minister. I'll let you know what day and time are scheduled."

Max said, "Okay."

The wedding was set for September 27, 1986. My mother and I planned the entire event. Max didn't want anything to do with it.

I went to the courthouse to find out about the marriage license. I was afraid there might be some legal issues regarding Max's birth certificate. You see Max was delivered July 3, 1959 by a local doctor who was also a local farmer. Dr. Field delivered Max late in the evening—my guess is that it must have been around 11:54 p.m. on July 3—but on the birth certificate the doctor wrote July 4.

On Max's sixteenth birthday, he took his birth certificate to the Secretary of State's office to get his driver's license. When he filled out the form and handed the clerk his papers, she handed them back to him and said, "Young man, don't you know when your birthday is?"

Max said, "Yes, it's July 3rd."

"Not according to your birth certificate it's not. It states here you were born on July 4th."

Humiliated, Max grabbed the papers from the woman and went to the funeral home to confront his mother. "You lied to me! My birthday is July 4, not July 3!"

Max said in anger.

"No, you were born on July 3, 1959. I should know, I was there!" Max's mother said. "Call Dr. Field and ask him about this."

Max called Dr. Field's office. It would appear that Dr. Field gave Max a birthday of July 4 because he thought it would be more fun to have a birthday on the Fourth of July. It was only a matter of minutes after all.

When Max told me this, I could hardly believe what he was saying. "Where I come from, that's called falsifying legal documents."

"Oh, Beth," Max said. "He didn't mean any harm. He was thinking about how much fun I would have on my birthday when I was a kid."

"I guess he should have told your mother then, huh?" I said. "All that falsifying for nothing!"

I told the clerk this story, and she laughed. As long as the birth date Max wrote on the marriage license application was the same as what was on his birth certificate, it was legal.

"If it works for you, then it works for me," I said.

The cake, the invitations, my shoes, and my dress were ordered. Things were moving right along. I took my sister Patty, who was my maid-of-honor, to be fitted for her dress. I wanted it to be similar to mine.

My dress was tea length and made of ivory satin. It was gathered at the waist for a fuller skirt. Small puffed sleeves fell slightly off the shoulders. Ivory satin roses adorned the top of the dress and were accented with small pearls inside. I had the same dress made for Patty, except her dress was teal, and her sleeves were smaller. Our dresses were beautiful.

Living in a small town didn't allow many options for a reception hall. There was an old country club five miles outside of Willow. I'd attended a wedding reception there a year earlier. It was on a well-groomed golf course, with seasonal flowers lining the entryway. It would be perfect for our wedding reception. I made an appointment with the event planner to see what my options were and if the date was available.

The event planner was able to hold the date. After much discussion, we decided to have a luncheon instead of dinner because the cost was dramatically less. I scheduled the luncheon for 74 people to be held from 1:00-4:00 p.m. The cost was $1,200, which covered a sit-down meal of chicken breast on a bed of wild rice, fresh steamed green beans, redskin potatoes, roll, and dinner salad. There was an extra charge for the cutting and distributing of the cake because I was having it brought in. The cost included tip. Max would be responsible for the bar tab.

My mother worked full time as a nursing director and would be paying for the entire wedding on her own, except, of course, for the rehearsal dinner and the bar bill. She was able to put aside $2,500 for my wedding. I was told this well in advance so I knew not to go over budget, and I didn't.

I had been married once before, so putting on a wedding seemed unnecessary and slightly embarrassing for me. I was on a tight budget; only close family and minimal friends could be invited—74 people, including the wedding party. That would give us each 35 people. I had asked Max to get me a list of people to invite, but, like everything else about the wedding, he was dragging his feet. Frustrated, I went to his mother and asked her for a guest list.

The word "prude" was designed for Max's mother, Irene. She was the kind of woman who'd leave her pearls on during a massage to remind you of how rich and powerful she thought she was. Her nose was naturally in the upright position, looking like she was continuously smelling the air; this, too, was a reminder you were beneath her. Irene's lips were pursed, and she never smiled. For the longest time, I thought she had rotten or missing teeth because she never showed them. And with all that going for her, I still made every effort to like her and to have her like me.

If I were casting the actress to play the role of Irene Edwards, I'd request Helen Mirren, and tell her to play Irene's character the same way she played Queen Elizabeth.

Irene and I sat at the kitchen table in the funeral home—that is where I could almost always find my soon-to-be mother-in-law—and created the guest list. Irene kept saying, "Well, what about Mr. and Mrs. Matthews?"

"We have no room," I said.

"We *have* to invite my cousin Bill and his friend Patrick," Irene insisted.

"You'll have to replace them with someone on your list if you really want them to come," I said.

"Who is paying for this?" Irene asked in a sharp tone.

"My mother is."

"Well," Irene said, "I'll take care of the rehearsal dinner, but really that is *all* I'm responsible for!"

I nodded my head and said, "Yes, I know."

I couldn't help thinking that my new mother-in-law was a pathetic snob. *This is her son's first marriage, and she knows it's my second. She also knows my family doesn't have the funds to do anything extravagant, and had this not been her son's first marriage, I wouldn't have a reception after the ceremony. We could just as easily go to the courthouse and get married by a judge.* I kept these thoughts silent and simply smiled.

Once the wedding invitation list was finished, Irene gave me her usual stoic look.

"You know you'll be expected to work for the funeral home?" she said.

"Yes," I said, "I'm looking forward to it."

"Really? I had no idea," Irene said. "No one gave me a choice. I wanted to be a teacher—I love little children—but I was expected to work *here*." Irene looked like someone had stolen something—her life—from her. If what she said was true, was she not able to stand up for herself? She looks and sounds capable. So why didn't she follow her dream?

"Why don't you go to school now and teach?" I asked. "It's never too late if you're passionate about it. My oldest sister, Marie, is still going to college, and she's 40-years-old. Marie is currently a dental hygienist, but she wants to be a physician's assistant."

"I'm 54-years-old. I'm too old to go back to school," Irene said, sounding a little irritated.

"I also have a cousin who's going to school to be a doctor," I said. "She's been going part time for years. Realistically, by the time she's finished, she'll be 50-years-old; which can be pretty discouraging. Marie told her, 'You're going to be 50-years-old anyway—wouldn't you rather be 50-years-old and a doctor?' Those few words from my sister gave my cousin the encouragement she needed to continue her education. You're never too old to go back school, or do anything you want to do, but you really have to want to do it," I said to Irene.

"Well, I've been here so long I don't know anything else," Irene said. I could see she didn't want to hear what I had to say. Sometimes it's easier to complain about something, rather than fix it. Clearly, I was sounding like "Little Suzie Sunshine," raining happiness all over her miserable day. I knew I needed to get out of there.

I still had a lot to do. Picking out tuxes was next on my list. I drove to Cadbury because our small town had no tux shop. I picked out a tux for Derrick and one for Zack, both gray. The tux I chose for Max was from the same collection, but in ivory and with tails. When I got home, I called to inform Max it was important for him to stop at the tux shop and give his measurements. His tux had to be ordered four weeks before the wedding to make sure the fit would be perfect.

As weeks went by, my mother and I were working as quickly as possible to tend to every detail.

"Max, the wedding is in three weeks. Your cousin Derrick, the best man has been fitted. Zack, the ring bearer, has been fitted. But the groom, that would be you, has yet to be fitted for your tux. Is there a problem? If you don't want to go through with this, you'd better tell me now. The ring still needs to be paid for, too," I said with stress. "I'm not going to mention this again. You're a grown man. If you show up to our wedding in a suit you wear for a funeral service, I will not be a happy bride. If you show up to the church and have no wedding ring with you, I will be more than a little upset."

The day before our wedding, Max came to my apartment. (I had moved into the apartment a month before our wedding day.) He was in tears. "What's the matter Max?" I asked with great concern.

"I don't know," he said. "This is the day before our wedding, and I feel sick to my stomach. I should feel good about what I'm about to do, and I don't. You are a sweet, beautiful woman. I couldn't be luckier to have you. Something just doesn't feel right." He sobbed and sobbed.

I tried to comfort him. "Max, we don't have to do this. If you feel in your heart you're doing the wrong thing by marrying me, then we don't have to go through with it. But I need to know now. We still have time to cancel. I'll call my mom and have her call my family and explain you've changed your mind. You can have your mother call your side of the family to cancel. You'll be expected to pay all expenses as a result of the wedding cancellation. I think that's fair, considering you're the one backing out."

"Beth, I don't want to do that either. It doesn't make me feel better to think about backing out. I love you, and I want to marry you. I don't understand why I feel so miserable," Max continued sobbing.

"Max, what you're feeling is called *cold feet*. I'm sure you've heard of this before, but never thought you'd be someone who'd actually experience it. It's like being afraid of the unknown. Many grooms and brides go through this. Some of them make it to the altar, and some don't. I want to do whatever I can to help you, but Max, this is the day before our wedding, and I still have a lot to do. If you want to call it off, I need to know within the next two hours. Right now, I'd like you to get hold of yourself. Think this through. Maybe talk to your mother. Let me know what you decide as soon as possible. I don't want you to do something you're not ready for. This is a big step."

"I want to do this," Max said, tears running down his face.

"Are you afraid I'm going to become a nasty wife, a monster?" I asked. "Or become big and fat? None of that will happen. And if I become a monster, you can divorce me; that's why they invented divorce you know." I smiled at him. Max wiped his eyes, gave me a hug, and said he'd call me later. I continued as though the wedding were still taking place.

Our wedding rehearsal was scheduled for 5:00 p.m. Max's mother was putting on the rehearsal dinner at 6:30 p.m., at the funeral home. It was now 4:00 p.m., and there was a knock at the door. It was Max. He had a bottle of champagne and a small bouquet of red roses. "Beth, I love you!" he said. I'm so sorry I put you through all of this. I want to marry you. But I don't understand why you want to marry me."

"Max," I responded, "You know I've been through a lot. I want to marry you because I love you, because I need stability, and my son Zack and I need security." I gave the honest truth. I wanted Max to know exactly what I expected from him.

Max reached into his pocket and pulled out my wedding ring, then opened the bottle of champagne. "Look, I picked up your ring!" Max said. "I think we should have a little sip to celebrate before we go to the church for rehearsal."

"I think that's a great idea!" I said. "And Max, I'll be a really good wife to you.  There's nothing to worry about."

The rehearsal went flawlessly. My family was a little taken aback by having dinner at the funeral home, especially since I had told them what a lovely home Irene had. But Max's mother and Aunt Lynn did a beautiful job setting the tables with linens, white porcelain china, silverware, and crystal water and wine goblets. In the center of each table was a lovely bouquet of fresh flowers. They served roast beef, mashed potatoes and gravy, scalloped corn, green beans, spinach salad, and rolls. It was delicious.

The evening went by quickly. I told Patty and Zack we needed to go home and be up bright and early for the big day. I kissed Max on the cheek, said I love you, and went home.

### *The Marriage*

We were married **September 27, 1986** without a prenuptial agreement. This surprised me. I had come into the marriage with nothing, so I had nothing to lose. Max had everything and a lot to lose.

The day I married Max, I arrived at his family's church. A special room was held for the bride so that the groom didn't see her before the ceremony. Peeking out the door, I could see Lewis Edwards, my soon to be father-in-law. He looked a little like Queen Elizabeth's son, Prince Charles, but instead of large ears, he had large teeth. I saw Irene Edwards. She was wearing something I had seen her in before, something I'd seen her wear to work; was she too busy to shop for something special to wear to her son's wedding? This was a woman who clearly felt her appearance was at the top of her priority list. You could see that about her at first glance. Irene usually looked like she'd jumped from a page of a fashionable clothing catalog. For her to show up in something common, something she'd given no thought to, showed how she felt, which made me feel awful. Wasn't her son important enough? Wasn't the event—her son's wedding—important enough? Or was it her son's marriage to *me* that wasn't important?

Most of the wedding pictures were taken before the ceremony. I couldn't see what difference it made. I hadn't seen my first husband before my marriage to him, and we had ended up divorced.

Once the ceremony was finished, Rev. Smith asked that Max and I, along with our two witnesses, sign the marriage certificate, which he would file at the courthouse first thing Monday morning. Max leaned over and said to me, "You can keep your name if you want."

Confused, I said, "Why would I do that? Do you really want me to continue using the last name of my ex-husband?"

"It doesn't really matter," Max said.

*What?* I thought. *Is my new husband being stupid, or sensitive? Who says that to a new wife? Maybe he's thinking of my son and his last name—if I kept the same last name as my son, it could be a nice thing, right?*

Before we went on to the reception, my new husband and I had a few more pictures taken. There was a lovely room with a fireplace located in the lower level of the church. Max and I had a beautiful photo taken with my family. Max had one taken with his family. "Shouldn't we get a picture with you, me, and your family?" I asked Max.

"No, that's not necessary," he said. "Let's go to the reception."

"But—" I started to say as I watched his parents getting ready to leave. I felt bad that I wasn't included in the photo taken with Max, his parents, and his sister Gladys. I decided to drop it. If it wasn't important to anyone but me, I suppose it wasn't important. If I persisted, Max could get upset with me, and this wasn't the day for that.

Max and I, along with the maid-of-honor, my younger sister Patty, and the groomsman, Max's, mullet-wearing cousin Derrick, went to the reception. We all got into one of the sedans belonging to the funeral home. Patty and I had placed a "Just Married" sign in the back window.

My blond-haired, blue-eyed, 5-year-old son Zack looked like he could have belonged to Max. Zack was a sweet little boy who desperately wanted a father. His own father left three years earlier, and we hadn't seen or heard from him since. I sent Zack to the reception with my sister Marie and her husband. He would spend the night with them while Max and I had a quiet, romantic night at home.

The reception was only five miles from the church. We arrived at the same time as our guests. I had hired a caterer to serve the luncheon. The food was delicious, and the cake was spectacular.

It was 4:15 p.m. The reception was over, and the guests had left. "Derrick and I will take the car back to the funeral home," Max said.

"Okay," I said. "Patty and I will take the gifts to my apartment, and I'll meet you there."

Patty was slim and pretty. Not only was she my sister, she was also my best friend. As little girls, we were often mistaken for twins. Patty had always been there for me. Marie had, too, but in a different way. Patty and I drove to the apartment and unloaded the gifts. She changed out of her dress and into her jeans and tee-shirt. She helped me out of my dress and then went home. I got into the shower, washed all the spray out of my hair and removed my wedding day make-up, blew out my hair, applied fresh make-up, and then waited.

And waited!

I had been home four hours. Where the heck was Max? I called the funeral home. It sounded like a party over there. "Why don't you come here," Max suggested. "My family all stopped after the reception. We're having leftovers from the rehearsal dinner."

I jumped in my car and drove the few blocks to the funeral home. Max's family was eating and chatting. I was directed to find Max and open the wedding gifts that were there. We ripped open paper and envelopes and thanked everyone present. It was now 11:00 p.m. I was tired and wanted nothing more than to take my groom home and go to bed. "Max, are you ready to go?" I asked.

"You take your car and go ahead of me," he said. "I'll be there in a minute."

I drove home, got into bed, and fell asleep. Max arrived sometime after midnight. The last time I'd looked at the clock it read 12:25 a.m. I shut my eyes and didn't wake until the next morning.

The first year of my marriage to Max was difficult, as most first years are. Even though I had known his family for four years now, adjusting to them as part of my family took some getting used to. The Edwards family was not warm and fuzzy. They didn't welcome me with open arms.

My family is Italian on my father's side and Scotch on my mother's. We hug and kiss hello. We hug and kiss goodbye. I didn't see anything like that going on with my new family. On the rare occasion that I did witness some form of minimal affection, it came in the form of a hug. An "air" hug. An air hug, while being patted on the back—the worst! The air between you clearly says, *I don't really want to hug you.* The patting on the back during the hug says, *Okay, that's enough, go away now.* I had read about prudish people like this, but thought they only existed in Victorian novels. Was I now part of a cold, unfamiliar novel, or worse, a family?

### *Buying Our First Home*

It was **1987**. Max and I had been married one year, and my apartment lease was about to be up. We started looking for a house. Purchasing a home for fifty thousand dollars seemed like a figure that was well within our means.

Everything we looked at needed so much work. Perhaps we needed to get out of our comfort zone and look for a home with a higher price tag. The only home even worth considering was around seventy-five thousand dollars. Every house we looked at, I could see potential in, but Max couldn't. Max thought it important to let his parents see every house we were considering. They hated them all.

Feeling defeated, I suggested to Max, "The next time you want to look at houses, take your parents and I'll stay home. I'm tired of being disappointed. It's their opinions that matter most anyway, not mine!"

There was a home for sale down the street from my in-laws. Irene really wanted us to look at it. I didn't want to go, but Max insisted we all go see the house together. Irene loved it. Max and I liked it, but, more importantly, we liked the neighborhood it was in. The house was located in a slightly older part of town, thought to be a prestigious location at one time. Wallpaper needed to be updated and painting needed to be done, but nothing more really needed our attention right away. It was a well-built house that could be really beautiful with little effort.

One of the ladies I worked with at the bank knew my husband and I were looking for a house. She told me she was getting a divorce, and she asked if I wanted to see her home before she put it on the market.

"I'd love to see it!" I said. "The house is located in the same neighborhood Max and I were hoping to live in. But my in-laws would really be making the final purchase decision. I'm pretty sure they're lending us part of the down payment."

She let me come over for a sneak peek. It was exactly what we were looking for, and it was a couple blocks away from my in-laws instead of down the street. That alone made the house more appealing. I decided to take matters into my own hands.

I drove over to the funeral home and asked Irene if I could speak to her for a moment. We went down the hall and into the kitchen. "There's a really wonderful house a couple blocks away from you," I said. "I really want this house. If you don't agree to it, I won't be able to have it. I don't think it's fair that you get to make the final decision on my home." Irene asked which house it was. She agreed that it was a nice home and, after all, it was in the right neighborhood. Irene would agree to it so Max and I could finally purchase our first home.

Even though Irene could be quick to criticize, she hated confrontation. And this conversation was considered confrontational from where Irene stood.

Max had saved twenty-five thousand dollars for the down payment. His parents lent us thirty thousand dollars in order to keep the mortgage payment low. Max wanted to apply for the mortgage and put it in his own name. Max's parents explained to Max that he had never established credit. Everything Max owned had been paid for with cash. "Beth has credit, and it will be her credit that gets you the mortgage," they said.

Emotionally wounded, I said, "I can't believe you don't want me on the mortgage."

“Well, it’s my money that’s paying for this house, why should your name be on it?” Max said.

“Oh, maybe it’s because I’m your wife!” I said.

The lender agreed that both of our names should be on the mortgage and the title to the house.

We lived there for eighteen years. Zack was raised there. We all loved the house and the memories we made there. When we moved, it was like leaving an old friend. I cried when I locked the door behind me for the last time.

### *The Adoption of My Son*

My ex-husband had been out of the picture since my son Zack was 2-years-old. In **1988**, he arrived back in town and called me at the bank to say he wanted to see his son. I was in shock. We hadn't heard from this man in years, nor did I receive child support payments, so why now? "I have the right to see my son," he said. "I know I've been away a long time, but I'm back and I want a relationship with Zack."

"You want a relationship?" I asked. "You haven't seen him in years. Zack doesn't know you anymore. And isn't there a warrant out for your arrest, for non-payment of child support?"

"Beth," he said, "talking to you has been real, and it's been fun, but it hasn't been real fun!" *Click.* He hung up on me.

I immediately called Max to let him know Zack's father was back in town.

And I called the Friend of the Court to inform them that Mr. Tragedy, my ex-husband, recently arrived back in town. They had already received a call, and a child support payment had been made. I was told I would be receiving a check in the mail soon, along with a scheduled date to discuss payment and visiting options.

"What visiting options?" I asked in total disbelief.

"How is it possible a man can drop off the face of the earth for five years without one word as to his whereabouts, or one dollar paid to support his son?

Now all is forgiven because he stopped by and made one child support payment? My son doesn't know this man; he was only 2-years-old when he left. I cannot, in good conscience, give my son to his father for a visit—his father is a stranger—regardless of what the legal consequences might be."

"Mrs. Edwards," the court representative said nicely, "we recognize it's been a long time since your son has visited his father. We would not want to subject your son to being with someone unfamiliar to him. Our suggestion is to go slowly. Your ex-husband should first send a card or two in the mail. Then follow up with a letter, a few phone calls, and, finally, a monitored visitation can be scheduled. You have nothing to worry about."

At least once a week, Mr. Tragedy called asking to see Zack. "You haven't sent your first card to him, as instructed by the court, and you think you have the right to see him?" I said, amazed at his ignorance. "You seem to think rules don't apply to you. That is why your life is the way it is."

Like a mockingbird, he said, "That is why your life is the way it is." *Click.* He hung up on me again.

*What an idiot!* I thought, as I put the receiver down. Instead of giving me a responsible adult answer, it was easier for him to be irresponsible and say something meaningless before he hung up on me. I'm sure he felt empowered by his childish ways. Some people never grow up, or accept responsibility. I found him sad and ignorant.

When Max came home that evening, I explained what I was being forced to deal with now that Mr. Tragedy was back. "What if I adopt Zack?" Max asked.

Zack and I were excited with the thought.

"We'll all have the same last name!" Zack said.

The balance owed in child support was around thirteen thousand dollars. I called my ex-husband and said, "If you allow me full custody and give permission to Max for the adoption of Zack, you will be forgiven all past child support owed. And, in time, as Zack gets a little older, I will allow you to see him, under supervision, until he gets to know you."

He said, "Okay!"

The adoption took place in **1989.** Zack was 7-years-old and his new name was Zack Edwards.

"Mom, I'm going to call Max 'Dad,'" Zack whispered to me in the kitchen.

"Okay," I said. "He is your dad now."

Zack walked into the living room, "Hi, Dad," he said nervously.

"Hi, Son," Max responded with sarcasm. "You don't need to call me Dad. It doesn't feel right. Just call me Max."

"Okay," Zack said. He came into the kitchen with tears in his eyes.

I reached deep inside my heart for comforting words. "It's okay," I said. "Maybe Max wants to be your friend instead of your father. That could be a good thing, right? You could become really good buddies!"

I did what I could to encourage a father-son relationship, but I soon came to realize that Max didn't really like Zack and wasn't interested in being a father. He only adopted him to keep my ex-husband away.

To Max's credit, soon after the adoption, he did take Zack on a father and son canoe trip with men from church. However, Max was embarrassed to see Zack at another family's picnic table having something to eat. Max hadn't cooked their food yet. Instead of pointing out to Zack that he should wait until the food they'd brought was cooked, Max got mad. Max didn't understand that children have to be taught. You can't expect a child to know something because you think they should. Zack was used to being at family gatherings. Everyone ate, without rules as to whose food you could and couldn't eat. Had Max explained this, he could have avoided his embarrassment. But really, do you think any parent would deny another child a hot dog or cookie? Really?

Over the years, other attempts were made—a couple of outings with Max and Zack alone, but mostly with the three of us. At the end of the day, Max was angry and impatient with Zack. I continued to hope for the best in a hopeless situation.

### *Mother-in-law and Furniture*

Max wouldn't allow me access to his savings account for seven years. When he wanted a new car, Max would simply pull the money out of his savings and purchase one. I took out a loan for my new car. Max paid the household bills. I paid for the groceries, decorating, and all expenses—day care, clothing, and dental—for my son and myself. This meant I was always in debt.

I wanted to quit working after Max and I got married, but Max told me he had to work, therefore, I had to work. It didn't seem to matter that I had a young son who could have benefited from having his mother at home.

A couple years into the marriage, my mother-in-law said she wanted to purchase some new living room furniture for Max and me. She had recently purchased some for her daughter Gladys, and Irene liked to keep her spending equal between her two children.

I found some contemporary furniture at Ester-Lynn's Furniture Store. I couldn't wait to bring my mother-in-law to the store and show her what I had selected. In my mind, I had it all displayed in my newly painted living room. All I'd have to save for was a new area rug. It would be so beautiful!

Outside, the sun was shining. Irene and I had a nice drive to the furniture store. It was a beautiful spring day. Irene parked the car, and we walked in. "There it is," I said with excitement.

"Oh," Irene said. She wasn't impressed. "Let's look over here at the Twinker Furniture. It's so lovely and rich looking."

"It's nice," I said, "but really not my style. Look at the taupe and black large plaid print on the armless chairs I've picked out. They go perfectly with the black leather sofa Max wants."

"No, that will go out of style really quickly, trust me," Irene said.

I was not up for an argument and stood silent while Irene pleaded her case. She went on and on about how traditional furniture is so wonderful and it never goes out of style. It's something we will have forever! *Gee, lucky me!* I thought. *Maybe the house will burn down and then I can purchase the furniture I want.*

"Irene, this is far too generous. Max and I really should purchase our own furniture."

"I have a wonderful idea," Irene said. "I'll purchase your coffee table, end tables, and entertainment center. I'll even combine an early birthday and Christmas gift by purchasing your dining room table and chairs. That way all your Twinker Furniture will match."

Clearly, this was not up for discussion. Irene was going to get what she wanted, whether I liked it or not.

### *Whose Family Is More Important?*

As time went on, things seemed to be working out for Max and me. The only stress I had was with my mother-in-law during the holidays. She wanted Max and me to spend every one of them with her family. This was unfair, as I had a family that only saw me on holidays. Max's family lived locally. He saw his parents every day at work, and his relatives often stopped by the funeral home to visit. None of this mattered much to Irene. She wanted her children on the holidays, and we were expected to be there. Sometimes, much to Irene's dismay, I would go to be with my family on holidays. Often I'd go around 5:00 p.m.; traffic was minimal at that time, and it was still daylight out.

Irene would ask, "How long will you be there?"

"Until 9:00 or 10:00 p.m.," I'd reply.

"Really?" she'd say. "Why not leave there at 7:00, and then you can be here with us at 8:00?"

"No. I only get to see my family once in a while and some of them only once a year. I'm not going to drive all that way, visit for a couple hours, and come back here. You see Zack and me all the time."

"You could leave there at 8:00 and be here at 9:00," she'd say.

"No," I'd reply, "that's not enough time."

"Well, what about 8:30?" she'd ask.

"I'll see what I can do," I said, realizing this woman was never going to let it go.

"Okay," she said, "we'll look forward to seeing you at 8:30!"

Every year I was given the same request, and every year I gave the same response. It was unfair and unrealistic to think I would take my son to my family's, hurry up and eat, then leave, just to make my mother-in-law, someone I saw weekly and sometimes daily, happy.

If it were only Zack and me going to visit my family, we'd stay until ten o'clock and then drive home and go to bed. Max, of course, would be at his parents'. He rarely came with me. He would claim he had to work. The excuse was frequent and annoying. When Max did come with me, he continually looked at his watch. After an hour or so he'd whisper, "Can we leave yet?"

If Max had a function for his side of the family, Irene always made sure the funeral job was covered so that Max and I could attend. Funny, it was important for his family to see us together, but not mine. If there was an event for my family, it was like pulling teeth to get Max to go. Didn't he like my family? He seemed to like them. My family was nice and made everyone feel welcome. *What's not to like?* I thought.

I do remember Max saying, "Your family all look alike—dark hair and dark eyes. I can't tell one cousin from the other." *What an ignorant thing to say,* I thought. *What are we, monkeys?*

My family eventually moved away, which made it easier to attend all the gatherings at my in-laws'. Irene and her sister took turns hosting the holidays. Irene called me when it was her turn. She'd ask me to help out before everyone arrived, setting up vegetable or fruit trays, cheese and cracker platters, or anything else she needed done.

Without fail, I was there, the ever-reliable, obedient daughter-in-law. I often wondered why it was me she always asked to help. She did have a daughter, Gladys. Gladys lived on a farm out of state, but attended every holiday as her mother requested. She could have come early or arrived the night before to help her mother, but she didn't.

Gladys's husband, Daryl, was talked to poorly by Irene, so he took pleasure in making sure things never went the way Irene had planned. I use to think Daryl was being childish and difficult. I later came to realize he was giving her exactly what she deserved. He was letting her know she was not going to control or push him around.

Gladys was two years older than Max and the apple of her mother's eye. She was naturally blond and had a small frame like her mother. When Gladys came home for the holidays, she'd wear her mother's clothes, which made her look frumpy instead of stylish. The clothes were far too old for her. Money was tight for Gladys, and she looked at her mother's clothing as something desirable to wear.

Gladys wasn't considered an attractive girl. She looked a lot like her father, especially in the teeth and gum area. She wore little make-up, and her skin was weathered beyond her years. She spent lots of time in the sun—not to get a tan, but to do things she loved, like planting a garden or riding her horse.

There was something sad about Gladys. She was a nice girl, but appeared emotionally frail. Did being raised around the funeral home have something to do with it?

When Gladys graduated from college, she moved away from home and rented a small house on a farm where she could own and keep a horse. She loved the outdoors and the simple life of farming, so it was no surprise that she married Daryl, a country boy.

Daryl was a farmer, from a family of farmers. He seemed to be the perfect match for Gladys. But Irene never liked him. He wasn't good enough for her daughter. This was a shame because Daryl's life fit Gladys's lifestyle perfectly. Maybe Irene didn't like him because he was as controlling as she was. Daryl liked to talk almost incessantly, and often he could be annoying trying to prove his point. Everyone has things about themselves others don't like, but this was Gladys's husband and she loved him, so Irene should have kept her mouth shut and put up with him for her daughter's sake. Isn't that what any loving mother would do?

Daryl wasn't aware that his wife called her mother almost daily to complain about him. Instead of Irene persuading her daughter to think better of her husband, the father of Irene's grandchildren, Irene took pleasure in complaining about Daryl right along with her daughter. I've often wondered how much complaining she did about me behind my back. It seemed Irene only wanted to destroy her daughter's marriage, instead of advising her on ways to remedy whatever the daily complaint was.

Daryl had high blood pressure. Irene and her daughter would joke about adding salt to his food and maybe he'd have a stroke and fall over dead. I didn't find that funny. It puzzled me how Irene and her daughter could talk this way and call themselves Christians. Did they learn that at church?

At one time, I felt Irene confided in me, telling me this terrible joke because she liked me. Maybe she wanted to be my friend? Years later, I found out that she not only didn't want to be my friend, but also that she drove in the wedge that destroyed my marriage. Christian, my fanny! I love and admire Jesus, but I've come to realize I don't like most people who call themselves Christians.

Irene complained about Daryl even before he married her daughter. Irene was upset that he was wearing cowboy boots to the wedding. Gladys didn't care as long as they were new. Irene took weeks finding the perfect outfit to wear to the ceremony.

When the minister said, "If anyone have just cause as to why these two should not be joined together, let him speak now or forever hold his peace," that is the point Irene Edwards should have stood up and said her peace, not only during her daughter's marriage, but also at her son's marriage to me six years earlier.

### *The Family Business*

Family-run funeral homes take over the lives of the families who run them. I could see myself working at Max's side. It would allow me to see him more, and that sounded good to me. But when I asked Max, he said, "No."

The funeral home was a member of a statewide funeral directors association. The association helped keep the information flowing between funeral homes and local government. It also helped to provide group health insurance and legal assistance related to the funeral business.

Each year, The Association of Funeral Directors (TAFD) held a convention in late summer. The person hired to do the seminars during the conference was meant to motivate, inspire, and educate the funeral directors. The directors could see new products: make-up, chemicals and fluids, equipment, caskets, vehicles such as limousines and hearses, etc. My first funeral convention was interesting, to say the least. TAFD also held a mid-winter conference every year, somewhere sunny and warm. Max and I went every year for many years. We traveled to several islands over the years for conferences and went on a couple of cruises, too. We looked forward to traveling to someplace tropical in the winter. It made the winter seem so much shorter. I'd never really traveled before I married Max. Doing it this way meant we only had to pay for half of the trip; Max's business paid for his half, since these conventions were considered a business expense. Max's parents paid my half, too—or did they take it out of his bonus?

One of the many benefits of traveling with TAFD was the ability to share stories with other funeral directors and their wives and learn how they successfully ran their businesses.

Every day at the pool, or in the evening at dinner, we'd sit and talk about the funeral business, its employees, and how to run a better company. Other topics of conversation were make-up tips and tricks and what brand of fluid to purchase to give the dead a more natural look. One of Max's tips was to add a lot of red dye to the embalming fluid because it gives the deceased a pink color instead of pasty gray and, therefore, less make-up is required.

Too much make-up had been a pet peeve of mine. I couldn't stomach looking at a body with too much make-up on it. It's nauseating! I suggested to Max that he not put powder in the ears, in the creases next to the nose, or around the fingernails. These areas were the first to get caked up, making the deceased creepy looking. *No one want's to look at that!* Fortunately, Max listened, and the bodies he presented were better than any other funeral home in our area. Max's business was considered the best because of their attention to the families, and now it was for their presentation of the deceased as well.

Max was given minimal time off. I couldn't understand this after talking to other funeral home directors who did the same amount of business with the same amount of full-time help. These funeral homes did, however, call upon other companies to make the nightly removals and hired part-time retired gentlemen to park cars before a funeral, or tend door in the evening.

I often wondered why Max's business couldn't run as smoothly as the funeral homes of some of the other owners I had talked with. Perhaps it was a trust issue.

Max's parents didn't want just anyone working in their business. I watched many secretaries leave over the years. As soon as the Edwardses would get one trained, she'd quit, often as a result of a conflict with Irene. Irene was a difficult woman to work for. She went through secretaries like I go through chewing gum. She'd chew them up and spit them out. This I'd learn firsthand. There was only so much Irene would let them do, and what they did do was seldom to Irene's liking.

Max came home and complained every day about his mother, father, or one of thcir employees. His mother was hard on everyone, including Max. Max took pleasure in lawn care and landscaping the grounds of the business because it got him out of the office and away from Irene. Max's father appeared to be an easygoing man who truly loved his job and expected everyone else to love it, too.

In **1991**, Max finally agreed to let me work for him in the office because his mother had chased off yet another secretary.

I was looking forward to my new job. On my first day of work, Max showed me what to do in the office. "Max, this is going to be great!" I said.

When payday arrived, Irene asked, "Well, how much do I *have* to pay you?" The tone in her voice was harsh and condescending.

*What?* I thought.

I explained, "The job I left paid me nine dollars an hour, and it was my understanding I would be making the same wage."

"Fine!" she said.

I thought, *what the hell? Is that any way to welcome your daughter-in-law into the family business?* I wanted to quit right on the spot.

As I learned each new task to its fullest, I'd ask for more work to do. Irene was hesitant to increase my workload because it would decrease hers.

The job became depressing. Not because of the families of the deceased, but because I was an outsider who was trying to belong. I was treated like a secretary instead of a member of the family.

A large number of funeral services were for elderly people. Most of their families were pleasant to work with. Well, pleasant unless they were fighting about the estate; that was an entirely different story.

The absolute worst funerals for everyone, family and employees, were the ones for the young. The loss of a young life is unbearable for all concerned, even the members of the funeral home.

I'd met a sweet girl when I worked at the bank. Her name was Jamie, and she looked like Mia Farrow when she had just gotten her pixie haircut. Jamie was a single mom in search of the perfect man.

I was working in the bank drive-thru, which was a separate building from the actual bank, when I received a call from the receptionist. There was a long distance call from Jamie to me, and the receptionist wasn't sure what to do. I told her to accept it and transfer the call to me.

"Beth?" I heard a faint voice ask.

"Yes, Jamie, where are you?" I asked.

"I'm in Jamaica," she said. "I was dating this guy, and he took me on this trip. We got into a fight, and he flew home without me. I have no way to get home. I don't have long to talk. I need to know if I have enough money in my savings account to be wired to my hotel."

I checked her account; she had fifty dollars. Not enough to get her home. "I wish I had money I personally could send you, but I don't," I said.

"You're very sweet, Beth, but I have a friend I can call and borrow the money from," she said before hanging up.

Within months, Jamie was dating a really nice guy, Rob. She was so excited to finally have a man in her life that she could trust. Jamie and I would go to lunch periodically and catch up with the happenings in each of our lives. Before too long, Jamie and Rob got married and purchased a small home together. Shortly thereafter, she became pregnant and had another son. I'd never seen her so happy.

Two years later, Jamie came into the bank with half of her head shaved and stitched. A large, white gauze bandage was taped to keep the area clean. "What happened?" I asked.

"I had a brain tumor and had surgery," Jamie said. "The doctor said he thinks they got it all, but I'll have to get medical treatments anyway, as a precaution."

A year went by and the doctors told Jamie she had brain cancer and there was nothing more they could do for her. Jamie, being the strong woman she was, found an alternative method of treatment. The treatment was not FDA approved and could only be obtained from the man who made it. The treatment extended her life, but, unfortunately, did not save it.

Jamie was my friend and a mother of two young boys when she passed away from cancer during my employment at the funeral home. She died late in the evening, so her boys were already in bed. Max went on the removal. I couldn't imagine my friend being put into a body bag. Even though she had passed on, the thought of it suffocated me. I explained to Max how important it was to leave the impression that he was taking the deceased somewhere pleasant. Using a cot with sheets and a blanket instead of a body bag could provide a better experience for all who might be watching. "Close the eyes and leave the face exposed, as though you are taking the deceased to the hospital, instead of the funeral home," I said.

That evening, Max did as I suggested. Jamie was on the rollaway cot, all tucked in as though she were on her way to the hospital. Her oldest boy, Adam, age 11, was woken up by the talking and walked into the living room as Max was about to take Jamie's body out the front door. Adam ran back into his bedroom and came out with a teddy bear. He asked Max if he could give it to his mom to keep her company. Max said, "Sure! Let me help you with that." Max took the bear and placed it under the blanket with its head sticking out, just like Adam's mom. Jamie's husband and sister were in awe.

The next morning, they came to the funeral home to finalize funeral arrangements. Jamie had pre-planned her funeral months before, just in case. Jamie's sister explained to me that Jamie had been talking to her boys about being ill and letting them know she would be going to heaven soon. When the younger of the two boys, Danny, age 4, got up that morning, he asked, "Where's Mommy?"

Jamie's sister said, "Mommy's gone to heaven, sweetie."

In his dinosaur pajamas, Danny ran to the window, looked up to the sky, and started waving. His small voice said, "Good-bye...good-bye Mommy...good-bye."

I was overcome with sadness and could not compose myself. Jamie's sister and I cried together and gave one another a hug. Max never used a body bag or covered a face again while making a removal. I had given him a suggestion that showed compassion for another human life. I never felt so proud. Max and I were going to be a great team.

Months passed. The job was becoming boring. Irene wouldn't give me enough to do. One day, after finishing all that could be done, I set up my own pre-arrangement. I selected a beautiful cherry casket lined with champagne colored velvet. I requested that only champagne colored roses be displayed and if any others were sent, they were to be thrown away. The smell of mixed flower bouquets can be nauseating. Many days, I'd walked into the viewing room to set up family flowers and felt sickened by the smell. I wanted to spare my guests that. Not only would it smell better, it would also be visually stunning. A funeral to remember. And it could be the start of something big, like *Better Funeral Homes and Caskets.*

Max was busy during the day and was, in fact, working. Irene, on the other hand, acted like she had all this work to do, but she wouldn't part with any of it. Perhaps it was a control issue, or maybe she thought I was going to kick her out of her job. I couldn't understand why she didn't take advantage of my employment there and take some days off to enjoy life a little. Irene spent every day at the office, from 10:00 a.m. to 10:00 p.m. Thc only time off she took was to shop with her sister Lynn, and that was a rare occasion.

Irene was the older of the two, but she never went out into the sun so her skin was milky white. Her face was flawless, and she was complimented regularly on her beauty. Lynn appeared jealous of Irene's beauty, financial success, and the freedom Irene had to purchase anything she wanted. By the amount of complaining Lynn did, it seemed as though she felt Irene took her shopping as a means of showing off how wealthy she was.

Lynn lived in the country, on property left to her from their father's estate. Irene also inherited property out in the country—38 acres directly next to Lynn's. Lynn and her husband built their home and raised their family on this land. Irene never did anything with hers, except rent part of it to a farmer. She said it allowed the property to be registered as agricultural and, therefore, made the property taxes less expensive.

Rarely did I see Lynn smile. To me, she looked like she'd been given sour lemons most of her life. I never understood this because she was a beautiful woman, far more attractive than Irene, but walking around with her sour attitude never allowed anyone to see it. The two sisters loved one another, as all sisters do, but there were years of sibling rivalry between them, and everyone could see it and knew the two sisters were only pretending to be friends.

Working with Irene was getting to be irritating. She seemed to waste a lot of time at work. There were endless phone calls with her daughter, and she did a single bookkeeping task three different ways because having it in one file just wasn't enough for her. All of this was frustrating to watch.

In **1992**, my in-laws decided it was time to expand the business and make the building larger. Blue prints were drawn up, and the building project was fast underway. Before I knew it, paint and carpet samples had to be selected. I took it upon myself to help with decorating options and went to Mayville Lumber and Decorating Center and spoke to one of their decorators. “Of course we can help you with your remodeling project,” the decorator said. “I’ll put a board together for you with carpet samples, fabric swatches, paint, etc. I’ll call you in a few days, and you can pick it up.”

“Great,” I said. “I’m sure this will be a big help to my mother-in-law. Thank you so much. I’ll wait to hear from you.”

When I told Irene what I’d done, she looked at me as though I’d just taken my finger and poked her in the eye. “Beth, why would you think I’d want to use Mayville’s Decorating Center?” Irene asked.

“Because they are the only local decorating center,” I said. “You should want to use local people, so that when they need your services they will come to you.”

“My friend and I are doing the decorating. Thanks for your effort, but we have other ideas,” Irene explained.

Feeling wounded, I said, “I understand.”

I picked up the phone and called Mayville’s to tell them I would not need their services after all. The remodeling project went on without me. I refused to give my opinion on anything. Irene was becoming more and more aggravated with the pressure to get things done.

Irene was gazing out the window one afternoon, and said, “Look at those people. What do they have on? Beth, come over here and look.”

"That's not very nice," I said. "Those people pay your bills." *Why did she think it was alright to judge people? When did she become judgmental and critical of others? Was she always this way*? I thought.

"I want to quit working at the funeral home," I said to Max. When he asked why, I told him that the office didn't need two secretaries. If his mother were taking time off and truly utilizing me, I could see a reason to stay; however, I didn't have enough to do. I couldn't very well tell my husband that his mother was a bitch who wasted time talking about people as she gazed out the office window, or that she acted like she is part of the royal family, now could I? She was the queen of this castle, an ice queen, and I *really* didn't like her. But disliking my mother-in-law would get me nowhere. She was the mother of my husband, after all.

Max talked to his mother and suggested she start taking advantage of having me work there. She needed to take a couple days off each week. "Beth is capable of running the office when you're off," Max said.

The following week, Irene took Sunday and Wednesday off. After that, it was Wednesday off. Within a month's time, Irene started to whine, "I have to take tomorrow off and I don't have anything to do. I feel like I'm being forced to stay home."

Going to work depressed me. I was overcome with dread as soon as I walked through the doors of the funeral home. Max could see a change in me and offered to make an appointment with Dr. Kay, a consultant and grief counselor he referred some of the families to for grief counseling.

Max took me to see Dr. Kay once a week. I really liked the doctor, and he seemed to understand my problem.

He told me I had dysthymic disorder, which is brought on by being in a certain place, or around a particular person, resulting in instant depression. The funeral home and Irene were causing my depression. Dr. Kay said, "There's a simple solution: you have to quit."

"Can you please tell Max?" I asked. "I'm afraid he won't believe me."

Dr. Kay called Max into his office and explained my disorder. "In order to clear up the depression, your wife needs to quit," he said.

Max said, "No problem. Beth doesn't need to work at the funeral home." I was surprised by how supportive Max was.

On the ride home, Max said I didn't have to go back to work at the funeral home, so maybe I could go back to working at the bank.

What I really wanted to do was go back to school.

### *Back To School*

I had gotten a job working for a title company as a representative. I'd drive to different real estate offices, mortgage companies, and law offices to pick up or deliver title work.

In the fall of **1992**, I decided to sign up for cosmetology school. This was going against Max, who felt no money could be made with this career choice.

One night, while out to dinner at our favorite pub, Emerald's, Max asked, "Who's going to pay for this schooling?"

"I plan to continue working and go to school at night, part-time. I will pay for it myself," I said.

"I don't know why you ever left the bank," Max said. "You were there twelve years. They wanted to make you assistant vice president. You could have stayed there until you retired. *That* would have been a *great* career for you."

"Listen, Max," I said, "I quit working for the bank after they merged with another one. The last two years there were difficult. Twelve years was long enough to work at a job I didn't really enjoy anymore. And the only reason I was offered the assistant vice president position, on my last day, was to keep me from quitting. I was never offered a management position. Now, all of a sudden, someone realized they screwed up. I had plenty of banking knowledge and experience, and they were about to watch me walk right out the door.

I believe part of this unremarkable offer had to do with the fact that I became your wife. Little do you realize, you hold status in this tiny town of ours. You are well-respected, you're an active member of the Commerce of Business, and you have money. The bank looked at our relationship as good advertising, plus, they wanted your business accounts. There's really nothing more to say on the subject."

It was my first day of school. I had been there all of one hour when the school secretary came into the instruction room to tell me I had a phone call. My first day of school, and already I'm getting a call. I was so embarrassed. I am not one to push the rules, and the rules stated, "NO PHONE CALLS!"

Max, on the other end of the phone line, asked, "Where's Zack?"

"He's at his friend Justin's house," I said.

"No, he's not there," Max said. "And Justin's mother can't find Justin."

"I'm sure he'll show up," I said. "If Zack doesn't check in within an hour, then give me a call back."

An hour went by. Max called again. "Justin's mother found a note that said he was running away. She thinks Zack is with him. What should I do?"

"Contact the police. I am leaving school as soon as I can explain to my instructor what's going on." I hung up the phone. No sooner had I finished explaining when I received another phone call. This time it was Irene. She was upset.

"They found Zack on the expressway," Irene said whimpering.

“Is he okay?” I asked frantically.

Irene said in a loud moan, “I don’t know, I can’t talk right now.” *Click.* The phone went dead.

*Oh my God! Was my son found dead on the side of the road?* I hurried to the funeral home. Max’s car was gone. I ran into the building. Irene was sitting at the kitchen table with Lewis.

“Where’s Zack?” I asked.

“He’s at the police station,” Lewis said.

“Where’s Max?” I asked.

“He went to the gym to work out,” Irene said in tears. “And if you weren’t wasting time at cosmetology school, you might know where your son is!”

“Just because I didn’t raise my son like you, doesn’t mean I’m doing it wrong!” I said, then turned around and walked out the door. It was the first time I ever got “ugly” with her.

Upon my arrival at the police station, Zack came running to me. I was so angry with him. He explained that Justin was running away and he didn’t want him to be alone, so he went with him to keep him company. Zack wasn’t running away, he was going to watch out for his friend.

Even though Zack was being a noble friend, I grounded him for two weeks. Trying to teach children the difference between right and wrong is a lifelong job. Lord, help me!

Zack had another friend, Benny. The two of them together were a regular comedy act. I preferred Benny to Justin. Like all mothers, I could tell one bad seed from another. Benny was a good seed, and we can all guess what kind of seed Justin was.

Zack spent a lot of time at Benny's house. Benny's parents were great people and treated Zack like one of their own. I knew Zack was safe whenever he was there. The two boys were balls of energy. Some nights Zack came home from Benny's still raring to go. I'd be tired and want nothing more than to go to bed and get some sleep, and Zack would still be eager to entertain.

"ZACK," I yelled, "go be funny by yourself!"

All was silent, for five seconds.

"BA-HA-HA," Zack burst out laughing. "Go be funny by yourself...Mom!"

Yep, I actually said that.

### *Max Makes Zack Cry*

In the early months of **1993**, I asked Max if he'd like a child of his own. We were both 33-years-old, and I wanted to be a young parent, instead of waiting until I was 40-years-old to give birth. Max said he didn't want children. His parents were never there for him as a child; they were too busy with the business. He didn't want to raise his child that way.

Zack was 12-years-old and having difficulty in school. Max said he would help him with his homework. The two of them sat in the kitchen while I went into the living room to watch TV. Approximately fifteen minutes into it, I could hear Zack crying. I went into the kitchen and asked, "What is going on in here?"

Max said, "Go back into the living room and don't question me in front of Zack." I did as I was told. Max was right, parents should never argue about a child in front of the child, especially when one parent is a stepparent. Yes, Max adopted Zack, but he was still considered a stepparent; he would never get the respect without the title of dad.

Max was getting frustrated with Zack. I could hear the anger in his voice. Zack was still crying and telling Max to "Stop it!" I could take it no more and went into the kitchen to witness Max curling his pointer finger under his thumb and flicking Zack in the head!

I yelled, "WHAT ARE YOU DOING? YOU NEVER HIT SOMEONE IN THE HEAD!"

Max scolded me, "BETH, GET BACK IN THE LIVING ROOM AND WE'LL TALK ABOUT THIS LATER!" Again, I did as I was told, but I was not happy about it!

Later that evening, I waited to speak to Max. "What are you thinking, thumping Zack in the head like that?" I asked.

"My father used to do it to me all the time when I wasn't doing what I should have been," Max replied. "I see nothing wrong with this type of discipline."

"Well I do!" I said. "Paddle his butt if you have to, but never, ever hit him in the head again!"

Within weeks, Max made a large wooden paddle and then drilled holes into it for extra sting. Max only had to threaten Zack with it; he never used it on him, thank goodness!

The following summer we were going to a wedding together as a family. I was running late and told Max and Zack to get into the car. I stood in the kitchen, putting on my lipstick in front of a large mirror. The mirror was opposite the picture window in the kitchen, which overlooked our driveway. As I turned around and grabbed my purse off the table, I saw Max push Zack with such force that he fell against the car, then to the ground. Zack met me at the door as I was opening it to leave. "Max pushed me!" he sobbed.

"I DID NOT," Max said. I was surprised by Max's need to lie, so I didn't say anything. My own husband had just lied to me, right to my face. I know men lie. I expected more out of mine.

I never allowed Max to discipline Zack from that point on. I couldn't trust him to do it in a parental way. Max had no tolerance for Zack, or any child for that matter.

I started asking myself, *Who is this man I married? If I'd seen this side of him, I don't know if I would have allowed him to adopt my son.*

It was clear to me that some people are not made to deal with children, especially other people's children. I encouraged Zack to spend the night at his friends' homes and discouraged his friends from staying over at our house. Zack grew up thinking I didn't like his friends. Better he thought that, than telling him the real reason. In my heart, I still hoped that one day Max and Zack would bond as father and son.

Through the years, Max only used the paddle as a threat. I actually used the paddle twice on Zack in his early teens. Something about hormones makes pubescent boys become "smart mouths." I had to knock him down a few pegs—at least that's what I was told by other parents who had been going through the same thing with their own teenagers. Others easily give advice, but I'm the one who had to live with the guilt of my actions. The paddle and its use gave me heavy guilt, and the memory of it still does today. I was once told a phrase that I've never forgotten: "We grow old to be reminded of the mistakes we made in our youth." There are other reasons to grow old: to teach, to learn, to remember the good, the bad—and yes, our mistakes.

As Zack grew older, the three of us didn't feel like a family. We would try family therapy and marriage counseling without success. Max wasn't honest in our sessions. He would only portray the man he wanted you to think he was, not the real Max. How do you help someone who refuses to think they need help?

## *A.D.D.*

I've had Attention Deficit Disorder (A.D.D.) my entire life. Back when I was a girl, they didn't have any idea what was wrong with me. I daydreamed all the time. The teacher would give directions, and my mind would fly into the clouds to think of pretty things, nice things, happy things. I was plunged back into reality when my teacher concluded her directions and said, "Okay, I'll expect your papers at the end of class."

*What? What did I miss?* I would panic and would feel the blood rushing to my face. My chest was hot. I wanted to cry. I raised my hand. When the teacher looked at me, she would press her lips tight and scrunch her eyes, looking angry and mean. "Yes, Beth, what is it?"

Shy and embarrassed, I would ask, "What are we supposed to do?"

The answer was always the same: "I just stood here and explained to the entire class what was to be done, but, like always, you weren't paying attention. So just do your best. I'm not explaining it again."

Eventually, I was placed into Special Ed. That was a fate worse than death back in the 1960s. Handicap and retarded children were in Special Ed. *Am I retarded? I bet I'm retarded and no one wants to tell me.*

I remember asking my father if I was retarded. Of course, he said, "No." *Maybe he just didn't want me to feel bad,* I remember thinking.

Even though I hated people knowing I had to go to Special Ed, I really liked the class once I was there and the door was shut.

The teacher was one of the nicest teachers I ever had. She always repeated whatever I missed, and she treated us like a really nice mom would treat her children—with patience and kindness. At the end of class, she would pass a tray of treats around: sometimes cookies, sometimes candy, sometimes both. This made being retarded almost tolerable.

In **1994**, I was diagnosed with A.D.D. I was 34-years-old. My son Zack was having problems in school, and I didn't want him to struggle the way I had. Max and I had him tested and, sure enough, he was classic A.D.D. Once Zack was tested, he was sent to a neurologist to determine if he had a chemical imbalance or some other disorder. Zack had a chemical imbalance and was prescribed medication to help him. He received 10 mg of it before school each day. After two weeks, I called the doctor because Zack was coming home every day after school full of anger. He reminded me of a girl with PMS.

"You must change his medication," I said to the doctor. "I can't live with Zack and his anger every day."

The doctor suggested I double Zack's medication. "What? Why would I want to do that?" I asked.

"The medication isn't working correctly for Zack because the dose is too low," the doctor said. "Please trust me and double the medication. If you don't see better results in a day or two, please call me right away."

I did as I was told. Zack became an excellent student. The only notes that came home from school praised his newfound brilliance and cooperation.

This blissful existence lasted only three short months. Then Zack returned to his old self. I couldn't figure it out. I gave him his medication every morning before school. I watched him take it. Something was wrong here. I asked Max his thoughts. "I think Zack is putting his medication down the drain," Max said.

"No, I give it to him and watch him take it," I said.

"You gave Zack his pills this morning?" Max asked.

"Yes, I did, about fifteen minutes ago," I said.

Max said, "Follow me to the kitchen." He put his hand down the drain and came up with two melted blue pills.

"I don't believe it!" I said. "Why would he do this? He obviously works better on the medication. I'll have to talk to him about it after school. Thanks, Max, I'd never have guessed that. I'm too trusting."

When Zack came home from school, I asked him why he threw his pills into the sink. "I don't like how they make me feel," he said.

"How do they make you feel?" I asked. "Do they make you feel sleepy, dizzy, fuzzy, numb, tingly, lightheaded, sluggish, silly, or angry?"

"No, they make me feel happy and sad at the same time," Zack said.

*What the heck does that mean?* I thought. *What is this medication doing to my son?*

One day when Max and Zack were out of the house, I decided that I would try Zack's medication. I needed to know how it was affecting him.

We lived two blocks from the hospital—the same hospital where I had given birth to Zack. If I took the medication and had an allergic reaction, I could go outside and lie down on my lawn. Someone driving by would see me flopping around on the grass in an allergic fit, pick me up, and drive me the two blocks to the hospital. All would be well.

I took 10 mg of Zack's medication. I waited. In forty minutes, I started to feel the effects. It was like an awakening, a feeling of alertness, like I suddenly had access to a part of my brain I wasn't allowed to use because it required a special key. The key was the medication. I waited, expecting to feel heart flutters or pounding, or jittery feelings like caffeine, but none of that happened. I did have energy—not enough to run around the block—but energy that made me want to clean something, make something, or learn something. This must be the "happy" side.

I also noticed a calming, soothing side of the medication. This must be the "sad" side, although I didn't feel sad. It felt more like a push me, pull me effect. The happy side allows one to have the energy, desire, and ability to learn or accomplish something. The sad side allows one to focus without distraction.

I understood all that Zack was feeling. But what about his learning experience?

I picked up a book and read one page. I read it through once and understood every word I read—without having to re-read it over and over again!

I put the book down in awe. This was a miracle. I'd spent my entire life wondering how people could read because I thought everyone read like I did, with no comprehension.

I'd read things over and over until I understood. There was too much going on in my own head to focus on reading. Now, for the first time, this special pill allowed me to focus, shut out the extra noise, and absorb new information like a sponge. Wow! I almost felt cheated—this is how normal people have been reading for years. I didn't know. I have A.D.D!

At the time, I wasn't aware that all A.D.D students were not the same. I now realize there are differences. My son is much smarter than I am, with or without the medication.

When I take my medication, I function like a normal person (whatever normal is). I can read something once and understand what I have read. I have the ability to start and accomplish tasks. The medication is only 50% of the reality. You are still the other 50%. So if you are in art class and you love it, you will excel. Unfortunately, if you are in math or science class, both of which you dislike, you'll be able to learn it and pass the class, but you'll not excel because it's not your passion.

For the most part, I enjoy life more while on the medication. Why, you might be asking? Because it makes me think like a normal person should. I am a smart person who spent years thinking I was below average. Without the medication, my thought process is so slow, I actually am below average.

The medication isn't something that has to build up in your system for several days. When I take it, I feel the results within an hour. Once I stop taking the medication (which I do once in a while to give myself a break), I go back to my old self in about forty-eight hours. I was diagnosed and received my medication through Dr. Gerald, a neurologist. My family doctor can also prescribe it for me.

I've heard people talk about their husbands or sons, wives or daughters, being lazy. Think about this: who really wants to be lazy? It's not a choice. It's an imbalance in the makeup of that person. The person has to be given the resources to make the choice to be normal...or not. There are several medications you can try to find the right one for you. Ask your doctor.

### *Ohio*

The year **1994** was a tough one.

My sister Patty and her family moved to Georgia because her husband Jason got a job flying for Value Jet. I love my sister and her boys as though they were my very own. The move was hard on all of us.

Zack asked if he could go to Ohio. Max's sister Gladys and her husband Daryl lived on an old, rundown farm there. Their home was in such disrepair one might think it was about to collapse or be condemned. Gladys and Daryl were about to have their first child. Farm work was becoming hard on Gladys as the pregnancy progressed, and Irene thought Zack could help out her pregnant daughter. I sent Zack to the farm for two weeks.

He called after his two-week farm vacation and asked if he could stay. "Sure," I said. "How much longer do you want to stay, and is it okay with Gladys and Daryl?"

"I want to stay here and go to school," Zack said.

"What? No! You can't stay there and go to school," I said. "You need to come home."

"No, Mom, listen," Zack, said. "We all talked about it. They want me to stay, and I really like it here."

"No, Zack, I'd miss you terribly!" I said.

"Mom, please let me stay," Zack pleaded. "Here, talk to Gladys."

Gladys said that Zack had been a huge help around the farm. She thought it could be a really good experience for him. "What does your husband think about it?"

"Just a minute," she said, and then put Daryl on the phone.

"If you're willing," Daryl said, "we'd love to have Zack start school here."

I asked that they let me think about it and call them back. I was beside myself. Maybe Max could shed some light on this and help me make a decision. This phone call had thrown me for a loop.

Max and I discussed it. He felt it could be a great opportunity for Zack. "If Zack or you have a hard time with him being away, we can always bring him home," Max said.

I called Zack. "It's okay with me if you want to stay. If you change your mind, all you have to do is call me. Now let me speak to Daryl."

"Daryl, I'll come down and take Zack shopping and get him enrolled in school. If there are any questions, I'll be there to provide whatever is needed. I'll leave here tomorrow."

I drove to Ohio alone. Max didn't want to go. "This will be better for you and Zack once you get there," Max said. "It will allow the two of you a little time together before you drive back home."

It was the first day of school. Daryl, Gladys, Zack, and I piled into the car and headed off to enroll Zack in eighth grade at Dellsville Middle School.

We arrived early and were directed to the office. The school smelled like all others on the first day—pencil shavings and fresh paint.

I was told that my brother and sister-in-law would need temporary guardianship papers in order for me to enroll Zack in school. Legally, it *had* to be done this way or they couldn't enroll him. "I've got an uncle who's an attorney," Daryl said. "He could draw up the papers for us."

"No, that won't be necessary," I said. "I'll have them drafted at home and send them to the school." The school secretary suggested I fax them and mail the originals as soon as possible. Zack could start school that day; thcy would wait for thc papcrs.

I drove back home alone and cried most of the way. The next day I went to the local courthouse and had temporary custody papers drawn up with an expiration date of "unknown." I drove to the post office and sent the papers by overnight mail to Zack's new school, then went home.

When I pulled into my driveway, I could see my friend Becca sitting on her front porch. Becca lived across the street. She looked like she could have been the sister to Annette Bening. She had just gone through a divorce. Her husband and her best friend, the previous owner of my home, were having an affair. It devastated her. How do you survive losing the two people closest to you? Somehow, through the grace of God, she prevailed.

Becca's daughter, Jessica, was a small blond version of Becca and had personality plus. Jessica was a friend and classmate of Zack's. They began their friendship in kindergarten and remained friends for many years. I wanted to update both mother and daughter on what was going on with Zack this school year. I sat on the porch next to Becca and told her, start to finish, how and why Zack was going to school in Ohio.

"I already knew that," Becca said.

Surprised, I said "What? How could you know that—it only just happened?"

"Your mother-in-law told me two weeks ago," she said.

"Are you sure it was two weeks ago?" I asked. "I've only known about this for a few days."

"Yes, I'm sure of it," Becca said. "I had a funeral to attend, and I stopped in the office to say hello to Irene. She told me all about it."

"What exactly did my mother-in-law say?" I asked, puzzled.

"She told me this would be a great help to her daughter because she is pregnant and having a hard time doing farm work," Becca explained. "Gladys's husband is insistent that she help out on the farm; he doesn't seem to realize Gladys's limitations due to her pregnancy. Irene thought this was a great idea, something that she and her daughter had been talking about since Zack arrived for his two week vacation."

"DO THEY THINK HE IS A HIRED HAND, OR SLAVE LABOR?" I blurted out.

"Irene also said she thought this would be good for you and Max, too," Becca said.

I was stunned. I felt sick—betrayed by my in-laws and possibly my own husband. Why would Irene and her daughter go behind my back and discuss my son without my knowledge? Plan this without my input? Did Max know about this? Was he in on it, too? Becca had no idea.

Zack called me every Sunday. Some weeks I couldn't wait until Sunday, so I'd call him before then. It was always so good to talk to him. He really enjoyed his new school and his new friends, and he liked working with Daryl, too. "Daryl is like a big kid," Zack said. "But I don't like that he won't allow me to spend time with my friends after school. I can't spend the night at anyone's house on the weekend either." Zack felt Gladys and Daryl were strict and didn't allow for any free time with friends unless they were there. Unless a cookout, birthday party, or gathering was being held, Zack was forced to have only one friend—Daryl.

"I'm sure they're only protecting you," I said. "You are not their child, so they are probably even more cautious about keeping you safe."

Zack and I didn't visit until Thanksgiving. Both of us needed time to adjust. I couldn't wait for him to come home for the holiday.

I asked Zack, "Are you happy there? Do you still want to stay with them?"

"Yes, I want to stay," he said. "It isn't as much fun as I'd hoped it was going to be. I really like the kids at my new school, but I can only see them at school. When I come home, Gladys makes me study, but Daryl lets me stay up late. We have ice cream every night while we watch Jay Leno."

"That sounds interesting," I said. "So Daryl is your buddy?"

"He's like a big kid, Mom. Sometimes I think he's my age," Zack said.

After the Thanksgiving holiday was over, Zack went back to Ohio with Daryl and Gladys.

Sometime before Christmas, I received legal papers in the mail from my brother-in-law's uncle. They were custody papers! I was confused and skeptical as I thumbed through the documents. *Why did he send me custody papers?* I asked myself.

I called Max. "I just got custody papers in the mail. They don't say temporary custody, they say *custody!* I don't want to sign them."

"Just sign them," Max said. "I'm sure it's fine."

"But Max, I don't feel right about this," I said. "It looks like this is for permanent custody of Zack."

"No one is going to steal your son," Max said. "If you want him back home, I'm sure they'll let him come home."

I called Daryl and asked why I received the custody papers. Daryl said, "If Zack wants to play sports, we need to have legal custody, just in case anything happens to him." I wasn't satisfied with his answer. Zack was only in eighth grade, and he had never expressed an interest in wanting to play sports. This situation was making me more nervous with every passing minute.

I called the courthouse and asked to speak to the judge who ruled over children's welfare cases. Surprisingly, I was connected. I explained my situation as quickly and briefly as possible. The judge told me *not* to sign the papers. If I signed the papers, it would mean losing custody of my son. Once I did that, I'd be giving up all rights and may not get them back. "Are you willing to do that?" the judge asked.

"No!" I said.

"I have to end this call. Having this conversation could be a conflict of interest if this ends up on my desk," the judge said.

I thanked the judge and hung up the phone. I called my son and told him I was coming to get him.

"Mom, could you please wait until Christmas break to move me back home?" Zack pleaded. "I'd like to have the chance to say goodbye to my friends and get their addresses."

After debating this with him, I gave in. "Okay, it's only a couple weeks away. I'll wait."

I never found out why Daryl and Gladys were really seeking custody. But I've always been grateful to the judge who helped me with her wise advice.

Becca said, "Women like Irene are only interested in keeping *their* family happy. She probably thought she was helping her daughter by sending Zack to help, and she must have thought she was helping Max by getting rid of Zack. This would take some stress out of your marriage, which would make Max easier to deal with at work."

That's what I love about Becca, she's the eternal optimist. I wish I could have been as positive.

### *A New Year*

It was a new year, **1995**, and I was happy to have my son back home where he belonged.

Max was stressed, so Zack and I were careful not to upset him. This was difficult, because Max seemed to get upset by everything and nothing. If he couldn't control a situation, or a person, he became angry very quickly.

"Mom," Zack said, "I'm afraid Max is going to blow up any minute and kill us."

"Don't be ridiculous," I said.

"Mom, you can't tell me you don't see the same anger in him that I do."

"Yes, I see the anger, but Max is stressed," I said.

"What is he stressed about?" Zack asked.

"I think Max is overworked," I said. "A person can't be treated like a robot and expected to operate twenty-four hours a day. Eventually, the person, like the robot, breaks down. Does that make sense to you?"

"Yes. But how do you get him to be nice? He's so mean," Zack said.

"It's his job that's stressing him. I don't know what I can do. We just have to stay out of his way and hope he'll get through whatever is bothering him," I said.

As usual, Max came home tense. That evening, after Zack had gone to bed, I asked Max what the problem was.

Max said, "You have the luxury of going to work and coming home every day, knowing that no one is going to call you back to work. I come home every evening, waiting for the phone to ring."

"Maybe this is something you need to discuss with your parents," I suggested.

"You don't understand," Max, said. "Why don't you just go to bed?"

"What did I do?" I asked.

"You're being crabby, and I don't want to listen to it!" Max barked.

"Crabby? What did I say that was crabby? Or how did I say it to make you think it sounded crabby?" I asked.

"Just go to bed!" Max demanded. So I went to bed. I didn't want to add any more stress to his evening.

The days and weeks to follow were more of the same. Nothing I could do or say helped. Max had Zack and me walking on eggshells. No matter what either of us said, Max heard it differently. We were afraid to speak.

The situation wasn't getting better, so I went to the funeral home to talk to Max's parents. "Do you both have a minute? I need to talk to you," I said.

"Yes, come and sit down in the office," Lewis said.

"I don't know if you've noticed, but Max has been extremely tense. My concern is that he's working too much," I said.

"Working too much? We try to let him go home every evening, while we stay here," Irene said.

"When I was Max's age, we ran an ambulance service and the funeral home," Lewis chimed in. "I worked many more hours than Max does now."

I could see I wasn't getting any sympathy. "Everyone is not capable of the same workload. You could handle all the work you were given, but I can see this is becoming difficult for Max," I said, directing my words at Lewis.

"What do you want us to do?" Irene whimpered.

"Can't you get more help?" I asked. "Put an ad in the paper, or contact a mortuary school?"

"Oh, we can't do that," Irene said. "If someone applied and we didn't give them the job, they could be upset and say bad things about us, or not use our services."

"Okay, I can understand how you might think that," I said. "I'm really not sure what kind of help Max needs. Is it another funeral director, or is it a couple of retired men to take over the nighttime removals? What about someone from church? Couldn't you put the word out or a note on the church bulletin board?"

"Yes, we've hired retired men in the past. We probably should look into doing it again," Irene said.

Many weeks went by. It was June now, and there'd been no follow-through with my suggestions. I couldn't take it anymore. No one seemed to want my advice. I didn't know how to help.

"Max," I said, "Can you hire someone, or does it have to go through your parents?"

"I'm not hiring anyone! If I hire someone, that's less money I get at the end of the year in my bonus," he growled at me.

"Don't you think it would be worth it to relieve some of your workload?" I asked.

"I make almost $80,000 a year. I don't want to give that up," Max said.

"I don't know what to tell you then, but living with you like this is becoming more than I can take," I said.

I needed a break. I called my sister Patty. "Patty, I'm thinking about bringing Zack to Georgia for a visit. Are you up for company?"

"Of course I am. I can't wait for you to see the new house. Is Max coming too?"

"No, just Zack and me," I said. "I'm going to see how soon I can get a flight, and I'll let you know what I find out."

"I'll let my boys know you're coming. I love you. Talk to you soon," she said before hanging up.

I let Max know Zack and I were going to Georgia to visit my sister for a week. My brother David also lived in Georgia, forty minutes away from Patty, on the other side of Atlanta. Zack and I would be taking a second week to stay with him. We were leaving in three days.

"I'll make sure the house is extra clean, and I can prepare some meals and put them in the freezer for you," I said.

"Don't go out of your way to cook for me, but if you'd like to make a meatloaf before you go, I'd really appreciate it," Max said and smiled. Meatloaf was Max's favorite. Every time I asked him what he wanted for dinner, the response was always the same—meatloaf. I hate meatloaf!

I spent the next two days making sure everything was perfect before I left. I changed the sheets, mopped the floors, scrubbed the bathrooms, and dusted everything in sight. Not only did I make a full dinner of meatloaf, mashed potatoes, and steamed green beans, but I also made a second meatloaf and put it in the freezer with a huge smiley face on it for Max.

I love to travel and so does Zack. He was usually left home with Irene and Lewis anytime Max and I went away. Zack hated staying with them, but I was grateful they offered to look after him. This time, it was just my son and me. It was rare that just the two of us travelled, so this trip felt extra special.

On our plane ride to Atlanta, I asked Zack if he would think about going to a Catholic all-boys' school. He could live there during the week and come home every weekend. If he became sick, the school was only forty minutes away, so I would be able to pick him up and bring him home. "This will keep you away from Max until things change," I said.

"Things change?" Zack asked.

"Yes, things," I said. "I'm not sure what I'm going to do, but you and I can't continue living in the current situation. Either Max gets help at work, or I don't know what I'm going to do."

"Can I think about it?" Zack asked.

"Of course," I said. "We can talk more about it when we go home."

The flight was less than two hours. Patty and her eldest child, 11-year-old Josh, greeted us at the airport.

Patty looked worn-out, and Josh had grown a foot taller since I last saw him. "Where are the twins, Ayden and Allen?" I asked.

"They're over at a friend's house playing. It was better to leave two 7-year-olds, than to drag them to the airport. We can pick them up on the golf cart when we get back," Patty said.

"You guys have a golf cart?" Zack asked. "Cool! Can I drive it?"

"No," I said. "We'll leave the driving to Aunt Patty."

Patty lived in Peachtree City. It was new, clean, and charming. Rows of trees lined the median and flowers seemed to be planted everywhere. It was visually the ideal place to live: sunny, pretty, and refreshing. Patty's neighborhood was built with airline pilots in mind. It was a planned community. There were golf cart paths behind all the houses, and the paths led to the grocery store, restaurant, video rental store, ice cream parlor, clothing stores, and several other places. It looked like a fun place to live.

We pulled into Patty's driveway. Patty gave Zack and me a quick tour of the house before we hopped into the golf cart. Away we went. The cart paths were shaded with large trees, and the air underneath them felt cool as we rode along. Zack and I both wished we lived there.

A couple days into the trip, Patty said she had a doctor's appointment and asked if I wanted to go with her. "Sure, I'd love to go anywhere you go," I said.

When we got into the car, Patty started to cry. "What's the matter?" I asked.

"I don't know. I've been so depressed. That's why I'm going to the doctor. I'm hoping he can give me something to make me feel better," she said. "The move from Silver Plank Road in Michigan, away from all my family, getting an apartment, waiting for the house to be done, and tending to all the details has been hard on me. Jason's no help, so it's all been on my shoulders."

"You need a break like I do," I said. "That's why I came to visit you. Max has become more than difficult to live with. Zack and I feel like we're walking on eggshells all the time. The littlest nothing sets Max off. I've offered suggestions, but they fall on deaf ears. When I go home, I'm filing for divorce. The current living situation is not fair to me, and it certainly is not fair to Zack. Max acts like he hates him. I can't allow this to continue. Zack deserves better, and so do I."

"I'm sorry to hear that, Beth. You've been through so much in your life already. It's sad to think you're getting another divorce, but I know you're strong and you'll be okay," she said. "Maybe you can move down here to Georgia."

"Wouldn't that be nice?" I said. "I can't plan too far ahead right now. We'll see what happens."

I waited in the reception area while Patty was in with her doctor. When she came out, she looked a little better and had a prescription in hand. "What did the doctor say?" I asked as we walked to the car.

"He said, from what I described, I have depression, and he gave me a prescription for Palixpam. It's an anti-depressant. The doctor said it takes time to build up in my system, so I should start to feel better in a week or two, depending."

"You'll have to tell me how it makes you feel," I said. "I've wondered about anti-depressants and what they do. Will they make you feel silly and giddy? Will you feel filled with happiness and want to dance? Hey, maybe you'll feel like you just smoked a joint!" We both laughed. Patty put her thumb and pointer finger together, as though she were holding something tiny. She then put her fingers to her lips, closed one eye, and pretended to take in the smoke from an imaginary marijuana joint. She took in a deep, long drag, pretended to hand it to me, and, while holding her breath, said, "'ere." We laughed so hard, we almost wet our pants. Ah, the good old days!

"Patty, you're my sister and best friend. We may not live in the same state anymore, but you know I'm always only a phone call away," I said. "And if you ever need me, I'm just a plane ride away. I'll always be here for you. Never forget that."

"I know," Patty said. "I wish I could take one of these pills and start to feel better today."

"Let's stop and fill the prescription, then drive-thru someplace for lunch," I said. "You can take your first pill now. The sooner you take it, the sooner you'll feel better."

The day Zack and I left for David's, Patty said, "I feel a tiny bit better today."

"A tiny bit is better than nothing at all," I said.

Visiting with David was relaxing, as always. He has a wonderful sense of humor and knows how to put everything into perspective. We talked about Patty and then talked about Max. David was sorry to hear about both.

My two-week vacation with Zack was over, and it was time to go home.

The first night at home was difficult. I didn't want to be there. I asked Max if I could talk to him before he went to sleep. "Max, I've made a decision while I was away. I'm going to file for divorce."

He didn't say anything, and we fell asleep.

Max had a way of letting things pile up on the dresser, if I wasn't around to clean up after him. As I organized, I found a handwritten letter from Max to me. He must have written it while I was away. He had used two different ink pens. Corrections were made, words were crossed out and re-written. It appeared that Max had the same idea as I did: he, too, wanted a divorce.

Almost a week had gone by, and Max was not his usual angry self. He was happy? I hadn't seen him this way in a long time. It was unnerving. Had I made him miserable all this time and not his job? Was the anticipation of our divorce shedding a ray of light and happiness over him?

I made an appointment with Mr. O'Brian, the attorney I'd hired for my first divorce, and went to see him.

"Beth, I've known you for some time now, and I know Max. He's a good man," Mr. O'Brian said.

"Yes, everyone says that about Max. But people don't know him the same way my son and I do. Max is not a very nice person, and he's less than nice where my son is concerned," I said.

"That may be, but think about it, Beth. Do you really want to go through this again? Give this more thought, and if you must, then come back and see me."

All I could do was think about it. I had watched a man I loved become miserable because of me. I didn't know what I had done. But since I'd asked for a divorce, he was happier than I'd ever seen him. Maybe he was having an affair? What else could it be? Could he be this happy just to be rid of Zack and me?

It had been two weeks since Max and I spoke. It was a Saturday, and for the first time in a really long time, Max didn't have to go into work.

"Do you want to go out to breakfast with me?"
Max asked.

"Sure," I said. We went to a local diner and sat at a small table for two. Sitting across from him, looking at him, made me realize I didn't want to be without him.

"Max, I don't want a divorce. I love you," I said.

"Let me give it some thought," he said. That was painful to hear, but I was the one who'd been making him unhappy, so what did I expect?

A couple more days went by, and I was getting nervous. My stomach felt like I had butterflies in it, which made me continually nauseous. *Either we're going to work at this or we're not. If it's fixable, let's get busy fixing it! What the heck is he waiting for?* I called Max at the office and asked if he had a minute to come home. He was there within ten minutes.

"I'm sorry to bother you with this, but it's been difficult waiting for you to tell me what the next step in my life is. I'm hanging on by a thread, and it's about to break. Please tell me you've made a decision," I pleaded.

Max stood there and looked at me. He took a deep breath and said, "I'd like to try and work this out."

I was so happy I could have screamed! I hugged him and jumped up and down. “Thank you, thank you, thank you! I love you!” I said.

From that moment, I felt Max and I were going to be happily married forever.

While putting towels away in Max’s bathroom one afternoon, I found a basket of medication, pulled it out, and noticed the word Palixpam on the bottle. “Max!” I yelled from the bathroom. “MAX!”

“WHAT?” he yelled back.

“How long have you been taking anti-depressants?” I asked.

“I don’t take anti-depressants!” Max said as he came into the bathroom.

“Then what are these?” I asked, holding up the pill bottle.

“Those are pills for my headaches,” he said.

“Max, these are anti-depressants. My sister Patty takes the same medication for her depression.” Max stood there for a minute, looking at me. I could see the wheels turning in his mind. BING! BING! BING!

“Oh my gosh, Beth! When you went to Georgia with Zack, I went to see Dr. Field because I was having headaches all the time. The doctor asked me a bunch of questions and then handed me a prescription. He said, “Try this.”

He continued, "It all makes sense now. The pills made the headaches go away and made me feel calmer, too. He knew I'd never agree to take anti-depressants. He's a smooth one, that doctor of mine. I'll have to stop by his office and thank him."

"Yes," I said, "and thank him for me, too!" Max was coping much better since he started taking the anti-depressant. He wasn't as tense and seemed more patient and understanding with me.

But, unfortunately, not with my son. You see Zack was in the middle of his teenage years. His hormones allowed him to say whatever he wanted to say and go and do what he wanted to do, when he wanted to do it. It was difficult for all of us.

Now, in addition to wanting to send Zack away to school to get him away from Max, I also wanted to send Zack to private school to get him away from his friend Justin. A mother can always tell a bad apple from a good one. Zack was at the age where he was easily influenced by rotten apples.

"I'm not interested in sending Zack to private school," Max said. "It's expensive and I don't want to pay for it."

"I was going to get a new car this year, but I'm going to do without it and spend the money on Zack's education instead," I said.

"Then go ahead," Max said. "I hope he appreciates what you're doing for him."

I enrolled Zack in a Catholic school for boys, where he attended his sophomore and junior years.

His grades were not what I'd hoped for, so I brought him home to Willow for his senior year. Zack graduated from Willow High School, but chose not to go on to college. He went to trade school and acquired a certificate in welding; later, he discovered he enjoyed carpentry more.

### *Hair of the Deceased*

In **1995**, I received my cosmetology license. I worked my first three months as an assistant to a hair stylist in Groverdale, Michigan. When I left that job, I decided to work for a local salon—one I could get to within fifteen minutes instead of one hour and fifteen minutes. Two years later, I had a large enough clientele to go into business for myself. Max and I renovated the basement in our home and made it into a salon. We lived in the Willow city limits, so I was able to acquire a business license with no problem.

My license and talent were a great benefit to the funeral home. I worked full time at home, but made time to do hair for the deceased as well.

It took a long time for me to be comfortable with the dead. In the early years of my marriage to Max, I had strange dreams that were similar in theme. I'd be in the living room of the funeral home, with two or three opened caskets. The people inside the caskets were sitting up eating bowls of popcorn and watching TV. It was as though I were throwing them a pajama party before they were buried the next day. I felt deep sadness while I handed out popcorn to the deceased. To think thcy could cat and cnjoy television one night, and be in the ground with the lid closed the next, made me feel sad beyond belief, as well as suffocated. Most of my dreams had to do with talking dead people. Not in a scary way—they were all very nice to me. It was the fact they were going to be buried, and I was afraid they were still alive. This was very disturbing to me. The dreams came often in the beginning, but went away with time.

I came to realize, the first time I did hair for the dead, that they are gone. I could actually tcll that the body no longer held a soul. All that was left was a shell, an empty corpse. No color, no movement, no breath of life. I found comfort in knowing that.

Max asked me to do my first head of hair. When I entered the prep room, the disinfectant smell was overwhelming. It's the kind of smell that makes you want to hold your breath. The room smelled clean and felt like an operating room. Everything was sterile. It was bright white with hints of periwinkle or powder blue splashed about. Max stayed with me the entire time. I asked questions about the equipment, and Max explained while I worked on hair.

"Max, how do you get the blood out and the embalming fluid in?" I asked. "I hate the word embalming. What an awful sounding word."

Max replied, "The word embalming isn't one of my favorite words either." He continued, "I use the machine over there." He pointed to a two-gallon-sized glass jar, which appeared to be upside down on a square base, with electrical switches and tubes coming out of it. It almost appeared to be a bizarre 1960s blender, or some kind of equipment from a sci-fi movie.

"Where does the blood go after you've removed it?" I asked.

"It's mixed with chemicals and disposed of down the drain," Max said.

"You pour it down the drain? That sounds like it would contaminate the water supply," I said.

"No. Think about what you flush out of your body every day. Where do you think it goes? It all goes to the same place; it's all treated, broken down, and made safe."

"I suppose it sounds different because it's dead blood," I said.

"What's that plastic thing?" I asked, pointing to the stomach of the man lying on the table."

"It's a plug I've inserted. It allows me access with a device used to prevent purging. If the deceased had a buildup of gas in his stomach, it could cause him to expand or foam from the mouth. If I don't use an aspirator on him, the stomach will expand, causing the deceased to smell. This is usually caused by undigested food. The aspirator is a vacuum-type unit that extracts the food or gas from the stomach," Max said. "If I see signs of purging, I take the proper steps to make sure it's taken care of before the family comes in for visitation."

"Does everyone need to be aspirated?" I asked.

"No," Max replied.

"How do you keep the dead from going to the bathroom?" I asked.

Max replied, "Upon death, everyone goes to the bathroom. The body relaxes, and it's a natural process. When they arrive here, one of the first things we do, is bathe them. If there is a concern about fecal matter escaping the rectum, a butt plug is inserted. It does exactly what you think it does."

"I don't think I want to be buried. I get claustrophobic just thinking about it. Can I be buried in my car? I wouldn't feel closed in, and if I should happen not to really be dead, all I have to do is honk the horn and someone will dig me up," I said cheerfully.

"You can't be buried in your car. The law requires that a casket, in this case your car, must be put into a burial vault before it's placed into the ground. And there is no burial vault big enough for your car. What you're really saying is you're afraid of being buried alive?" Max asked.

"Yes, that's what I'm saying. Don't you think it's strange I should marry a funeral director when I have such a phobia?" I asked. "Being baked to a crisp sounds even less attractive to me than burial. In the end, when I'm 125 years old, I hope to die alone in my home in the early months of winter. When I'm found in the spring, all they will find is a skeleton and a little patch of hair," I said smiling.

"I have another question. Do you glue the eyes and mouths shut?" I asked.

"Sometimes, but not always. There is a thin, louvered circle I place on the eye. It's similar to a contact lens. I verify that the ridges on the lens are in the proper position before placing it on the eye. Once there, I pull the lid over the top of it. The ridges keep the eye from opening. It's rare, but if needed, I've added a little glue to a corner of the eye. We don't want any peeking," Max said, being silly.

"And for the mouth, I give them braces," Max claimed. "I use thin wire and go in and out through the teeth, then tighten the wires to pull the teeth together. This assists in closing the mouth. And, again, sometimes I have to add a dab of glue.

"Here is something you might find interesting," Max said. "Several years ago, a 12-year-old boy was playing in a large hole dug near his home for a repair in the sewer system. The hole caved in, and the boy was killed. When the parents made the funeral arrangements, the mother said, 'Do not glue my son's mouth shut! His mouth was never naturally closed.' Maybe he was a mouth breather, or his teeth were large. Whatever the reason, I was asked to leave the mouth alone, and I did. He looked more natural that way, and resembled every photo taken of him. It was the first time anyone ever made that request, but in the end, it was a good suggestion."

"Interesting," I said as I added a few more curls to the hair.

Over the years, Max stayed with me whenever I needed his company in the prep room. Sometimes there would be as many as three bodies in there. Irene usually did all the old ladies' hair. She was a pro at tiny roller sets and comb-outs. Irene couldn't quite get the hang of the younger styles, and she didn't want to attempt them.

I never really liked doing hair at the funeral home, but I liked being with Max. If he called me to do hair for the deceased, it didn't seem so terrible because I felt I was helping him out. When Irene called, she manipulated me into doing it. There was always a condescending tone to her voice, and I resented her for this. "Hello, Beth, how are you?" Irene would ask. "What are you doing today? Do you think it might be possible to come down to the funeral home and do some hair for me? You do such a beautiful job of it, far more beautiful than anything I could ever do. P-l-e-a-s-e," she'd whine into the phone. It was so annoying!

Doing hair at the funeral home ruined my day. The disinfectant smell of the prep room would saturate my clothing and my nostrils. No matter how many times I blew my nose, I couldn't get rid of the smell. Whatever shampoo, conditioner, or hairspray I used on dead hair, I could never use again outside the prep room without getting grossed out.

I wore rubber gloves each time I touched the dead, even if it was just to sweep the bangs over the forehead. My mother-in-law did hair without gloves. It made me sick to think about it. Max, too, was comfortable touching the dead without gloves. Perhaps it was just my phobia. The bodies were clean, prepared for viewing, and dressed, but I felt bacteria could still be collecting under Max's nails. And I didn't want my husband to touch me with the bacteria. It became my mission to get them to put on the gloves *always*! I talked about bacteria and the unsanitary practice of touching anything in the room without gloves. Max kept everything sterile. He was obsessed with the sterilization of the prep-room. I finally got them to understand you can't see bacteria, and when I was around, they would put on gloves. When I wasn't, who knows?

I remember several high school-aged girls I did hair for over the years. They had died from car accidents, suicide, drug overdose, cancer, or other illnesses. There were also several accidental deaths from autoerotic asphyxiation. This activity was more common among college students. They put something around their neck to cut off circulation while pleasuring themselves. When the moment of climax arrived, something went wrong, and instead of passing out from pleasure, they died.

I spent hours on their hair, getting every curl perfect. When Max and I were done with make-up and hair, the dead looked alive, like they were taking a nap, but would get up for the party any minute.

I often felt this was a disservice to the families. There should be some death in the look of the dead. Maybe this is the cause of the strange dreams I've had. Maybe not.

One day, Max accidentally shaved a mustache off a gentleman he'd gotten from the nursing home. The family hadn't brought in a photo. Max thought the man was simply unshaven; he didn't realize the man wore a very short mustache. In a panic, Max called me to see if there was anything I could do. I clipped some of the hair from the back of the man's head. Then, picking each hair up with tweezers, one by one, I applied glue and attached them to the man's upper lip. I spent eight hours doing this.

Years ago, I'd purchased some human hair extensions. The hair could be dyed to match the color of the deceased. The funeral home benefited from not only my styling ability, but hair cutting and coloring skills as well. Families whose son, daughter, father, or mother had passed away from brain surgery, aneurism, etc. and had arrived at the funeral home with a partially shaven head, were surprised when they viewed their loved ones at the funeral home with a full head of natural looking hair—the color and cut blended, as though nothing had ever happened.

It was always a proud moment when Max came home with rave reviews.

### *Another Holiday with Max's Family*

Between Irene and her sister Lynn, they covered all the holidays. Lynn hosted Christmas in her home, and Irene hosted Easter and Thanksgiving at the funeral home.

Lynn was the mother to Max's cousin Derrick, who was a year younger than Max and me. Derrick and Max hung around a bit together after Max got out of college. Derrick appeared to be threatened by Max's success and good looks. I was never sure if Derrick's attitude came from jealousy, or if he was a naturally difficult individual. You know, the kind of person you can never make happy. I could easily imagine Derrick as a grumpy old man, drooling from the side of his mouth. I picture him tied to his wheelchair for being an obnoxious patient. "I don't like peas! Give me mashed potatoes, damn it!" he'd slur as he threw his peas.

When Max and I were dating, Derrick was really nice to me for about six months. I have no idea what I did to make him mad. Maybe, like a sea monster, it just took that long for the real Derrick to come to the surface and rear his ugly head. Derrick acted like a spoiled brat most of the time. He'd demand we leave a bar or a party because he wanted to go home, for no reason, other than to make us miserable. Max, never wanting confrontation, allowed his cousin to have his way, and we'd take him home.

Max and I had been married for a few years. We attended Christmas at Lynn's like always. This was the year Derrick had finally moved out. He'd gotten a job setting up sound systems for traveling play performances through a state college. His mother didn't see him much, as the job kept him busy.

When Max and I arrived that year for Christmas dinner, Derrick was taking a nap. I remember thinking, *Who takes a nap when guests are coming to dinner?* When Derrick got up, he was a crab and yelled at his mother, "When's dinner? I'm hungry!"

Lynn replied nicely, "In a little bit. I'm cooking the gravy."

"Well, I'm hungry now," barked Derrick.

"Be nice," I said to him. "It's Christmas!" Derrick glared at me.

We were all seated and ready to eat. "Where are the rolls?" Derrick barked.

"I'm getting them out of the oven. Give me just a minute," Lynn responded.

"Can you get them now before my food gets cold?" he barked again.

"Derrick," I said, "it's Christmas. You should be nice to your mother."

Derrick, so obviously irritated with my need to spread kindness on Christmas, yelled at me, "LISTEN, YOU'RE A GUEST, AND THERE'S THE DOOR! YOU DON'T LIKE IT, LEAVE!"

I was mortified. The room was silent. No one defended me. What kind of family lets people act like that? It was as though they were all afraid of him. He had no power—he was just a big-mouthed, thin guy with red hair and crooked teeth.

I didn't know if I should cry, leave, or give him a scolding and a much overdue spanking in the form of a black eye. I got up and went into the kitchen to collect myself. Not even my own husband came in to see if I was okay. I stood in the kitchen alone, drinking ice water, until I collected myself, then returned to the dinner table and ate silently. Little was said. We all finished our meal, and I asked Max if we could go home. Fortunately, he said yes.

### *The Business and the Attorney*

It was **1998**. Max and I had been married for twelve years. One evening, Max informed me he had an appointment with his parents to meet with their attorney to discuss matters about the business. "What matters?" I asked.

He said, "Well, if anything happens to my parents, I will take over the business."

"And what if something happens to you?" I asked.

"Then it becomes yours," Max said. My mind raced, jumping to that moment in time where I have just buried my husband and someone says to me, "Well the business is now yours, what are you going to do?" I panicked at the thought! "What if smart decisions weren't made over the years? What if owning this business was going to make me financially responsible for something or someone I didn't want to be responsible for?"

"Max, don't you think I should be at that meeting?" I asked.

"Why?" Max asked. "Are you afraid you won't get something?" Humiliated, to say the least, I quietly said no. I left the room, went into the bathroom, sat on the toilet, and cried.

Max had his meeting. He never discussed with me what was said or signed, or anything else about the meeting. All of it took place while I was in the hospital recovering from a full hysterectomy due to endometriosis. It was pre-scheduled surgery. I went in on December 29, 1998 and returned home January 1, 1999. While I lay in the hospital, Max went with his parents to see their attorney.

During my twelve-week recovery, my friend Lea, the wife of Max's friend Craig, called and invited me to lunch. Max and I stood up for Craig and Lea when they got married. We were all the best of friends. The guys had grown up across the street from one another. Craig, like Max, worked in his family's business.

During lunch, Lea told me that she and her husband had been arguing. Apparently, Craig and his parents were going to their attorney to talk about the business and legal issues. Lea said, "Shouldn't I be there?" Craig said no. The argument was regarding decisions that were made at the attorney's office that could affect Lea. She wanted to be part of those discussions. She didn't want to wake up one day and find that she was left with a business that could financially ruin her.

Lea was in tears. "Then, to top it all off, Craig said to me, 'Are you afraid you won't get something?' "

I could not believe my ears! I told her that I had the same thing happen just months before. The more she talked, the angrier we both got. By the end of our lunch, we both felt betrayed and dismissed by our own husbands.

As time went by, Lea and I hoped for the best with regard to decisions that were made without us, and simply moved on. The four of us were inseparable and were now doing almost everything together: we met for dinner several times a week, traveled, went to movies, attended social events, and were occasionally invited to one another's family gatherings. Most of our friends were from the same social circle, so we knew all the same people and were invited to the same parties. Max and Craig knew everyone in town, and both of them belonged to the same social and networking groups.

### *POA, Wills, and the Family Farm*

Shortly after I recovered from my surgery in **1999**, Max told me we had an appointment with Mr. Roberts, his parents' attorney, to set up some legal documents. *It's about time you included me,* I thought.

We went to the attorney's office one morning to discuss setting up our Wills and to sign previously prepared our Durable Powers of Attorney Medical and Durable Powers of Attorney General (POA). This meant Max had the authority to sign medical and financial documents on my behalf, should I become unable to do so myself, and I would have the same authority to sign for him.

Max let the receptionist know that we were there, and within moments, an obese man came to the lobby and asked us to follow him into his office. He introduced himself as Stewart Roberts and extended his hand to me. I shook it and said, "Mr. Roberts, I'm Beth, nice to meet you."

We were invited to sit down in front of Mr. Roberts's desk. I signed some documents and Max signed some documents.

Mr. Roberts informed Max and me that Irene and Lewis were *never* going to retire. This statement surprised Max. It seemed odd news coming from an attorney. Why didn't they tell us themselves? Their plan was to work until they died. This meant Max would continue working for his parents forever. They would continue to have full control. Have I mentioned what great health Irene is in?

Max and I then discussed our Wills. I felt that Zack, not being a bloodline of Max, should receive 50% of the estate upon the death of Max and me. The other 50% would be left to Max's nephew and niece, the children of his sister Gladys.

I felt this was fair. Mr. Roberts said he would have the Wills typed and would inform us when they were ready to be signed. In the meantime, he'd make copies of the POA documents and see that we received the originals.

Several weeks went by. I asked Max, "Are the Wills done yet?"

Max said, "I don't know. I'll stop by the attorney's office and ask." After work, Max told me he stopped at Mr. Roberts's office. "We have an appointment to sign our Wills on March 3rd."

We arrived that afternoon, and many papers were signed. Mr. Roberts said he'd have our signatures witnessed and he'd put the documents in the mail with our POA documents. I believed him and didn't think anymore about it.

That summer, Max started spending every spare minute at the family farm. It's not really a farm, but it used to be. I believe Max felt this was a place where he could escape. A few years ago, he'd had a 1600-square-foot pole barn built there, and every chance Max got, that's where he went.

In order for me to see more of Max and share his love of this land, I would go to the farm and plant perennials, clean out weeds, and do landscaping around the pole barn. Sometimes Max would help and sometimes I'd be there alone while Max worked in town at the funeral home. I learned about flowers and weeds, what to grow and what to avoid. This was a new hobby for me, and I was having fun with it.

Another hobby of mine was scrapbooking.

Irene had given me one hundred or more photos to scan, edit, print, and scrapbook for her, and then to put a scrapbook together as a Christmas gift for her daughter Gladys. In order to put the book together in the proper timeline, I had to ask many questions. In doing so, I not only was given the time frame of the photos, but this story as well:

*Many years ago, in the late 1800s, a father and son worked a 300-acre farm. The father was Max's great grandfather, Charles, and the son was Max's grandfather, Ned. This would be Irene's father.*

*The father, Charles, and son, Ned, worked hard on the farm, side by side, for many years. There were also two daughters, but they married and moved away. In time, Ned married and moved across the road from the farm, where he and his wife raised four children: two boys and two girls. Irene was the third child in the lineup.*

*Charles, the owner of the farm and the grandfather to the four children, lived across the road from them. He wasn't a very nice man and had no tolerance for children. Instead of giving them loving smiles, he scowled at them and even tripped them when no one was looking. He took pleasure in sticking out his foot to watch them stumble over it. He took great joy in watching them cry.*

*When Grandfather Charles died, he left everything to his two daughters. The son, Ned, who had stayed and worked the farm, side by side with his father, got nothing.*

*Ned then had to purchase the farmhouse, barn, and 300 acres from his sisters. He and his wife, along with their children, continued to farm the land. His wife died, and as time went on, Ned sold parts of the farm for income to live on.*

*When Ned died, he left all he had—150 acres and the house and barn—to his four children and asked that they divide it equally amongst themselves. The four children put four pieces of paper into their father's hat. Written on each piece of paper was one-quarter of the land. One piece of paper had the land, plus the house and the barn. It was the oldest boy who got the piece with the house and barn. He wasn't interested in living there, so he sold it. The second child, also a boy, kept the acreage he received. Many years later, he and his wife built a home on it and lived there until his death. Around the early 1970s, the youngest daughter, Lynn, and her family built a modest home on her land. She and her husband, Ben, still live there.*

*The third child, daughter Irene, held onto her land, hoping to one day live on the land she had grown to love. Irene married Lewis, whose family had a local funeral home business in town, just seven miles from her land. Irene and her husband had a daughter, Gladys, and a son, Max. Though Irene had always wanted to build on her land, her husband had no desire to live on a dirt road out in the country.*

As Max grew up, he spent time out at his mother's property. When Max was in his early twenties, he started racing dirt bikes. He even bought a used bulldozer to move the earth into hills and berms for his own private dirt bike riding course. Throughout our marriage, Max would often go to the property and walk it, mow it, and think about it. He remembered his grandfather there. He imagined his mother as a girl there, along with her siblings. Max thought about his great grandfather and how unfair he was to his son. Max would look at different areas and think, *Perhaps one day I'll get to build my house right there.* Max loved this land and all the stories that went with it.

One year for Christmas, Irene gave Max and me a book. The story takes place on a farm similar to the one she grew up on and is about a gift purchased for a wife around 1900. The gift was an organ. The story tells how the organ was put on a sled and pulled by horses to transport it to its recipient. Back in the day, one had to pump the pedals of the old-style organ, while stroking the keys to get the right sound to bellow out from it. Not like the organs of today.

I saw an antique organ, like the one mentioned in the story, in one of the upstairs guest bedrooms of the funeral home. When I asked what it was, Irene came up and played it for me; it looked like a lot of work to play one song. Irene told me the story, and she gave Max and me the book that very Christmas.

## *Marriage and Drama*

In the year **2000**, my sister Patty and her son Ayden came to visit between Christmas and New Year's. Max and I had been invited to a New Year's Eve party. I called the host of the party and explained that my sister was in town, and, unfortunately, I wouldn't be able to attend the party. I hoped the host would suggest I bring my sister, but an invitation was not extended, and I would never be so impolite as to ask, or to show up with an uninvited guest.

When Max got home that evening, I told him we weren't going to the party. There was no way I was leaving my sister at home. Oddly enough, he still wanted to go. I told Max to call so they knew to expect him, and he did.

At 10:00 p.m., after only two hours had passed, Max was back home. He looked shook up. "Why are you back so soon?" I asked.

"Can I talk to you in private for a minute?" Max asked.

"Sure," I said, following him into the bedroom.

Max explained, "I was standing off to the side, having a beer, and I witnessed some creepy guy, a friend of Craig's, standing behind Lea and gently rubbing his fingers up and down her spine."

"Where was Craig?" I asked.

"Standing in front of Lea, talking to her and the creep," Max said.

"So Craig obviously didn't see this going on," I said. "What was Lea doing while this creepy guy had his fingers up and down her spine?"

"Nothing!" Max said. "She just stood there and let it happen!"

"Was he cute?" I asked. "You know what I mean, the creepy guy?"

"I don't know, no, maybe...Yes, I guess you'd say he was attractive," Max said.

The next day Max went on and on about this, obsessing about it. There had always been some harmless flirting between Max and Lea, as well as Craig and me. As a matter of fact, I remember one evening while the four of us were out to dinner, Max introduced the three of us to someone he hadn't seen in years. The introduction went like this: "Hi, I'd like you to meet my wife Beth, my friend Craig, and my second wife Lea." Of course Max was only kidding, but the comment stung me right in the heart.

I started to think maybe Max was seeing things. My grandmother always said, "Don't believe anything you hear and only half of what you see." She also said, "If you look for shit, you'll find it."

This didn't sound like something Lea would allow to happen. And, two days later, Max wouldn't stop talking about it. "Max, this is really upsetting you," I said. "If you are positive about what you saw, then confront Lea about it."

"Really, do you think I should?" Max asked.

"Yes," I said.

The next morning, I couldn't shake the fact that Max had let this supposed flirtation between Lea and some creep take over his life. *Why is Max so upset by this*? I asked myself over and over.

*Oh my God, does he have feelings for her beyond friendship? Is Max jealous?*

Before Max went to work, I had to ask. "Max, do you have feelings for Lea? You have obsessed about this situation far beyond one friend being concerned over another. Are you in love with her?"

"*No*, I'm not in love. Well…I don't think I'm in love with her," Max said.

I tried to play it cool. Right now, I needed answers, not confrontation. "It's understandable if you are," I said. "We do everything with them—travel, dinner, socialize. We all do some harmless flirting. Maybe you've gotten caught up in it all. Lea is beautiful inside and out. I could understand how you could have fallen for her." The words flew out of my mouth. I didn't want to lose my husband, but I needed to know on what ground I was standing. Was it shaky or was it firm? I needed to convince Max I was not going to judge him. He needed to know he could confide in me.

"Oh my God, maybe I have fallen for her," Max said. "You don't know this, but she's always putting her nose in my neck and telling me how good I smell and how handsome I always look."

*No,* I thought, *I don't know any of that. Is this really true? Where was I when this was going on?*

"Have you been seeing her outside of our socializing?" I asked.

"No, of course not," Max said.

"So, are you in love with her?" I asked.

"I'm not sure," Max said. "But it's possible I am."

The morning was passing quickly. I had to get my sister and her son to the airport, and Max had to get to work. I told him to go. He'd been gone a couple minutes, and I remembered he was going to call Lea today. The more I went over it in my head, the more I felt Max should mind his own business. It was not his place to confront her. I called his cell phone. "Max, I've been thinking about this. Please do NOT call Lea."

Max said okay.

Lea was my best friend, and I wasn't ready to let Max ruin our friendship. Max had spent his entire life being overdramatic about everything. If someone said something in a disagreeable tone, Max said this person was ready to get into a fistfight with him. Max complained every single day about someone or something. I had been married to Max long enough to know that what he says and reality are not the same thing.

When I started dating Max, his parents worked him from morning to night. Even after we married, they overworked him for years. But in the past ten years, I had come to realize that Max wasn't being called in the middle of the night anymore, and he was able to take some time off. He now came home in the evening and was usually there for the night, but that didn't seem to lighten up his complaints. Night after night he'd complain; night after night I'd counsel him and see what creative ideas I could come up with to help. Max never took one of my ideas and tried to fix the problem. It was easier to complain. Looking back on it now, I should have told him to quit his whining and take it like a man. But I would never do that. I loved Max and knew he was overly sensitive, and I didn't want to bruise his feelings.

I was a great wife. I cooked, cleaned, and usually looked great for him. The word "no" was not in my vocabulary.

Anything he wanted was all right by me. Unlike some of my friends, I never even said no to sex. Realistically, it takes less than twenty minutes, so going through the process was better than living with Max being miserable for longer than the twenty minutes I would be giving up. Make it good, make it quick, and you'll make him happy!

Max called me at home and said, "I did it! I confronted Lea!"

"What? I asked you not to!" I said.

"You did? When?" Max asked.

"When I called you on your cell earlier, just after you left here," I said. "You agreed not to call her."

"I don't remember that," Max claimed.

"Can you come home so we can talk about this?" I asked.

"Yes, I'm on my way now," Max said.

When Max arrived, he was like a middle school boy who'd asked the prettiest girl in the class to the school dance and she said *NO!* Max was not a happy man; he was bitter and angry. He explained that he had called Lea and told her he needed to speak to her. She was feeding the dogs and horses for some mutual friends and asked Max to meet her at the Robinson farm. When she arrived, Max told her what he had seen. Lea denied it and told Max she couldn't believe he would say such a thing. She told him he'd better not say anything to Craig about this because it never happened!

"Lea asked if I had talked with you about this," Max told me. "I said, 'Yes, Beth thinks I'm in love with you.'

"'WHAT?' Lea said. 'That's ridiculous.'

"That was about it," Max said. "She wanted to make sure I never told Craig. I think that Lea is a liar and somewhat of a slut. She's always flirting with men. She acts like it is all innocent. I don't trust her."

*You don't trust her?* I thought. *I don't trust you!*

"Okay, Max," I said. "It's all possible, but you do realize that the relationship between the four of us now has to change? We will no longer be traveling with them. I would feel far too uncomfortable on any beach with the two of you. I would be assuming you were looking at her and desiring her, whether you were or not. I'm not willing to put any of us through that mental torment. Also, in order *not* to alert Craig, we will start going to dinner together less and less, until we are not going at all."

I couldn't bear to call Lea. What must she be thinking?

Then the phone rang, and it was Lea. "I am so upset with your husband," Lea said. "How could he make up such a story? When Max called and asked me to meet him, all I could think was something's wrong with Beth and he needed to tell me away from everyone because no one knew yet."

"Max is overdramatic," I said. "I don't know what he saw; I only know what he thinks he saw. Max became jealous because it wasn't him running his fingers down your spine."

"That's just gross!" Lea said. "No offense, Beth, but I'm not attracted to Max that way. He kept probing me, asking me, 'So what do you think? Do you think I'm in love with you, and what if I am?' It was sickening!"

“I’m so sorry,” I said. “I could tell he had fallen for you, and I needed to know for sure.”

Lea said, “I told Max, ‘How dare you try to destroy my friendship with Beth. She is my best friend!’ So please, Beth, don’t let this ruin our friendship. We can still hang out and do things without the guys. I couldn’t stand it if you weren’t in my life!”

“Lea, I’m sorry it went this far,” I said.

“As soon as I got home, I told Craig about it,” Lea said. “He couldn’t believe it. And I have to tell you, Beth, when Max called, my niece was over. I told her, ‘If I don’t call you in one hour, call the police.’ Needless to say, I was a little freaked out as to why Max thought he needed to see me alone. Sometimes he gives off strange vibes.”

“It’s interesting that you told Craig, because Max said you wanted to make sure he never said anything to Craig,” I said confused.

“I never said that,” Lea said. “It sounds like he’s trying to put me in a bad light to take away from the dark seeded thing he tried to do.”

“Don’t worry. It’s all over, and we’ll stay friends,” I said. “Let’s go to the movies next weekend, just the two of us. We’ll find a good chick flick to watch.”

Lea said, “Absolutely!”

Even though I tried to play it cool, I felt like I’d been shot in the heart. In the past years, I’d heard of husbands falling for their wives’ best friends, but I never expected mine to be one of them. Knowing what I know now, could he be trusted?

### *Lewis Has a Stroke*

In the warmer months of **2002**, I was designing our new home. One day Max and I would build that home. I worked hours on it, sitting at our home computer designing it inside and out; using the floor plan from our current home, I added additional space where needed. Max would give me details as to what he'd like to see in a new home, and I would add them in, hoping to make it a reality with every key stoke.

One night around 10:00 p.m., the phone rang. Max answered. It was Irene calling. "Please come over and help me get your father out of the bathtub," she said.

"Did he slip and fall? Is he bleeding?" Max asked.

"No, I just need you to come over now," she said. "I need your help!"

"I'll be right there," Max said and hung up the phone.

We only lived two blocks away, so I expected Max to be right back. Two hours went by before he returned. He got into bed around midnight.

"What happened?" I asked.

"My dad was taking a bath," Max said. "My mom asked him if he was ready to get out, and he didn't respond. She kept asking him if he could hear her, but still no response. That's when she called me. I asked, "DAD, CAN YOU HEAR ME? He finally said yes after I yelled at him three times.

"Where is your dad now?" I asked.

"We got him out of the tub and into bed," Max said.

"YOUR DAD IS IN BED? Don't you think you should take him to the hospital? It sounds like he's had a stroke," I said.

"Yes, that's what I think, too," Max said. "He's comfortable now, so I'm not going to disturb him."

"Well, he's your father, not mine," I said, "but I think he should go to the hospital."

"I'll take care of it tomorrow," Max said.

The next morning, I called my sister Marie, who's a physician's assistant at a hospital, and explained what happened in the night.

"WHAT? They need to get him to the hospital right now! There is no time to waste. It may be too late already!"

I yelled into the bathroom while Max showered. "Max! You have to get your father to the hospital right now! I just got off the phone with Marie, and she said you should have taken him last night. If you take a person who's suffered a stroke to the emergency room within three hours of the stroke, the doctors can remedy it. If you don't take him right away, the damage to the brain can be permanent."

Max dressed, called his mother, and went to the house to pick her and Lewis up. Max drove them to the hospital. It was too late. The damage had been done. Knowing this, the doctors had them sit and wait all day long. Tests were taken with no urgency. A hospital room was finally given to Lewis at 11:00 p.m., before Max came home.

Lewis had suffered a stroke, but x-rays showed he'd been having mini-strokes for years.

This last stroke didn't harm any of his motor skills, but it did affect his short-term memory. The once chatty, socially inspired individual now had nothing to say. Worst yet, he couldn't remember anyone outside the immediate family, and, at times, that was questionable.

I did research to see what I could find out. Rehabilitation can help people who suffered a stroke or other brain damage. It's very possible that some or all of their normal thinking skills can be restored, but it depends on the person's natural ability to heal or repair the affected area. From what I read, it could take six months to two years. The recovery can't be predicted because it's dependent on the individual.

When Lewis came home, Irene had someone come to the house to help Lewis with his rehabilitation. The help seemed to fade away with time. I'm not sure if it was because Lewis had only shown a limited amount of progress or if Irene became tired of the process.

Max came home every evening telling me about his dad. Irene continued to bring Lewis into the office, where the only task he was capable of doing was opening the mail. Every time the phone rang, someone had to grab it before Lewis did because for Lewis, every day was like the first day at a new job. He didn't know what to say or how to respond to the questions asked. Max and the employees tried to fix this by unplugging Lewis's phone. As soon as Lewis was alone in the office, he somehow knew to plug his phone back in. I'm the only one who found this amusing.

I went into the funeral home one afternoon and asked Irene if I could make an appointment for Lewis to meet with my neurologist. She was hesitant, but agreed it could be helpful. I made the appointment and was asked to bring the most recent set of Lewis's brain x-rays if they were available.

I picked up Irene and Lewis from the funeral home, along with the x-rays, and drove them to meet my neurologist, Dr. Gerald. Dr. Gerald asked Lewis a series of questions—what day is it, what year is it, that kind of stuff. He asked what kind of man Lewis was before the stroke. Between Irene and me, we gave the doctor a clear picture of the man we lost compared to the man that was with us today.

"There are some medications that may help Lewis; some that may even give a bit of his old personality back," Dr. Gerald said.

"Lewis is already on a handful of medications," Irene said. "Is one more pill really going to make that big of a difference?"

"We won't know until we try," Dr. Gerald said. "Give me a list of what Lewis is currently taking. Maybe I can help by prescribing a drug that can combine two or more of his current medications and deliver the same effect."

We made another appointment, received the new prescription, and I took Irene and Lewis back to the funeral home.

Over the next several months, I took Lewis to see Dr. Gerald. Each time I picked up Lewis, I could see an improvement. Irene and Max could not. Maybe the improvements were less noticeable to them because they saw Lewis every day. Maybe they were expecting miracles. I felt the progress with Lewis was a miracle. Now, Lewis tried to have a conversation and pretended to know everyone. That part was sad. But the fact that he was joining in and speaking with others was a huge improvement, whether he recognized them or not.

### *Irene Wants a Trust*

Irene said she wanted Max and me to go to her attorney and set up a Trust. She would pay for it, and it would be part of the Family Trust.

Max set up the appointment, and he and I went to see the Edwards's attorney, Mr. Roberts. We were told that Lewis and Irene had divided their estate between Max and his sister Gladys.

Irene knew that Max and I wanted to build a new home, so she had deeded 5 of her 38 acres to Max and me. This was a nice surprise. I wondered how this gift to Max and me could be legal after Lewis's stroke. But maybe Lewis didn't have to sign because it was considered Irene's property.

"The remaining 33 acres will be used as you wish to use it," Mr. Roberts said. "Upon Max's death, the property will go to Gladys."

"Who is going to pay the property taxes on the 33 acres?" I asked.

"You and Max will because it will be your land," Mr. Roberts said.

"But you just said the 33 acres goes to Gladys upon Max's death," I said.

"Yes, that is correct; however, you will be enjoying the property. You can even farm the property if you want," Mr. Roberts said.

"Okay, let me see if I get this straight," I said. "I will be able to farm the property if I want. I will enjoy looking at it out the window. Max and I will be paying taxes on the 33 acres, and when Max dies, I give it to his sister?"

"Yes, that is correct," said Mr. Roberts.

"Well, then I don't want it. Why would we pay years of property taxes on property I would never personally own? Let Gladys pay the taxes. It's basically her land anyway. I can still look at it out my window, but it's not going to cost me anything to do it," I said.

"WAIT A MINUTE! Do you mean to tell me my mother has given me 5 acres and my sister the other 33 acres?" Max said angrily.

Mr. Roberts said, "Your parents have divided their estate and feel that because you will receive the funeral home, your sister Gladys will receive all of their personal assets. This includes their home, belongings, bank accounts, and the 33 acres."

Max stood up. "ABSOLUTELY NOT!" She is doing the same thing to me that her great grandfather did to his son. I have worked by my parents' side every day since I can remember, and where was my sister? She was always away, living in another part of the state or out of state. I have been the one who stayed and worked my entire life and did as I was asked. I'll be dammed if my mother is going to leave MY PROPERTY to my sister!"

"Max, it's not that important," I said.

"Oh, yes it is," Max said. "I will be confronting my mother about this."

Max and I continued answering questions for Mr. Roberts about our estate and the plans we wanted to make regarding it.

I still felt that upon our death, Zack should receive 50% of our estate and Max's niece and nephew the other 50%.

After our meeting with Mr. Roberts, Max drove me home and dropped me off. "I have to go talk to my mother," Max said. "There is no way she's giving that property to my sister."

When Max came home, he said that his mother understood and would make sure she deeded the 33 acres to him.

"Max, you may want to ask your mother about the funeral home *building*," I said. "As I recall, the business is separate from the building. Your parents once mentioned they pay themselves $3,000 a month for rent. You will get the business, but Gladys will own the building."

"No, that's not true," Max said. "The building and the business are all in one."

"Okay," I said, "just thought I'd mention it. You know more than I do. I'm only telling you what they once told me.

"Max, can you do me a huge favor?" I said. "Please make sure that the pole barn is on the 5 acres your mom is deeding to the both of us. I'm afraid if you precede me in death she'll somehow see that Gladys gets it."

"Oh, you're being ridiculous," Max said. "But I'll see what I can do to make sure the pole barn is on our deed."

Max had the land surveyed and included the pole barn and landscaped areas in the 5 acres we were planning to build on. I quit doing hair, except for the funeral home, and put all my energy into finishing the designs for our new home.

The weather was cold now, and we were expecting snow. It was **December 2002**. Max told me we had an appointment to finalize our Trust documents.

We walked into Mr. Roberts's office. Before I had a chance to take off my coat, I saw Mr. Roberts flipping through a yellow legal pad. Looking at Max, Mr. Roberts said, "So, is the boy still being cut out of everything?"

*I was shocked. Was he referring to Zack?* I looked at Max and whispered, "If you don't leave 'the boy' at least $10,000 dollars, you will destroy him beyond repair!"

Max turned red and looked guilty as sin. He said, "No, no, I never said that. You must have written that down wrong." Listening to Max, I was suddenly reminded of a used car salesman. *Trust me, really, it's just like new; only driven to church on Sunday by an old lady. Really! I wouldn't lie to you.*

Mr. Roberts said, "Max, this is what you said to me when you were here last. But I can change it if you like. Is the boy, Zack, now in good favor?"

"Yes, yes, take that out of there," Max said. "You must have misunderstood."

Mr. Roberts said he'd have the changes made and call us to could come back and sign the final documents.

### *Friend or Enemy*

On **March 1, 2003**, Max and I had an appointment to sign the final paperwork. We sat down in Mr. Roberts's office. He handed us the finished documents. My husband, being the animal lover that he was, had asked that the beginning of both of our Trusts read: "Upon my death, $10,000 will be donated to the Pet & Wild Animal Society."

"I think I want to change that," I said.

"You can change it anytime. You don't need to do it now," Mr. Roberts said.

I quickly flipped through the pages and noticed my sister-in-law and her children's names instead of Zack's. "I think I need to change this!" I said.

"Let's have you sign the documents today," Mr. Roberts said. "I'll make copies and mail you the originals. You'll be able to take your time and read through the documents and note what changes you'd like. You can come in anytime and make any changes you like," he said with a condescending tone in his voice.

The attorney flipped to the back of the document and said, "Sign here." I signed and started to date it.

"OH NO! Don't do that! You'll mess everything up! I'll have the date put on there for you," Mr. Roberts said.

I didn't give it any thought. I trusted him. He was the person who made it known to me that Max was trying to cut my son out of the Trust. Clearly, Max had visited this attorney's office without my knowledge. My hope was that Mr. Roberts was looking out for me.

When all the signing was done, Mr. Roberts asked if I had any questions. "What if I need to change something?" I asked.

"When you receive the documents in the mail, read them over. You can change them anytime," Mr. Roberts said again. "I'll have someone in the office witness your signatures, make copies, and put the originals in the mail to you."

*How could someone witness my signature if they didn't see me sign?* I thought.

Max and I signed many pages that day. I couldn't tell one from another. I left feeling a little confused. How many times did I sign and what exactly was I signing?

We received two large envelopes in the mail about a week later. An invoice was dated March 10, 2003. I opened both envelopes to see what was sent. It looked like our Trust, Wills, and POA (Power of Attorney) documents. I flipped through the Trust and could see it would take some time to read and decipher what it said.

I glanced through the remaining documents. There were two extra:

1. **POA General, from Max to his <u>father</u>, dated March 3, 1999**

On March 3, 1999, while I gave Max a Power of Attorney that would allow him to legally sign my name, Max sat right next to me and gave his Power of Attorney to his father? Why would he do this?

Then, after his father's stroke in 2002, Max signed a new POA that gave the power to me, so he must have known what he was signing. The documents also listed Max's address as that of the funeral home.

What does this all mean you might be asking? Prior to 2002, if Max had been in an accident that put him on life support, I would have had the legal authority to shut off that life support with the POA Medical I was given by Max. However, if there were many bills to be paid and I had personally run out of money while Max was on life support, I would have had to go to his father and ask for approval to access Max's funds. Max's father had the authority by Max's POA General to tell me yes or no.

*I wonder what the other surprise document is?*

**2. Last Will for Max, dated December 30, 1998**

Max had signed a Will that said: "I hereby nominate and appoint as Personal Representative of this, my LAST WILL AND TESTAMENT, **my parents**, Lewis Edwards and Irene Edwards, or the survivor of them." If they are unable, Max gives it to the Trust Department of Willow Bank & Trust.

Wow! I felt like someone had just opened my front door and threw me out into the snow, homeless and abandoned.

I flipped through each Trust to verify the dates.

"Beth L. Edwards, Revocable Trust, dated March 1, 1999." That's weird, because I didn't sign it until March 1, 2003.

"Maximilian B. Edwards, Revocable Trust, dated December 30, 1998."
Max and I signed the Trust at the same time, on the same day—March 1, 2003. What is going on here?

I immediately copied all documents and put the originals in our safe.

When I approached Max with the newfound information—the POA to his father, and the Will to his parents, as well as the signature dates—he said, "It was done that way because of the business."

"But, Max," I said, "you don't own the business, your parents do."

"They told me to sign it, so I signed it! What, are you afraid of—you're not going to get something?" Max said in anger.

"How dare you! I am your wife! When you signed those documents, we had been married for twelve years, not twelve months. What did you think I was going to do?"

Max stood silent and just glared at me.

I continued, "Every time I might need money, if you were unconscious or on life support, I would have to go to your father and ask for it. What were you thinking? Then there is the Will issue—I'm not even going to ask about that right now—and you have the nerve to ask if I'm afraid I won't get something! I have stood by your side for seventeen years. I don't want the business. I hate that business. It has sucked the life right out of you! Sell it, give it away, burn it down for all I care. I never want to hear about it again!"

I could see that no one, not even my own husband, was looking out for my best interest. I became enraged and couldn't control myself.

"Max, you might want to rethink me as your medical POA person," I yelled. "At this point, I'm so incensed by what you've done, if you end up in a coma, I will do everything within my power to see that you are made well. Then, I will find the nastiest, stinkiest nursing home I can find in the deep, dark ghetto of Detroit and put your ass in it! No one will visit you. Upon your death, I will have you cremated and flush your remains down the toilet! Have you never heard the saying, 'HELL HATH NO FURY LIKE A WOMAN SCORNED?'"

The look on Max's face was priceless. He had not taken into consideration what I would or could do in my anger. I could see him asking himself, *Would she really do these things?*

In the days, weeks, and months to come, I tried to put it behind me. Even though Max had, at one time, given powers to his parents, it looked as though he had re-visited the lawyer's office and made the correct changes after his father's stroke. Maybe it was his father who requested these documents in the first place. At this point, it didn't matter. Max and I were about to build a new home together. Once our home was built, Max would be happy to come home to it every night, as it would be on the property he loves so much.

### *Building Our New Home*

The blue prints to our new home were finally ready. The architect followed my design and made minimal changes. I quit doing hair entirely, except for cutting Zack and Max's hair. I no longer wanted to go to the funeral home if I didn't have to. The building project would take most of my time, and we would soon be living miles instead of blocks from the funeral home. Irene whined about me quitting, but I didn't let her get to me.

Max purchased a used backhoe to help with the digging of the new basement. He staked it out to see where everything would be. "Oh no, this looks too small," Max said. "I think we should make it bigger."

"Bigger? No! It's big enough," I said.

"But it doesn't look very big," Max said. "If we need more room, we should do it now, before we start. What if we add just four more feet?"

"No, it's not necessary. Remember, I drew up the plans using the layout and measurements from our current home. I added square footage to every room, including the basement. Now think about it, if the new basement was as big as our current home, don't you feel that would be big enough?" I asked.

"I guess so," Max replied.

"It's not the same size, it's bigger," I said. "There's nothing to worry about."

Max started digging.

With every scoop he took, it was apparent the basement was not only large, it was too large! Max and his backhoe looked like a toy in a child's sandbox. I looked at the blue prints. The basement would be 2,452 square feet with 9-foot ceilings. The first floor would be the same, and the second floor was going to be 1,174 square feet. That, in my opinion, was more space than two people need. Especially since the house we currently lived in was 1,150 square feet total.

"Max, I didn't realize how big this was going to be," I said. "When I designed the house, I used graph paper, with each square representing one square foot, and then I added a couple feet here and there to each room, to give us exactly what we needed. But this is too big!"

"No, it's not," Max said. "We'll be living on the first floor. The basement will be used for storage, and we won't be finishing the upstairs right away because we don't need it."

Being put into a nursing home in his old age was a fear Max had. Building a home to accommodate one or both of us if we were limited to a wheelchair was part of my design. The hallways were four feet wide. The doorways were three feet wide. The master shower was a five-foot square walk in. The house was no mansion, but in comparison to the bungalow we had lived in for eighteen years, it felt like it was. I had designed the upstairs to accommodate two bedrooms, one full bath, a kitchen, living room, and small office. This space was not intended for our use, but as living quarters for a young couple who might be interested in taking care of Max and me in our old age. I had thought of everything.

Working on our new home was a labor of love. Max was the general contractor, and he found time to lay marble floors in the foyer, guest bathroom, and first floor laundry room.

I shopped for deals on cabinets, doors, counters, flooring, etc. I also stained all of the wood trim and doors, then primed and painted the interior of the house. It took a year and a half to finish the project. When it was done, it was beautiful!

We moved the old Twinker Furniture Max's mother purchased for us years ago into the new house and planned to paint it black. The home was an empty palette, and I was excited to decorate. I wanted to do it once, do it right, and never have to do it again.

Decorating is expensive, and we had money to do it, but I continually had to pull it out of our savings. I asked Max, "Can you please increase your weekly paycheck? I feel extremely guilty pulling the money out of our savings."

"No," Max said. "I like getting the huge check at the end of the year. The money is in the savings, use it."

Thousands of dollars were spent each month for many months to give our home the feel of an English Tudor. Pulling out large sums to pay our credit card overwhelmed me with guilt. Instead of taking a large sum of money out of the savings to pay the card off every month, I'd pay the minimum and wait until the credit card balance built up to $15,000 or more. Then I'd withdraw a large sum all at once and pay it off.

Max didn't understand my bill-paying method, but he wouldn't listen to me either. He deposited $3,600 a month into our checking, but our expenses were $5,200 a month. He kept out over $1,000 a month for miscellaneous expenses for himself. Max had been giving me the same amount of money for the past fifteen years. His salary had not increased from $65,000 a year, but the bonus had grown many times over that.

He had a company car and gas card, so he kept this Money for what—daily lunch and pizza for us on Fridays? I didn't care what he did or didn't do with his money, but the fact that he questioned me about spending and wouldn't take over the bill paying frustrated me.

We never went out anymore, once we moved. I cut Max's hair and purchased his clothing, undergarments, white dress shirts, sox, and shoes. His mother paid for Max's custom suits—Max had a muscular build and finding a suit to fit his wide shoulders, well-built arms, and small waist was difficult.

Sure, I shopped for myself as well, but I shopped the outlet. Max wasn't paying attention to me anymore, now that we lived in the middle of nowhere, but I still took pride in how I looked for him. My efforts were in vain; Max looked at me less and less.

### *We Moved In!*

We moved into our new home on **October 4, 2004**. Our first night there felt strange. Not like the cozy home we had just left.

The very next morning, I heard Max whisper, “Beth.” I had been sleeping on my back. *Was I snoring?* When I glanced over at Max, I saw our tiny black cat Zelda between Max and me, lying on her back like a little person, with her head poking out from underneath the covers and her paws curled over the blanket. Max and I giggled. It was the cutest thing I’d ever seen. She’d never done this before and, unfortunately, never did it again.

I spent most of the first year decorating and getting used to a larger space. The house was more beautiful than anything I’d ever expected to live in. But I never felt at home there.

Max’s parents lent us money to build the house. We used the proceeds from the sale of our old home to partially pay them back and gradually repaid the remainder by depositing payments into a savings account opened in the four of our names. This would allow for accurate records to show when we paid off the loan.

Zack moved in for a couple weeks and then moved to Idaho with his friend Benny. They were gone several months and returned home by spring. This time, Zack stayed with Max and me for one month and then finally moved out on his own for good.

Our new home was built next door to Max’s Aunt Lynn and Uncle Ben. Ben came over many times during the building project to see what progress was being made.
It took Lynn over a year to stop by because of her jealousy.

I had made brownies for Christmas, and Lynn was returning my platter. She tried to hand me the platter at the door, but I encouraged her to come in. When Max and I were building, I had envisioned Lynn and me becoming friends. I had a couple of hobbies I could see myself teaching Lynn how to do. In my mind, we'd laugh and chat while I'd show her how to make stained glass windows or mosaic tile stepping stones.

I showed Lynn around Max's and my new home. She didn't say a word. I could see disgust on her face. "I know the house is large," I said, feeling like I needed to make excuses, "but Max is such a hard worker. He's worked very hard for this home. He wanted it, and I feel he deserves it."

"Well, Beth," Lynn said, "lots of people work hard and they don't live like this!"

I was speechless. All my happy thoughts about us becoming friends and doing things together just blew away. What a bitter thing to say. This was her nephew, for goodness sake. How about being proud that he could accomplish such a goal, and that he had a wife who worked on the house day and night to help make his dream more affordable? How about saying, "This is nothing more than you and Max deserve!"?

Why bother with these thoughts? People are who they are. Lynn left, and my bubble had been burst.

Even though Lynn and Ben lived next door, we could not see their house from ours. I could stand at my front door and scream as loudly as I could and no one would hear me. I felt like I lived out in the middle of nowhere.

The upside of this location was that we built on the highest point of the property and water could be seen from the front and back of the house. Looking out the library window at the front of the house, we could see across the road to Raccoon Lake. From the back window of the four-season room, we could see beautiful green trees, wetlands, and Blackberry Lake beyond that. While looking out the same window, we could see, off to the far left, the 33 acres Irene wanted to go to her daughter, after Max's death.

Max and I had lived in our new home a year now. I had my routine, and Max had his. Mine included making sure the house was clean, the laundry was done, and dinner was prepared. I would shower, blow out my hair, and apply my make-up before Max came home around 6:30 p.m. every night. Max's routine was to come home, say, "Hello, I'm changing my clothes and going down to the barn. I'll be back in around nine." He was quickly becoming a stranger to me. This was supposed to be our dream home, the place that could bring us closer together. Why was this move to the country, onto land that my husband loved, taking us further apart?

Night after night, I was burdened with sadness to think my own husband didn't want to spend time with me. If I wanted to talk to him, I had to follow behind him through the house as he continued to walk away from me. If, by chance, he came in after work instead of going to the barn, he'd usually go into the four-season room to watch TV, while I watched TV in the great room. Being at home by myself all day and in the evening, too, was making me lonely. I decided to look for a job. I needed something to do and people to talk to.

I cooked dinner every night. Max never wanted to eat right away. Around 10:00 p.m., he'd put his food in the microwave. It didn't matter that it takes time to prepare delicious food; he wasn't going to eat it until he was ready. No matter what time I presented dinner—7:00, 8:00, 9:00 p.m.—he never ate it when it was fresh and ready. Did he think microwaving made it better? I could never understand his process. And despite what you may be thinking, I was a good cook!

Was he overstressed? Max had suffered a couple of emotional breakdowns in the last few years. I tried to encourage him to find another career—one that could make him happy—but he refused. "I could never make what I make now," Max said. "Not anywhere! And I'm not willing to give that up."

"But you are miserable! You hate what you do!" I said.

"No I don't," he replied.

"You always say that, but you've done nothing but complain about that business since the day I met you. You're not fooling anyone but yourself," I said.

"One day I'll have the chance to do what I want," Max replied.

"Chances aren't something you have, chances are something you take! If you're waiting for your mother's life to end so that yours can begin, you'll be waiting a very long time," I said.

Max had been fighting and swearing in his sleep, and it was getting worse. He thrashed and punched in his sleep now, too. He hit me twice while sleeping. I told him if it kept up, I'd have to move to the guest room.

### *No Love for Max*

It was **2005**. Max and I were standing in the four-season room, looking out the window at all the deer on our property. There were so many does and fawns. We both smiled and laughed at them playing. We noticed one of the doe mothers protecting her slightly wounded baby as another fawn wanted to play. "Look, Max, that mother is taking care of her baby," I said. "I bet she's saying, 'I will love you and protect you, don't you worry!'"

"I don't ever remember my mother telling me she loves me," Max said.

"Never? Really? Did she at least hug you?" I asked.

"No, I don't ever remember her hugging me, either," Max said with sadness.

"That is the saddest thing I ever heard," I said. "I wonder if it had anything to do with your grandmother's death. Your mom said her mother died shortly after you were born, and your mom was so devastated she couldn't get out of bed for weeks. Maybe she had some kind of breakdown and couldn't care for you the way you deserved."

"I don't know. It's possible," Max said.

One day awhile later, I had the opportunity to talk to Irene in the funeral home kitchen. "I have something to say, and I'm not saying it to hurt your feelings," I said. "My fear is that someday, something will happen to you or Max and you'll be left with the consequence of not telling him that you love him."

"Oh, I used to tell him all the time when he was a baby," she said. "And besides, my parents never said it to me."

"That doesn't make it right," I said. "You're not getting any younger. If something happens to you and Max doesn't hear you tell him you love him, I don't know what it will do to him."

"Does Max think I don't love him? I always treat Max the same as I do Gladys," Irene claimed.

"Yes, as far as money goes, you do treat them the same," I said. "However, when Gladys comes to visit, she gets a hug and an 'I love you' before she goes back home."

"Well that's because she approaches me and says it first," Irene said.

"Max mentioned this to me and said he doesn't remember his mother hugging him or saying 'I love you.' This has been weighing on his heart for a long time."

Irene opened her mouth as if to say something, but nothing came out, and she closed it. Then she asked, "What do you want me to do?"

"Sometime in the near future, opportunity will present itself. Give him a hug and tell him you love him," I said.

"Okay," Irene said.

"And, Irene," I said, "I love you."

"I love you, too," Irene said.

I wanted to show Irene how easy it was to say these three important words.

This was the year Lewis and Irene would celebrate their fiftieth wedding anniversary. They celebrated it with Irene's side of the family only. Irene didn't invite Lewis's side of the family. I questioned her, "Why aren't you inviting the other side of the family? They invited all of us when Lewis's brother and his wife had their fiftieth."

"Lewis's brother and wife are in an assisted living facility," she said, "and the rest of them are all too busy. Most likely they wouldn't want to attend anyway."

"I bet they would want to come, but this is your choice. If Lewis's brother and his wife and family find out that you didn't invite them, feelings could be hurt. I don't want anyone to think it was Gladys or me because we were helping you with the invitations," I said.

"Oh, you worry too much," Irene said.

The day of the event, everyone from Irene's side of the family was there. Irene was always trying to impress her family, but when it came to Lewis's side, Irene never went to the same great lengths. This never made sense to me because Lewis came from a really nice family. Even Max preferred his father's side of the family to his mother's. But this wasn't my event, so I wasn't going to force the issue.

After dinner was over and desserts had been eaten, it was time to leave. Irene's nieces and nephews were lining up to say goodbye and thank her for the invitation. Irene hugged each one and said, "I love you." She did this while looking at me, look at her. But no attempt was made for her only son.

A few months later, we had the conversation again.

"Did Max tell you we hugged in church?" Irene asked.

"No, he never mentioned it," I said.

"Well, we did," she said, "And my parents didn't tell me they loved me!" She sounded like a spoiled brat instead of a dignified lady. I waited to hear her say, "So there!" But it was never said.

Again I said, "That doesn't make it right."

A few months went by. Irene fell from a ladder and broke her elbow. Max spent all day at the hospital with her. I remembered Lewis's joint replacement surgery years ago. Irene had dropped him off at the hospital and never gone back. Not to visit him or pick him up. Max and I visited, and Max picked Lewis up when he was released a week after his surgery. What kind of wife does that? Was Irene made so emotionally disconnected by her own parents that this cold-hearted behavior seemed normal?

Fall was approaching. For the first time since my sister Patty moved to Georgia, got a divorce, and remarried, I was able to talk Max into making the trip with me. We would spend a long weekend visiting Patty, her new husband, Dennis, and my three nephews, then fly to Florida, where my dad and his wife had resided since retirement and visit them. The trip would end with Max and me in Disney World. He had never been, and I wanted to show it to him. Everyone should see it at least once.

The weather was so much warmer in Georgia than what we'd left in Michigan. Patty and Dennis showed us Centennial Park in downtown Atlanta, where the Olympics had taken place. From there, we went to the CNN building; we took a tour and watched, through a thick glass window, broadcasters report the day's events. We went back to the house to pick up the three boys for dinner.

Dennis had three children of his own, and having all six children under the same roof was becoming stressful for everyone. Much to Dennis's disappointment, shortly after Max and I left, Patty chose to take the equity from the sale of her home, given to her in her divorce, and put a down payment on a home for her sons to live in. She felt it wasn't fair that her boys suffered from her divorce from their father or her marriage to her new husband. Patty was trying to do the right thing by her children. Purchasing a home would allow her boys to remain together and not be forced to live with Patty's new family members.

Patty's oldest boy, Josh, was 21-years-old and in college. He had to get a job to help with the expenses. Patty provided her three-year alimony check to help Josh with the financial responsibility of the house. Within six months, the twins, Ayden and Allen, turned 18-years-old, and Josh felt he was providing more than his fair share to the support of his brothers.

Ayden called and was terribly upset. Josh had told him to pull his weight or move out. Ayden had worked since he was 14-years-old and continued to maintain part-time work. The chemistry between Josh and Ayden had never blended; they were like oil and vinegar. Josh had a good relationship with the other twin, Allen, but took pleasure in tormenting Ayden to the point of insanity.

"Aunt Beth," Ayden said on the other end of the phone, "I can't live here anymore. I'm depressed and tired of being abused by my brother. I'm going to look for an apartment."

"Apartments can be expensive," I said. "Do your best to get along with your brother and try to find a better job."

"Maybe I could move in with you and Uncle Max," Ayden suggested.

“As much as I would like that,” I said, “Uncle Max wouldn’t. Keep me informed,” I said. “I’ll do whatever I can to help.”

Ayden found a better job, and moved into the basement of a friend’s house. This lasted almost a year, before he realized this was not the ideal living situation, either. Ayden called me. “Aunt Beth, I need your help. I need to get my own place.”

“Do you have any money for your security deposit?” I asked.

“No,” he replied, “but I have enough for a month’s rent.”

“I’m coming for a visit. I’ll help you look as soon as I get there,” I said.

Within a month, I was in Georgia at a hotel in Peachtree City. Ayden came to the hotel every day after work. He and I drove around looking for an affordable place for him to live. “I think you should buy a condominium,” I said.

“I can’t afford to do that,” he said. “I don’t make enough money.”

“All the more reason to do it now,” I said. “If you make under a certain amount of money, you can qualify for a low payment loan. This loan is for first time homebuyers. There are certain requirements your home will have to meet in order to qualify, but you should be able to purchase something with no money down and a reasonable monthly payment. Talk to your bank. They’ll be able to direct you better than I can. I’m just going from memory.”

“Let’s do it!” Ayden said. We drove around looking for condominiums. Ayden drove, and I kept a log of addresses and real estate phone numbers. He called on a few, but they were too expensive or had already been sold.

“Start looking at everything you can for comparison,” I said. “I have to go home. I’ve decided to look for a job. Let me know what you find.”

### *Changes to the Trust*

**2006** – I had wanted to look for a job, but couldn't decide what I wanted to do. A friend of mine worked for a television station and said they could use more volunteers, if I were looking to do something just to keep busy. I took her up on the offer and went in once a week to help out in shipping. I really liked it there. Three months into volunteering, a job was posted that I qualified for. My friend urged me to apply, and I got the job as a customer service specialist.

Four months later, I got another call from Ayden.

"Aunt Beth, I found a townhouse! I've filled out all the paperwork, but the bank is telling me I need a co-signer or co-borrower. My mom can't sign because she has her name on Josh's house, and my dad said he wouldn't do it. That leaves you."

"Of course I'll help you," I said. "Let me talk to Uncle Max, and I'll call you tomorrow."

That evening, I talked to Max about Ayden's situation.

"That's not a good idea," Max said. "What happens if he can't make his payment?"

"I will help him out," I said. "The income I'm currently making is spent on miscellaneous nonsense. At least this way the money could go to helping my nephew. It's not like we need my income to live on. I only took a job out of boredom. It won't be forever, and I will help him set goals."

"And what if I say no?" Max asked.

"Then I will do it anyway," I said. "'No' has never been in my vocabulary, and you shouldn't be introducing it into yours. We are not poor! I can help my nephew, and I'm going to help him. I've not asked you to help, and I won't use your money to do this."

"Before you sign the mortgage papers, I want to see them," Max demanded.

I called Ayden and told him I'd co-sign. We were able to take care of almost everything through fax. The actual mortgage documents were sent overnight to me at work. I took the package home and handed it to Max. "Here are the mortgage papers you asked to see," I said as I handed him the package.

Max tossed the package across the table. "I don't want to see those," he said.

I closed my eyes, took a deep breath, picked up the package, and put it under my purse. "I've signed and will send it back by an overnight service tomorrow," I said. "If you decide to look at them, you have until morning to do so."

The next morning when I arrived at work, I called my nephew.

"Ayden," I said, "Uncle Max isn't happy about this, but that's not your worry. He has a nephew and a niece. They are too young to need his help. I hope one day he will help them with college, if nothing else. He will then find the joy one gets from giving. Unfortunately, Max has never experienced that joy. Your signed mortgage papers are on the way."

* * *

Max went away on a trip with his friend Burt, who had his own airplane. Burt enjoyed going to air shows out of state and many times asked Max to go with him. I encouraged it because Max needed to get away from the stress of the business. Burt and Max always had a great time together. Max had good stories to tell each time he came home from one of these trips.

One weekend, while Max and Burt were away at an air show, I remembered I still hadn't read the Trust documents Max and I had set up. I had forgotten there were things I wanted to change. I pulled the documents out and began to read...

This was not good. I'd have to remind Max that it made me uncomfortable that the first line of the documents read, "Upon my death, I leave $10,000 to the Pet & Wild Animal Society." It didn't feel right. Animals are not more important than people. Why would my husband want this on the first page of the last thing we say? Taking out an ink pen, I crossed out the words "the Pet & Wild Animal Society" and wrote in the name of my favorite nephew, Ayden. It would be nice to leave him something and Zack would understand because he would be getting everything else I left behind. Besides, if I were going to give money to the Pet & Wild Animal Society, I'd prefer to do it while I was alive.

The language used in the Trust was difficult to decipher. I might as well have been reading Chinese, because I don't understand that either.

I flipped through the pages hoping to read something I might understand. The first thing I noticed was that my Trust was dated March 1, 1999, but my signature was witnessed and notarized on March 1, 2003.

The topic of a Trust wasn't brought up to me until after Lewis had his stroke in 2002. Why would my Trust be dated this way? Max and I set up POA and Wills, and signed them on March 3, 1999, but we never received them. We discussed setting up a Trust in 2002 and finally signed the Trusts on March 1, 2003.

*Maybe I'm being paranoid, but something isn't right here.*

I pulled out Max's Trust for comparison. It appeared to be exactly the same as mine. After Irene deeded 5 acres to Max and me in 2002, she deeded the 33 acres to the Maximilian B. Edwards Revocable Trust, dated December 30, 1998.

*I'm so confused. Why does my paperwork list Max's sister? It should have my son Zack's name there. And what does "per stripes" mean?*

Later, I learned that, basically, "per stripes" represents the children of Gladys, Max's nephew and niece. Maybe Max wasn't aware of what the Trust states. This was the first time I was aware of it.

I hoped this was a mistake. Maybe it was a setup by Irene and her attorney. Maybe it was just another document slipped in among the others to be signed. But if that were true, Irene would be risking her relationship with Max. She'd never do that. Irene needed him to run the business; she couldn't do it alone, and how would she ever explain to the public Max not being there? My mind raced, trying to make sense of all of it. I couldn't.

Zack had been deeply scarred by Max never wanting to be his father. Max tried to cut Zack out of the Trust, and it appeared he may have succeeded. How much damage could a person cause before recognizing what he'd done?

Max came home from his trip on Sunday. I waited until Monday evening before bringing this new information to his attention. I also needed to go to the township hall and see why we hadn't received a tax bill for Max's 33 acres. It would be better to address all issues at once.

I went to the township with my checkbook in hand and said, "I'd like to pay the taxes for the 33 acres listed on this tax ID number. The land was deeded to my husband, but, I'm afraid, because he didn't change the billing address, the taxes haven't been paid."

The clerk looked up the taxes for the property and said, "I can see it's owned by your husband's Trust. The bill was sent to the funeral home address, and the taxes are paid up to date."

"Oh good, I'm so relieved it's paid," I said. "My husband is so busy he must have forgotten to mention it. I'll talk to him about changing the billing address. Thank you."

When Max came home that night, we'd need to discuss this.

"Max," I said, "I'm going to change some wording on my Trust. It looks to me as though I'm stating that animals are more important than people, especially when it's the first thing you see when you read the Trust. Aside from you, I would rather leave all that I have to my son and leave the $10,000 to my nephew, who has always felt like a second son to me. If I have extra money in my lifetime, I will give it to the animals then."

"Also," I continued, "I am removing Gladys and her children from my document. It doesn't feel right and I don't want to send the wrong message to Zack should he be the one reading my Trust after my death."

"And Max," I said, "Why is your mother still paying the property taxes on your 33 acres? I have never seen a bill for it? Is the bill going to the funeral home, like everything else you're keeping from me?"

"My mother is paying for it because it's my mother's property," Max answered with anger.

"No, it's not!" I said. "It's yours!"

"Well, you seem to know more about it than I do!" he barked at me.

"Oh, come on, Max! You can't be that stupid! The bill goes to the funeral home, and it has *your* name on it!" I replied. "The property is listed in your Trust!"

"Yes, I guess I've seen a bill from the township addressed to me," he sheepishly said. "I opened it and gave it to my mother, and she paid it."

"Why, are you poor and can't pay your own bills?"
I asked.

"NO! She's doing it to be nice," he yelled. "It's a gift! Why are you complaining about someone doing something nice?"

"Because there is something wrong with all of this, and I need some answers!" I said.

Max threw the Trust document and started waving his arms, screaming, "I'm done, I can't take it anymore, and you are paranoid! I've had it!"

"Well that makes two of us!" I said. "I need to know who is responsible for ruining my marriage! Is it you or your mother?"

Max calmly and slowly said, "Beth, I don't want you to get that property, I don't want Zack to get it, I don't want Gladys or her children to get it. I want the property to be left alone. I'm going to donate it to the Pet & Wild Animal Society so the deer have room to roam. There is not enough land for the deer to roam!"

After closing my mouth, which was hanging open in shock, I said, "So, animals *are* more important than people?"

Out of the 33 acres, at least 15 of it is good usable farmland. It was currently being rented to a farmer. I had no idea for how much, as Max's mother still took charge of it all and continued to pay the property taxes on the land she had deeded to her son's Trust.

I said, "You have the right to do with the land as you please. It belongs to you. I don't like that you want to give it away, and I don't have to like it. But don't be hasty with this. You don't know what the future brings, and you may decide to farm the land yourself one day. Or, what about going to the township and giving them the land in exchange for no property taxes for the rest of our lives?" The exchange of land for no taxes was a great idea, something that would have benefited both of us for many years to come without disturbing the land or the animals that roam there.

But, like always, no response from Max.

### *Strange Vibes*

I made changes on two pages of my Trust and copied them. I put a copy in the mail to Mr. Roberts and asked that he make the changes and call me as soon as possible for my signature.

Mr. Roberts called and said my amended Trust was ready to sign. He told me to stop in and sign on **December 1, 2006**, which I did.

"Does Max know you're here?" Mr. Roberts asked.

"I mentioned it, but whether he remembers or not, I don't know," I replied.

"What does Max think about this?" Mr. Roberts asked.

"I don't know what he thinks, but I think people are more important than animals and my son is more important than my sister-in-law or her children, and I don't trust this TRUST!" I said with frustration.

"We won't mention it to him," Mr. Roberts said, waving his hand back and forth in a hush, hush sort of way.

My face must have given my thoughts away: *That's a strange thing to say to me.* Mr. Roberts started to tell a story about a family in Waters Bay.

A young couple—he knew the family, too—had gotten married. The bride's mother-in-law took it upon herself to clean the newlyweds' home once a week. This disturbed the young wife, as her mother-in-law was washing personal things like sheets and undergarments. The young wife felt this was an invasion of her privacy and asked that the young husband tell his mother she must stop doing this and return the house key because she could clean her own house. The young husband felt he couldn't and wouldn't do this to his mother, as it would offend her. After many arguments on the subject, the marriage ended in divorce.

This time, my expression was of confusion and mistrust. All I could think was, *What is he talking about and why did he just tell me that stupid story?*

Quickly, Mr. Roberts asked, "So what's your opinion of your mother-in-law?"

*Why is he asking me this? Does he think we're friends?* I told him the same thing I would have said had she been standing right in front of me: "I think she is controlling and overdramatic, just like Max," I said.

The attorney laughed. "This is just between you and me," he said. "Your mother-in-law and Max call me all the time with the littlest of issues. Sometimes I wonder if they just look for things to complain about." He sounded irritated by their actions.

*Mr. Roberts is forgetting that he is, in fact, their attorney and is PAID for the legal counseling he provides. Instead of complaining about how much they call, he should be charging them for his time, regardless of how trivial their questions or concerns are.* I kept these thoughts to myself.

Mr. Roberts then called in his son Daniel to witness my signature. "Daniel, Max doesn't know his wife is here, so we aren't going to mention it," he said to his son, again waving his hand like my presence should be a big secret.

*This was beyond strange, to mention this not once, but twice. And why was he having his son witness my signature? No one ever witnessed my signature before. What's going on here?* I was too dumbfounded to speak.

I left that office very confused. *Why was he acting like he was my friend? Was he really trying to let me know he was looking out for my best interests despite what the Edwardses were trying to do?* The more I thought about it, the more skeptical I became. While still in the parking lot at Mr. Roberts's office, I pulled out some paper and wrote down everything that had just happened. I felt like I was going crazy, or was stuck in a game show called, "Let's Make Her Mental!"

The next evening after work, Max arrived home and said, "Did you go to the attorney's office yesterday?"

I started laughing. "Funny you should mention it, because, oddly enough, Mr. Roberts said he wasn't going to say anything to you."

Max looked at me as though I were lying.

"He has to tell me, because if I don't sign your changes, they're not legal!" Max claimed.

"Not legal?" I said. *What was going on here, this doesn't make sense!*

"What changes did you make?" Max asked.

"You never seem to listen to anything I say. I told you what changes I was making. My nephew Ayden is getting the money, *not* the animals. And I know you don't want my son to get everything you leave behind, but he is MY SON and he has the right to receive everything I LEAVE BEHIND!" I said.

Max sat clenching his teeth and didn't say a word.

"If I had married anyone else, anyone but you, the outcome would still be the same. You knew I had a son when you married me; you even adopted him! You did this on your own—no one asked you to adopt him! Now you want to leave it all to your sister and her children?

"We need to see a different attorney; I *do not* trust this one!" I said. "He was talking crap about you and your mother; it was totally unprofessional. I would like to write him a letter and fire him!"

"What are you talking about?" Max asked with annoyance.

I said, "My letter would read as follows:

*Mr. Roberts,*
*You gave me your personal opinion about the Edwardses, and I gave you mine. The Edwardses don't pay me for my opinion, therefore, it is irrelevant. The Edwardses do pay you, and, therefore, your personal opinion should be kept to yourself.*

*The Edwardses are not educated in law, you are. That is why you are their attorney, and that is why they call you with every legal concern. To complain about the numerous or silly things they call for is not only unprofessional, but also unjust. You are their lawyer, and that is what they pay you for. And for that you are fired!"*

Max shook his head and refused to acknowledge anything I had said.

Weeks later, he bought another life insurance policy, thinking this would pacify me. While in the office of the insurance company, I watched Max set up a one million dollar life insurance policy. The beneficiary was his Trust.

The insurance man said, "I will need the original copy of your Trust before I can process the paper work."

"I have it at my office; I'll drop it off this afternoon," Max said.

I started to feel sick. Had I just swallowed a bowling ball? There is only one original Trust and the attorney told me he had sent it to the house. So if I have the original, what does Max have? I didn't say anything. I needed to wait to see how this would play out.

Apparently, Max had an original of his Trust at the office. What exactly did that one say? And when would I be privileged with that information? I couldn't start asking questions again. Every time I asked about the Trust, I was made to feel like I was stealing the family jewels.

After my appointment with Mr. Roberts on December 1, 2006, I personally received an invoice from his office, and I paid him myself, with a check signed by me, dated December 17, 2006. Didn't this make Mr. Roberts obligated to me as his client now? I was under the impression that once an attorney accepts payment from you for his services, he is obligated to you by some code of ethics or code of professional responsibility. Perhaps I was wrong.

### *Cold and Confused*

**January 15, 2007** – After going to the grocery store, I stopped at the mailbox at the end of our driveway and picked up the mail. I looked through it quickly and noticed a handwritten envelope from Willow Bank & Trust. Was I overdrawn on our checking? I opened it to see what it was.

It was a bill from Willow Bank & Trust for the payment of two life insurance policies listed on the "Maximilian B. Edwards *Irrevocable* Trust U/A dated December 31, 1998."

My heart started pounding. I had no knowledge of an Irrevocable Trust. I kept telling myself to think about this with a clear head. I placed the letter on the kitchen counter and tried to think clearly as to what this could mean.

Revocable means the document *can* be changed at anytime.

Irrevocable means the document *cannot* be changed. Whatever this document has in it, it will be unchangeable by anyone, even the person who had it drafted. One must be absolutely sure of his decision before creating an Irrevocable Trust.

I couldn't think clearly. *Who is doing this to me? And why do they think I deserve this? Is it Irene and Mr. Roberts? Or is it Max?*

I felt like I was losing my mind. I called my sister Marie. First crying, then sobbing, I said, "I don't know what's real anymore. Nothing is making sense. Max has created legal documents behind my back. I need help and don't know what to do."

Marie said, "I have a friend who works for the law firm of Buckley and Long. Let me call her and see what she has to say. I'll call you right back."

Within minutes, Marie called me with a phone number and told me to call and set up an appointment. I called the number. Marie's friend answered, and I explained my problem. She set up an appointment with Mr. Simmons, an attorney she worked for. In the meantime, she told me to write down my questions.

To keep busy, I spent the day cleaning and thinking. I decided to make stew out of the uneaten roast beef from last night's dinner. *Even though I'd rather dump it over Max's head, I should still make him dinner because I am a good wife who cares for her husband. Actually, I'm a stupid wife, who continues to take care of a shitty husband! Never mind the fact that my husband is setting up legal documents behind my back. Don't think about it; pray about it!*

I keep a bottle of holy water on a shelf in the library, next to my Bible and religious books. I poured some over my fingertips and blessed myself. I closed my eyes and prayed.

*Dear God, Jesus, Blessed Mother, and Joseph. You are a family. I need help from all of you.*

*Joseph, you raised a son that wasn't your own, just like Max. Would you have done things behind Mary's back to keep your legacy from Jesus?*

*Blessed Mother, you gave birth to a son, just like I did. We spend our lives protecting our son from pain, and come to realize it's an impossible task. I have stood by my husband, as you stood by yours. Help me to recognize the good in my husband. Unlock his secrets and let them be known to me.*

*Jesus you were raised by a man who wasn't your father, just like Zack. Would you forgive Joseph for going behind your mother's back to leave you with nothing?*

*I ask you all for help, as one mother to another, as one family to another. I need answers. No matter what the outcome. I have to know what is going on. My life is falling apart and so is my mind. Please help me find the truth. In the name of the Father, Son, and Holy Spirit, Amen.*

I had a sudden urge to talk to Max!

I drove down the long driveway between the house and the pole barn. Max's truck was parked outside, so he was already home from work. I took the letter inside. "Max, please read this and tell me what it is," I asked.

"Well, you said you wanted things to be sent here instead of the funeral home. This is a bill to pay for two life insurance policies. One is on me and the other is on my father. When he dies, I receive life insurance to pay my mother for the business," he explained.

"Okay, but why is this labeled as "Irrevocable"? When did you change your Revocable Trust to Irrevocable?" I asked, shaking with anger.

"I don't know anything about that," Max claimed.

I yelled at him, "HOW COULD YOU NOT KNOW ABOUT IT? THIS IS YOUR DOCUMENT! YOU SIGNED IT!"

Max yelled, "WHAT DO YOU THINK I'M DOING? YOU'RE JUST PARANOID!"

"None of this is making sense," I said. "There are too many unanswered questions, one of which is, why, in Mr. Roberts's office, did I so trustingly sign documents without a date to later find it dated 1999? You and I both know I didn't set up a Trust until after your father's stroke in 2002. Only Last Will and Testaments were discussed, and a POA signed for each to the other."

"I don't know, maybe you should ask him?" Max said.

I left the pole barn, went home, opened the safe, and took out all the documents, including the copies I had made. I threw them in a box and put them in my car. Then I drove to Nora's.

"Nora, can I please leave a box with you for awhile, until I have a chance to figure things out?" I asked.

"Of course," she said. "Are you alright?" I told her I was okay and would explain when I came back for the box.

On the way home, I was shaking. My life felt like it was falling apart. Max was still at the pole barn. I drove by and went straight to the house. Within minutes Max was home. I was irritated. The phone rang. Caller ID showed it was the funeral home. I picked it up. "WHAT?" I yelled into the phone.

Shocked by a tone Irene had *never* heard from me, she hesitated. "Is Max there?"

I yelled with sarcasm, "MAX, IT'S YOUR MOTHER!"

Max took the call in the bedroom. When he came out, he said, "A friend's brother just passed away. I need to go to the funeral home. Will you answer the phone if anyone calls about it?" I ignored him and his request.

I had nothing nice to say, so I wasn't saying anything at all. Besides, what did he think? I wouldn't answer the phone? I just answered it, didn't I?

Max stormed out. "THANKS A LOT!"

That night I slept in bed, and he slept on the sofa.

The next morning, Max said, "I'm going to work." I said nothing.

Later in the day, I decided to call him at work and ask him where the Irrevocable Trust and life insurance policies were. "At the funeral home," he said.

"Please bring them home. I have never seen them, and I feel I have the right to. I would also like you to bring home any other life insurance policies and all of our tax returns that you keep there under your mother's lock and key."

Max knew we had a secure place to keep important documents, but he insisted on taking our personal paperwork to his office.

### *Christmas Traditions*

**December 25, 2007** – My son Zack had become engaged in October. He was bringing his fiancée, Tina, to meet Max's family for the first time on Christmas Day.

It had become family tradition that Christmas morning would be spent at the Edwards home. Gladys and Daryl brought their two children on Christmas Eve and would stay until New Year's Day. It was also tradition that I would bring an assortment of quiches and oven-baked rosemary potatoes for breakfast on Christmas morning. Irene usually had cereal, bagels, and some kind of fruit.

Zack and Tina were running late, so we ate without them. The children were getting anxious waiting for Zack, so we let the kids open gifts. I wasn't exactly sure what time to expect Zack; I only knew he was bringing Tina this morning to meet everyone.

Irene was sitting on the floor next to her daughter, watching her open a gift, when we heard a knock at the door. "It must be Zack and Tina," I said. It was not my home, so I didn't think it was appropriate for me to answer the door. Irene, however, made no move to get up and answer her own front door. I kept looking at her, and she wasn't moving. We couldn't leave them out in the snow on Christmas morning, so I got up and answered the door.

"Merry Christmas," I said to them. "Come in. Let me take your coats."

I took them into the living room, and Zack made the introductions.

"Can I get either of you something to eat?" I asked.
"No thanks, we had breakfast at home," they replied.

This was Irene's home—shouldn't she be the hostess here? Has Miss Manners been steering me wrong my entire life? Irene never got up off the floor. She spent the entire morning chatting with Gladys and her grandchildren. She did, however, manage to muster a "thank you" when she opened gifts from the rest of us. What had I done, or Zack for that matter, that pissed off the Queen today?

### *I'm trying to Understand*

I loved my husband and I hated my husband. Max, I believe, took this as a sign of bi-polar disorder. I tried to forgive him, but every time I thought about it, I was crushed beyond repair. I did have issues regarding Max, his mother, and her attorney. Unfortunately, I always felt Max's interest was in his family's estate instead of his marital legacy.

At this point, I was considering therapy. I needed help to understand my anger and get beyond it, and if I couldn't get beyond it, I'd need help with that, too. I hated the thought of being manipulated into believing some lie.

I would never want something someone didn't want me to have. To take something in that regard would be taking something that is stolen or cursed. Nothing good would ever come from it.

All those years ago, a father didn't want his son to inherit land he had worked so hard for. That son defied his father's wish to give the land to his sisters and purchased it from them anyway. There must have been a reason why the father left this land to his daughters instead of his son. It's my belief the land is cursed. No one has been made happier by living on it.

I thought about how miserable Irene and her siblings appeared. What happiness has this land brought to any of them? Lynn was married to a wonderful man who truly loved her. That alone should have provided her with all the happiness she could ever want. Instead, she looked bitter because of jealousy and envy of her sister.

Her brother lived down the road, with his loving and caring wife. He was an ornery individual, a grumpy old man. I know she loved him; I just don't know how she tolerated him. And what happened to my own husband? I no longer recognized him. His mother didn't want him to have the property, either; she wanted Gladys and Gladys's children to have it. I believe the legacy lives on.

I also believe that Irene loves her daughter more than her son. Max has tried to gain favor with his mother his entire life, without success. I hope, after all is said and done, he accomplishes this lifelong goal.

### *I Need Legal help*

On **January 17, 2008**, I went to meet with an attorney at Buckley and Long Law Firm, considered by some to be one of the best legal offices there is.

The entrance alone was impressive: granite floors, wooden walls, beautiful artwork hung perfectly. Ahead of me was a desk with a receptionist, to the right of her, a long hallway with bookshelves. Law books covered the wall from floor to ceiling.

When the attorney came out, he shook my hand and introduced himself, "I'm Mr. Simmons." He was a sharp-looking middle-aged man. We walked down the hall into a conference room, sat down, and I started talking. He wasn't interested in hearing my conspiracy theory. He only wanted to see the facts: the Trust.

Mr. Simmons explained that a Trust is usually set up as a tax shelter. By having a Trust, you can avoid inheritance tax and the lengthy probate process. He said, "Pull your chair over and let's go through this together." Mr. Simmons asked me several questions.

"Have you been married before?"

"Yes."

"Do you have children from that marriage?"

"Yes, I do."

"Do you have children from this marriage?"

"No, but my husband adopted my son."

"Did the attorney who drew up this Trust recommend you have separate counsel?"

"No."

"Well, he should have. It's a conflict of interest. You're interested in leaving a legacy for your son. Your husband may or may not have the same intention," he said.

He read aloud, quickly, every bold-faced phrase and explained everything I had underlined. He saw no problem with my husband's Trust.

When he opened mine and started reading, he said, "*What?* Your Trust appears to be an exact copy of your husband's, except the names have been changed."

"I noticed that also," I said, "so I had an amendment done to change it."

"Thank goodness," he said, "because if you hadn't, I would have suggested it!"

I explained about the day I went to sign the amendment and how the attorney called my husband to tell him of the changes.

Mr. Simmons said, "You can changc your Trust whenever you want. No one needs to know about it. There is no clause here stating your husband needs to be notified of any or all changes."

"What about the date?" I asked. I explained the issue I had with the dates.

"I have no idea why he would backdate this document, but I find it odd that your Trust is dated March 30, 1999, your signature is dated March 1, 1999, on one page, and March 1, 2003, on another. That just goes to show you the incompetence of the person who prepared this document," he said. He handed me my papers. I could tell my time was up. I asked what I owed, wrote a check, thanked him for his time, and left. I felt pretty good about my meeting.

A few days passed, and Max said, "I need your code to look at the credit card statements on-line."

"The statements are all in the library desk," I said.

The next morning, before I went to work, I checked the desk for the credit card statements. They were gone. Max must have taken them to work. I didn't know what his problem was. Maybe he thought I spent too much money? Before Max complained about *my* spending, he needed to take a good look in his pole barn at his bulldozer, backhoe, new dump truck, tractor, along with parts that drag behind it for who knows what—plowing fields?—one of those circular lawn mowers, a four-wheeler, a couple snow blowers, power washers, ark welder, plasma cutter, some kind of metal bending thing; and the list goes on. I do realize some of this equipment is used to take care of the funeral home lawn, but most of it isn't, and if he is storing items belonging to the funeral home, why aren't we charging them rent? He is a funeral director—not a construction worker, not a farmer, not a professional welder—a funeral director! So give me a break Max! There were no diamond rings or fur coats on our credit card statement. So why the sudden curiosity?

### *My Marriage Is Falling Apart*

**February 2008** – I received the savings account bank statement, the one used to pay back the money we borrowed from Max's parents for the construction of our home. Irene had closed the account January 31, 2008.

Why would she close it? Max still owed money to them. Maybe Irene closed the account and was collecting the balance from Max's *huge* bonus she gave him every year? It never made sense to me that we didn't pay off that debt sooner. I didn't like it hanging over our heads. But when I had suggested to Max that we pay it off, he had said "No!"

Given the fact that Irene closed out the account, I assumed the debt was paid in full.

**March 2008** – Max and I were invited to a fiftieth wedding anniversary party for his Aunt Lynn and Uncle Ben. I really didn't want to go, but Max insisted. When we arrived, there was a chill in the room. And I'm not referring to the air temperature. It was as though everyone knew something, and that something had to do with me. I guessed it was because I answered the phone and was short with Irene a few months ago. Irene and her sister talked about everyone, so I was sure this was a juicy tidbit for their tea and crumpets social hour.

When Max and I arrived, we took off our coats, handed them to the coat check girl, and walked into the reception hall. It was a beautiful old lodge next to a lake and several old cabins. It was called Waverly Woods and was established many years ago on campgrounds. Still today, people rent the old cabins for weeks at a time, and for many it's a summer family ritual. I had always wanted to stay there, but never took the time to do it. The cabins have to be booked far in advance in order to guarantee your stay. The old lodge is booked up as well, for wedding receptions and parties.

I walked up to Lynn and Ben. “Congratulations! Lynn, you look lovely. What a great place to have your anniversary party. It’s so warm and cozy with the roaring fire in the stone fireplace. The old wood wainscoting panels are absolutely beautiful!”

“Have you been here before?” Lynn asked.

“Yes, I’d been here once when I worked for the bank. We had our Christmas party here. It’s really beautiful at Christmastime. They have it all decorated with garland and large red velvet bows, white lights on everything, and a huge Christmas tree. I remember when I walked in for that party, there was a smell of pine in the air. It was like stepping back into time. So beautiful. I’ll never forget it.”

“It sounds beautiful,” Lynn said.

“I was here at night, so I never realized you could see the lake out of the windows. It makes it even more enchanting,” I said.

Lynn and I walked over to the windows and looked out over the lake. It was March and very cold out; the wind was blowing hard. I could see the effects of the wind on the water.

I continued to look out the window, and Lynn went to greet her guests. I turned around to locate Max. He was at the bar getting a drink. *I need a drink,* I thought, and started walking in that direction.

Irene appeared out of nowhere and was suddenly standing right in front of my face. "Hello," Irene said.

"Hello," I said, then turned and walked away from her to get a drink.

I couldn't stand there and make small talk with a woman who was single- handedly (well, with the aid of her attorney) ruining my marriage. What kind of mother-in-law gives her son a gift of land and doesn't include his wife? This gift created a huge wedge, not because of the land itself, but more because of the manipulative way it was given, compliments of Irene Edwards. Was this the Christian thing to do? Whatever happened to "two shall become one" or "a man shall leave his parent and cleave to his wife"? When she was at church, didn't she pay attention to what was being said?

Had Irene and Max sat down with me and discussed the land, they would have had my cooperation in whatever they wanted to do. Instead, my feelings were never given consideration. My marriage had slowly been destroyed by the orchestration and manipulation that had taken place.

Let me be clear on this: *I'm not upset because of **WHAT** they did, I'm upset because of **HOW** they did it!*

Do you think if Lewis had done any of this to Irene, she would have sat back and said nothing? Would Irene have ignored her husband going behind her back and setting up legal documents with his mother, without taking Irene into consideration? I don't think so!

**April 2008** – Max and I went to Paris with some friends who were celebrating their thirtieth wedding anniversary. We had a great time visiting museums, churches, cafés, the Palace of Versailles, etc.

Ah, April in Paris! Fountains flowing, the smell of freshly baked bread in the air, streets made of stone, historic beauty everywhere! Paris is the most romantic city in the world! Unfortunately, when Max and I were alone, the trip totally lacked romance. No lovemaking, kissing, or even handholding.

Towards the end of our trip, we visited the Eiffel Tower. While standing underneath it, I looked up and said, "Max, kiss me." He looked at me (like I had three heads) and gave me a quick peck on the lips.

"Well, we'll always have that!" I said with great disappointment.

Within days of our return home from France, I decided it was time to get help from a professional therapist. I wanted to find someone to help me understand the anger I felt. Had I created all of this in my head? No matter what Max had done, he was my husband and I should try to forgive him. I wanted to forgive him. Could I forgive him?

In my heart, I felt Max's mother had betrayed Max, as well as me. He deserved someone who would love him and be there for him. I think I understand Max like no one else. At least that's what I tell myself. Everyone deserves someone who knows and understands you, who can give you love and kindness, so that you can have a happier life. I wanted to be that person for my husband. I wanted to help create happiness for him. Don't we all deserve happiness from our spouse? We all deserve it, regardless of who we are. Well, don't we?

Researching on-line for a therapist was easy. I pulled up my insurance provider to see who was listed. I printed the information, and, on the following Sunday, I called a few of the numbers and listened to the voices on the answering machine. I wanted to make sure I didn't get someone young, but rather someone with "life experience." Finally, a voice sounded mature and sincere. I left a message asking the therapist to please call me back so I could schedule an appointment.

This could be life changing; at least I was hoping it would be. The sooner I got beyond this, the sooner I could attempt to be a good wife again.

Dr. Shaw returned my call, and I scheduled an appointment with her. The earliest available date wasn't until June.

### *Exchanging Letters*

**May 1, 2008** – Out of the blue, I received a letter from my mother-in-law. I stared at it. It was addressed to Beth Edwards. Why would she write me a letter? Can't she pick up the phone if she has something to say to me? Confused by it and the possibilities of what it could say, I finally opened it. The letter read:

*Beth,*

*Whatever happened to the Beth I used to know and will she be back? The one who stood in my kitchen and said, "Irene, I love your son so very much." That statement alone gave me more happiness than you could imagine. Where is Beth and will she be back? The one, who came to family gatherings, laughed, had nice things to say, and was fun to be with. Where did Beth go and will she be back? Beth who had empathy for a dying neighbor, and gave joy by doing her hair; the one who put time aside for weekly prayer in her church, and nursed a sick deer. Where did Beth go and will she be back? The one who has made many family scrapbooks, enjoyable scrapbooks, we would never otherwise have had. Where did Beth go and will she be back? The Beth who would stop at the office to chat, who cared enough about her father-in-law's brain condition to see that he got to a neurologist for evaluation. Where did Beth go and will she be back?*

*The happy 50th celebration, with all of my family together, was marked with your obvious brush-off. Where have we failed you Beth? Is there a kinder or more understanding family out there for you somewhere? Where has Beth gone and will she be back?*

*Irene*

My first thought was, *Is she for real?* I read this letter over and over. I didn't show it to Max. This was between Irene and me. My mother-in-law expected a reaction, so I gave her one. I wrote:

*Irene,*

*Whatever happened to the Irene I thought I knew?*

*The mother of the man I came to love so much. The mother who stood in her kitchen a few short years ago and told me she would NOT tell her son she loved him because her parents never said it to her. The mother who chose to say three important words to her daughter, but not to the son who has worked with her and for her, for many years. The mother I later witnessed saying those three words to her nephews, but not to her own son. THIS has given me more sadness than you could ever imagine.*

*Whatever happened to the Irene I thought I knew?*

*The wonderful, happy celebration of Christmas, where you met Zack's fiancée for the first time, was marked with sadness. The once gracious hostess who used to make everyone feel welcome, couldn't be bothered to get up off the floor and express a welcoming gesture.*

*I was taught that if you can't say anything nice, don't say anything at all.*

*With that said...*

*I remain,*

*Beth*

I felt like I was at war with Irene. What was her problem?

In my anger, I remembered that Max hadn't yet brought me the documents I'd asked for. Having asked several times for him to bring them home, I called him again.

"Max, please bring home your Irrevocable Trust, insurance policies, and our tax documents. Get them and put them in your truck *now*, please!" I said.

To my surprise, Max finally brought them home, and I was able to look at his Irrevocable Trust. I have never read legal verbiage so thick. It would take time to understand what it said.

The first thing that stood out very clearly, and also disturbingly, was that Max had cut Zack (his adopted son) out of any inheritance. That, in itself, was hurtful on many levels. Had he told me this, I might not have been happy about it, but options could have been discussed.

Max asked if I looked at the document. I ignored him.
He stood in front of me and said, "The Irrevocable Trust was set up for the life insurance policies, to make sure they would be paid. So if I become a drug addict or become mentally disabled, the bank has to contact you or my mother for payment. Once my father is gone, this money will pay for the purchase of the funeral home from my mother. Do you have any questions?"

I looked at him and said nothing. Silence is golden. This time I felt smarter for *not* saying anything. Every time we argued about legal documents before, Max felt I always understood and was, therefore, in agreement. The conversation was over, so all questions should have been answered. I kept bringing it up because Max wasn't fully answering the questions I asked, and without a full explanation, it didn't make sense.

*It's time to investigate this and get to the bottom of it.*

### *Questions Need Answers*

I made a list of questions for Mr. Roberts and asked Max to drop them off when he had time. Several weeks went by before I received a response. It came in the mail addressed to me. I opened it and started to read.

*Dear Beth,*

*Max dropped off a list of questions from you, and in this letter I will answer them for you.*

*It appears you have concerns regarding your or Max's Trust. You may have misunderstood the meaning or significance of the Trusts. Please call me if you ever have questions about the Trust, and I will answer your questions clearly and honestly. Know that if your husband should meet with me, I consider this private and won't discuss with you or the family, the contents of that conversation. The same shall apply to you; anything you and I discuss remains within my office and is not discussed with Max, or any of the family! I pride myself on confidentiality. If you think I'm too close with Lewis and Irene Edword's or Max Edword's, there are two other attorneys in my office who can meet with you if you prefer to meet with them confidentially. They would never discuss with anyone your issues or concerns. The attorneys in my office never discuss conversations they have with clients, unless it involves public matters such as litigation. We represent many families and individuals. Each interest of his/her process remains confidential, and the same goes for you.*

*Below are the answers to your questions:*

1. *WHY'S THE DATE ON BETH'S TRUST 1999?*

*The date you signed your original Trust is March 1, 1999. I notarized your signature that day. The original Trust can be amended at any time. You did your First Amendment December 1, 2006.*

2. *IS MY TRUST LINKED TO MAX'S IRREVOCABLE TRUST?*

*No...December 30, 1998, Max signed his Revocable Trust (ILIT). It was set up to reduce estate taxes regarding the life insurance, as it's considered a portion of gross taxable estate. Max's life insurance is owned by his Trust, and the Trustee must be a third party, which is the Trust Department of Willow Bank & Trust. Beth, you are the beneficiary, not the Trust Department. Because you are Max's wife, no estate tax applies. You would receive all proceeds from the life insurance outright.*

3. *BETH DID NOT SIGN TILL AFTER 2000. IS THIS LEGAL?*

*All documents have been reviewed. Your signature and dates are legal and valid.*

4. *WHY DID MAX SIGN THE AMENDMENT TO BETH'S TRUST?*

*Max is the First Successor Trustee...it had nothing to do with the content of your Amendment, and the content is not, nor should it be, Max's concern.*

5. *MAX AND BETH'S TRUST ARE SEPARATE, NOT JOINT?*

*Correct...Your Trust is your personal information, and you are in control of the assets in your Trust. Max has no control over your Trust, and cannot tell you what to do with your assets. The same applies to Max's Trust. You have no control over the assets or his Trust.*

*6. THERE'S NOT A CLAUSE THAT MAX NEEDS TO SIGN BETH'S CHANGES?*

*Correct...Max has no say about changes to your Trust. Max signed your Amendment only in his capacity as the First Successor Trustee. This means he acknowledges the terms in the Amendment and has to abide by them.*

*7. WHAT PURPOSE DID IT SERVE?*

*It only acknowledges Max as your First Successor Trustee. Max was notified, and knows you made changes to your First Amendment to your Trust. Max must accept the Amendment terms. You signed Max's Trust dated December 30, 1998, as First Successor Trustee, just as Max is First Successor Trustee of your Trust.*

*Please feel free to call my son or myself, if you have any questions. If you prefer someone unfamiliar with the Edwards family, there are two other attorneys in this office who would be happy to help you and clarify anything you might not understand.*

*The attorneys in my office will deal with you as an individual and will not discuss confidential matters.*

*Yours Very Truly,*

*Stewart Roberts*

Mr. Roberts stated that he'd gone over all my documents and verified that all dates were correct. I looked at the Amendment to my Trust. My signature was dated December 1, 2006, and the second page where Max signed was notarized by Mr. Roberts on December 27, 2005, one year earlier. Mr. Roberts was either incompetent, or he was messing with me on purpose.

I also have Mr. Roberts's bill/invoice, dated March 11, 1999. The bill was for Last Wills and Testaments, and Durable Powers of Attorney, General and Medical. Had I drawn up a Trust, shouldn't it have been listed on this bill?

Why had life insurance been put into an Irrevocable Trust to eliminate estate tax? There is no tax on life insurance, estate or otherwise. Have the laws changed? Taxes are paid on the insurance premiums when payments are made, not when the policy is cashed out. Again, this made no sense.

Does he think I'm an idiot? Am I an idiot? Am I really losing my mind? Am I paranoid? Am I obsessed and don't have a clue about reality? The attorney wrote me a letter wanting me to trust him and his confidentiality. Didn't the attorney break that trust with Max when he told me something I didn't know—that Max wanted to cut Zack out of any inheritance? And didn't this attorney break confidentiality again by telling me he wasn't going to tell Max I'd been in his office, then calling Max to tell him exactly that? Was this man trying to manipulate me, or the situation? Is there a legal term for mental cruelty? If what this man was doing wasn't against the law, it certainly should be.

I left the letter on the end table next to the sofa and put a pair of reading glasses on top of it so Max could read it when he came home.
Max came home, sat down, and pushed the letter and the glasses to the side to make room for his beer.

"I got the letter from your attorney. Aren't you going to read it?" I asked.

"No, I'm tired," Max said. "Did he answer your questions?"

"Yes," I said, "he answered my questions."

"Do you feel better now?" he asked.

"No. There are still things that don't make sense," I said.

Max glared at me, shut his eyes, and shook his head. Then he opened his eyes, rolled them to the television, and began to watch.

To remove the uneasy feeling I got from his glare, I decided to change the subject. "Did you eat?" I asked.

"Not yet," he replied. I reheated his dinner in the microwave and handed it to him. We watched television together and no more was said.

### *The Beginning of Therapy*

**June 12, 2008**, **Therapist 1** – My first appointment went really well. I told Dr. Shaw my life story as quickly as I could, while she took notes. We scheduled a month of appointments in advance; I went once a week.

In the sessions to follow, Dr. Shaw and I discussed everything from my childhood to the issues I have with the Trust documents and all that went with it. I even brought the Trust in to show her why I questioned it.

Dr. Shaw was very supportive of me.

"You have every right to be angry and mistrusting," Dr. Shaw said. "Your husband's first obligation should be to you, but, clearly, this is not the case. This is not the first time I've heard a story like yours," she said. "It's very common when a business is owned by a family that greed takes place. No one wants to give away something they have worked hard for. You are not blood, so you are not family."

I explained, "The family business was owned by Max's father, whose family started it in the early 1900s. One would think that Irene was sole owner. She found a sense of entitlement to the business as the owner's wife, but I wasn't allowed that same sense."

After two months of visits with Dr. Shaw, I stopped my sessions. The appointments were becoming a repeat of the last. How many times could I go over the same thing? Complaining about Max and his mother on a weekly basis seemed unproductive.

The therapist felt the issue was really an unhealthy relationship between my husband and his mother.

Max's mother came first, and I would always come second. This was not news to me; I knew I was second, but hearing it gave it new meaning. I decided to forget about it for the time being and focus on making my marriage better—focus on the positive instead of the negative.

I went to Nora's to pick up my box of documents. Nora and her husband Andy sat quietly while I explained what was going on.

"The thing with the dates is really bugging me," I said.

"I think the date must be linked to something else," Nora said.

"You could be right. Max's Revocable Trust is dated December 30, 1998, and the Irrevocable Trust is dated December 31, 1998—one day apart. Why not date them both the same day? My guess is that the two Trust documents have something to do with each other," I said.

Finally, something I could wrap my brain around; it sounded logical. Whether this was accurate or not, it made more sense than anything else I had thought of. I was so tired of being obsessed with this—tired of putting pieces of the puzzle together. I wanted nothing more than to put it all behind me.

The following weeks went really well for Max and me. I was putting everything I had into my marriage. Max and I were going to be okay after all. We were on our way to starting over.

Or so it seemed.

### *I Want a Divorce*

It was **August 17, 2008**. I had left the mail from the day before in the car, as I often do, too tired to look at it. The next morning, I brought it in and opened all of it. To my surprise and horror, there was an invoice from Mr. Roberts's Law Office. *What was this?* Over a dozen items were listed.

*01/07/08 Conference w/Atty. Roberts started to draft Amendment to Trust & prepared memo to Atty. Roberts*

*01/08/08 Corrected draft deed. Listened to Atty. Roberts's dictation, prepared Certificate of Trust & 2nd Amendment to Trust*

*01/09/08 Worked on Second Amendment to Trust*

*01/11/08 Met w/Max & Irene, prepared Certificate of Trust & deed*

*01/25/08 Phone call to Irene (2): Revisions to Max's Trust with a 1st and 2nd Amendment RE: Farm & Zack*

*02/01/08 Listened to Atty. Roberts's dictation; & prepared draft #2 of First Amendment to Trust & memo to Atty. Roberts*

*02/04/08 Revision to Trust & Amendments*

*02/07/08 Prepared draft #3 of Trust Amendment & made changes to Certificate of Trust*

*02/27/08 Finalized Trust Amendment & made appt. w/Max*

*02/29/08 Met w/Max Edwards*

*03/24/08 Reviewed documents & prepared memo to Atty. Roberts*

*04/29/08 Review & correction to First Amendment*

*06/02/08 Started dictation RE: letter to Beth Edwards*

*06/02/08 Finished draft letter to Beth Edwards & completed 1st draft of modified First Amendment to Trust (Max)*

*06/04/08 Corrected letter to Beth Edwards. Finalized - Letter to Beth & First Amendment to Max's Trust*

*07/01/08 Proofread drafts of Codicil, POA-General, POA-Medical, & finalized all documents*

*The cost is $2,197.50*

Conversations between the attorney, Irene, and Max? Changes made to Max's Trust, with a first and second amendment regarding the farm and Zack? A new Trust? I wonder what this one says? And what kind of deed are they drafting now? One for Max's half of the house? Or a new deed, transferring my share of the house with the use of the POA I gave Max?

*Not again!* My heart began to pound so hard I feared it would leap from my chest. A heat wave came over me like a hot flash I'd never experienced before. I became numb from my head to my toes and couldn't breathe. I felt sick. I bent over the counter so I wouldn't collapse to the floor. I thought I would pass out, but started to cry instead. I went into the bedroom, curled up on the bed, and sobbed for hours.

When Max came home, I confronted him with the invoice. "Max," I said calmly and slowly, "what are all these legal documents for?"

"I don't know what all the documents listed are for," he said.

“What do they say Max?” I calmly asked.

“I don’t know,” he said nervously.

“Where are the documents now?” I asked calmly.

“I don’t know,” he said frantically.

He kept repeating, "I’m so mad at that attorney! I’m so mad at that attorney!" I’d ask a question, but instead of giving me an answer, Max buried his face in the invoice and kept repeating, “I don’t know. I’m really mad at that attorney!”

I was getting nowhere, so out of nowhere I asked, “Max, will you take me to the movies?” With a huge sigh of relief, Max perked up and pretended none of this had just happened; he was following my lead. I wanted to let it rest until morning. I had lost all respect for him and knew in that moment he was nothing but a coward. Perhaps one more evening of pretended normalcy would somehow fix things.

Neither of us had eaten dinner, so Max took me to dinner first. We sat across the table from one another, and Max started talking to me. Nothing important was being said. He was doing all the talking for fear I’d start and bring up the invoice. For a moment, it seemed like old times. I’d forgotten how Max and I used to look at each other, and how at one time he had wanted to hear what I had to say, like he was interested instead of frustrated with me. Max never treated me like crap, he just didn’t know what to do with me. Perhaps he thought, *If I just ignore her, maybe she’ll go away.*

How did he go from being that man to the man he is today? Why was he running from me instead of to me? Had I been a bitch all these years and chosen not to see it? Had I created all of this drama in my head? What about the invoice—the extra Trust document I'd never seen? I didn't know what to do.

Max took me to the movies that evening and nothing more was said.

**August 18, 2008** – I'd gotten up earlier than usual because I couldn't sleep. I told Max I was going to Mr. Roberts's office that morning to find out what this was all about. "That's not necessary," Max said. "I'm going over there. I'm so angry with him!"

"Good," I said, "Then we can go together."

"No, you don't need to go there," Max said.

"Well, Max, I can go there alone, but I'm certain Mr. Roberts will call you as soon as I walk into his office," I said calmly.

"Just a minute," Max said as he walked into the bedroom.

When he came back he had some typed papers in his hand. "What's that?" I asked.

"Just some notes," he said. "I'm not like you and can't think of what to say when I'm backed into a corner. You know I don't like confrontation."

"You don't like confrontation because you tell lies. People who tell the truth are never backed into a corner; it's the lies that back you into that corner. It's too bad you still haven't learned this," I said, drained of emotion.

Max skimmed his notes and said, “As you know, several months ago we weren’t doing very well, and I was considering a divorce and wanted to find out my options. I don’t think I need to discuss that with you.”

“I agree,” I replied. “A visit to an attorney for a divorce does not need to be discussed. But why him of all people?” I asked.

“Because he knows his stuff!” Max yelled.

“Oh, yes, and that’s why he lies to me, and misspelled your last name in my letter. I hope you’re not going to pay him the $37.50 he charged you on the invoice for this *non-correction,”* I said out of anger. “What about the other things listed?”

"The attorney took it upon himself to draw up legal documents,” Max claimed. “He wanted me to sign them. I said, ‘Absolutely not! I'm not signing that!’ Then a bill arrived at the funeral home with only an amount on it. I called Mr. Roberts’s office and told him not to send me a bill with only a dollar figure—I need to know what I’m paying for, break it down! So the attorney broke it down and sent it to the house instead of the funeral home.”

“Don’t you find this interesting?” I asked. “Mr. Roberts knew I knew nothing about the documents listed in his invoice. Max, the attorney knew I would be upset by this.”

I went from angry to heartbroken and started to cry. “What kind of game is being played, Max? This is my life, and it’s being ruined. I can’t trust you anymore. Every time I turn around, you and your mother are skipping off to the attorney’s office to get another legal document.

What was the outcome of all of this, what did the documents say, and where are they? Why was your mother involved? Why does it mention Zack? Have you not done enough damage to him, or our marriage?"

"Max, did your mother ever tell you about the letter she sent to me?" I asked.

"Yes. And my mother loves me, and she told me she loves me! Your response to her was childish," Max said.

"Childish or not, it was well worth it to get her to say 'I love you' to you after all these years," I said. "Do you realize what mental issues could have come to you had she not said these words before she died? Regardless of what you think, I'm happy I could do that for you, even if you choose not to see it."

Max just glared at me and let me continue.

"I've loved you and watched you go through three emotional breakdowns, and you still go back for more," I said, tears running down my face. "That business is killing you."

"That's why I'm planning to retire when I'm 55-years-old," Max said.

"Your mother has got you by the balls! Do you think for one minute she's going to let you retire? She'll guilt you into staying. She'll never let you walk away from that business."

"She may not have anything to say about it," Max claimed.

"How do you figure that?" I asked.

"I'll sell it," he said like a defiant child.

"Do I have to keep reminding you, Max, you don't own it?" I said.

Out of left field, Max said, "You don't like my friends, you don't like my family, and you hate my business. Why do you stay?"

I stood silent for a moment while the last four disappointing years bounced around in my head. "You're right," I said. "Maybe this has come at a good time. Maybe it's time to do this."

I looked at the clock and said, "I've got to go to work" and left.

On my way to work, I called my boss to tell her I wouldn't be in. I needed to stop at the bank. I waited in line behind a woman who appeared to be around 85-years-old. I think the teller called her Mrs. Perkins. Mrs. Perkins had filled out a withdrawal slip, and the teller was questioning her. "I gave you $200 yesterday," the teller said. "Why do you need more money today, Mrs. Perkins?"

"Groceries," Mrs. Perkins replied.

"That's what you said yesterday," the teller said. *Why is the teller questioning this poor woman? It's her money—just give it to her! I have my own mess to deal with. I wish they would hurry up!*

When I finally got up to the counter, I paid off the credit card and asked the bank teller to issue a cashier's check from me, made payable to Dr. Clifton, a plastic surgeon Marie spoke highly of. I had always wanted rhinoplasty (a nose job) and putting $1,500 down on surgery Max said I could have years ago shouldn't make him angry.

I then asked the teller to cut another cashier's check to me for one-half of the account's remaining balance.

Next, I stopped at the office of an attorney recommended to me by Nora and made an appointment to file for divorce. There was no other option. I could no longer be married to someone who would never look out for my best interest, someone who never cared about me enough to have a conversation, someone who's dedicated to his mother and what she wanted in life instead of to his wife and what she wanted. It was time for me to take control of my life before there was nothing left of it.

My appointment was with attorney Harold Jones. I took the Trust document with me. Sitting in the waiting room going over my papers kept me busy until Mr. Jones came out and introduced himself. At first glance, I couldn't believe his resemblance to actor Patrick Stewart. If they were standing next to each other, I'd swear they were related. He asked me into his office. For the first time, I felt a ray of hope; someone was going to help me. He thumbed through the document.

"There's nothing in it," he said.

"Excuse me?" I said.

"Do you understand what a Trust is for?" he asked.

"I've been told they are used as tax shelters, but from what I've just been through, it appears that a spouse can remove assets from the other by playing a legal document shell game. One document leads to the other, which directs you to a fake, while a new Will and Trust, with all the answers, has been hidden away in your husband's desk drawer at work," I said sarcastically.

"I don't know what that was all about," he said, "but I'm sure it has something to do with why you're here today. Let me explain," Mr. Jones said. "I can answer questions when I'm done."

"This is how a Trust works," he said. "There is a husband and a wife. One day they have a question: I wonder what will happen to us when we are old and can't take care of ourselves? What if I die before you or you die before me? What about Grandmother's pearls and Uncle Bill's gold watch? I don't want my children to have control over my assets because they will spend it all and put me in a nursing home.

"The husband and wife sit down together with paper and pen. They write down all the assets they have together, and all the assets that are separate. Together, they decide what they'd like to do with these assets. Who they'd like to see get the pearls and the watch. The Trust becomes an extension of them. The husband and the wife now, together, put everything they have into the Trust—savings accounts, retirement accounts, the deed to their home, everything; and what they don't cover with the Trust, they can cover with a Will. The Will can list all the items in their jewelry box and the fifty people they want each piece to go to. Their savings account will now read, for example, 'The Max Edwards and Beth Edwards Revocable Trust, Savings Account, or Checking Account, or IRA Account.' The deed to their home will read the same way. They will sign a Quit Claim Deed from Max Edwards and Beth Edwards, to The Max Edwards and Beth Edwards Revocable Trust. Everything they have—*everything*—becomes part of their Trust. Do you understand?" he said.

"Yes, I think for the very first time, I do understand! Thank you," I said.

"As I look at your Trust, I wonder why this was set up with nothing in it. My guess is, it was set up to keep you from getting something. Perhaps it's this piece of land?" he asked.

"Yes, Max and his mother didn't want me to have the land," I said. "But I never wanted it. The Trust was set up in such a manipulative way. It's not what they did; it's how they did it. They continued to scamper off to Irene's attorney, who played such head games, I'm afraid I'm losing my mind."

"Irene's attorney, Mr. Roberts, was doing his job," Mr. Jones said. "And his job was to protect the assets of his client. Not you, but his clients, Lewis and Irene Edwards."

"Because of this Trust, I can no longer trust my husband," I said. "I'm afraid he will *Trust* me out of everything we should have together, and I will be left with 50% of a home I won't be able to afford to live in. For all I know, he's already quit-claimed his half of the deed, and mine, from the two of us to his Trust. I need to make the POA I previously signed void, so it's one less thing for me to worry about," I said. "Is this something you can do for me?"

"Yes," Mr. Jones said. "I will take care of it today."

"You want to know something? I actually prayed for answers, and they were sent to me in the mail! Who knew God would use the postal service?" I said, trying to make light of it. "My mother always said, 'Be careful of what you wish for, for you surely could get it.'"

"Is there any chance the two of you will reconcile?" Mr. Jones asked.

"No," I said. "I really don't want a divorce. I love my husband, but Max is forcing me to divorce him. I'm afraid if I stay married, I will wake up one day with nothing because he will Trust it all away to his sister's children or the Pet & Wild Animal Society. Never did I believe something like this could be possible. I was under the impression the legal system was set up to insure fairness. But as my mother also used to say, 'Whoever said life is fair?' "

"Beth, women always want to be fair; men don't," Mr. Jones said. "You will find this out during your divorce: you will want fairness, and he will want it all."

* * *

I told Max I filed for divorce and moved into the guest room. He didn't even care.

In the days to come, Max and I didn't speak. On the rare occasion when we did, I took great pleasure in telling him to "Fuck off!" Max thought it offensive if I said the word "fuck" to him outside of the bedroom. Now that I was divorcing him, I let it fly out of my mouth whenever I felt the urge. Like a new bird taking flight, I said the word for the sheer enjoyment of watching Max clench his teeth in anger: "Fuck-off!"

I was given a packet of papers to fill out for my attorney by September 26, 2008. There were over fifty questions. Each question needed an answer or document to support the answer. I had to supply information from the past two years. They asked for bank statements, pay stubs, insurance documents, a list of monthly household expenses, etc. I purchased a large three-ring binder and dividers to keep the information organized.

This started out to be a good idea, but it was difficult to separate the questions and answers to keep them neat. I ended up typing all the questions so I could give my answers in a neat and organized manner. When I delivered the binder to the attorney's office, Mr. Jones was impressed. I gave him copies of everything I had, including the Irrevocable Trust. Mr. Jones felt this was not his area of expertise and sent it on to an estate planner with another law firm.

"This is fantastic. Everyone should present his or her information to me this way," he said. "I could actually take *this* to court."

"Good," I said, realizing that I'd gone above and beyond what was expected of me.

One of the questions asked me to explain the breakdown of the marriage. I spent many hours preparing six typed pages that explained, in great detail, the facts that led to the destruction of my marriage. I wanted the judge to understand how I had been manipulated. Little did I know, the judge would never see anything I'd written. I found out later, from my attorney's assistant, that we were only allowed to submit to the judge a short paragraph for each question askcd. How do you sum up the destruction of a 22 year marriage in a paragraph? Most of the hours I spent organizing and answering everything asked of me turned out to be a total waste of my time. I was extremely disappointed.

Our pre-trial was set for 1:00 p.m. on Wednesday, **October 1, 2008**. The judge informed us she wanted the divorce finished in ninety days. My attorney stated that thcrc was a possibility that Max was hiding assets, and he would need time to investigate.

The judge replied, “Mr. Edwards, if you are hiding assets, I will see that anything uncovered is given to your wife. Do you understand?”

“Yes, your honor,” Max said.

### *Gossip*

Every town has a busybody, and ours was no exception. Some busybodies are prudish, sly, or even funny. This one was a short, creepy, little bald man with beady eyes and glasses. He took pleasure in spreading gossip from one end of town to the other, stopping in at the insurance office, coffee shop, chiropractor, and anywhere else someone had time to listen to his current line of bullshit. His name was Wilbur Jeffers. He never gave any thought or consideration to the damage he did to the people he gossiped about. To him it was sheer entertainment.

Mr. Jeffers never liked me, and I never understood why. Max told me that Mr. Jeffers called me Brunhilda behind my back when he referred to me. I had only spoken two sentences to Mr. Jeffers through the years, so his ugly comments towards me were unjust. I had never had cross words or any type of argument with this man, so why would he call me names? And, more importantly, why did Max let him?

Shortly after I filed for divorce, I called my friends to let them know.

“Hi, Becca. I wanted to let you know I filed for divorce,” I said.

“Did you just file?” she asked.

“Yes,” I said. “The papers were actually filed with the court on August 20.

“Were you going to get a divorce earlier this year?” Becca asked.

“No, why do you ask?” I replied.

“Because earlier this year, I went to get my back adjusted at the chiropractor’s office and they told me that you and Max were getting a divorce.

“When was this?” I asked.

“It was around the beginning of the year—January or February. I asked them who they heard it from, because if you were getting a divorce, you would have called me,” Becca said. “They clammed up and didn’t say another word about it after that.”

“Aha, this is starting to make sense,” I said. “I had a bank account with Irene, Lewis, and Max. Irene closed it out at the end of January. It didn’t make sense at the time, but now it’s all becoming clear. Also, I got this invoice from Irene’s attorney, Stewart Roberts, which, miraculously, got sent to me by accident, if you can imagine it. There were several entries from January and February—visits Max and Irene had with the attorney. Max said he had thought about divorcing me at the beginning of the year. It sounds like he did more than just think about it,” I said. “Often, Irene and Max hire Wilbur Jeffers, that little troll, to tend door, make a removal, whatever. I bet in all off Irene’s excitement, she spilled the beans to the little creep, and we all know he can’t keep his mouth shut. Apparently, Irene can’t keep her mouth shut either.”

Becca later went back to the chiropractor and said, “Well, you must be in tight with someone who could have supplied you with information so privileged that Beth Edwards herself didn’t know.”

They gave no response.

### *Therapy Is Making Me Crazy!*

**September 12, 2008** – It had been several weeks since I filed for divorce.

For the most part, I had always felt like a strong person. I made my decisions and proceeded. But reality about the divorce had set in, and I began to feel desperate and remorseful about the life-changing event that I was so sure would make me happier.

One evening while Max was in the pole barn, I went there to talk. "Max we've been married for twenty-two years. We have to try and work through this. I love you and don't want to get a divorce. Please, can we talk about this?" I asked.

"No," Max said, "I'm good with this."

I walked back to the house, hopeless, sobbing. I felt like I'd just been kicked in the stomach. I got into bed fully clothed and cried myself to sleep.

* * *

I was at my bi-yearly check-up at my neurologist's office so he could evaluate my progress with my A.D.D. medication. Dr. Gerald stepped into the room and said, "So how are you doing?"

I burst into tears. I seemed to have no control over them now. "Terrible. I'm getting a divorce," I said sobbing. I explained the situation as quickly as I could because I knew he had other patients waiting. Dr. Gerald could see right away I was a mess. My eyes were puffy, and my nose was red. I hadn't put on any make-up in days because I only cried it off.

"Would you like to try an anti-depressant?" he asked

"I never thought about it," I said. "Depression is for other people."

"I can prescribe something that would work well with your A.D.D. medication." I agreed to give it a try. My doctor also wanted me to take some time off work, if it were possible, to help me with the adjustment of my new life. I was given a one month medical leave, with a re-evaluation in one month.

After my appointment, I went into work with the medical leave slip filled out by my doctor. I knocked on my boss Marcy's door.

"Hi, Beth, you look terrible. Come in and sit down," Marcy said.

"I'm sorry to do this to you, but I have to. My life is falling apart. I'd been coming to work every day and crying while I work. I'm in so much pain, I feel like someone is ripping my skin off. I've never felt anything so excruciating in my life. I want to die. My stress is high, and my nerves are shot. My daily fear is that someone will stop by my desk and need something from me, and I'll break down in tears. I can't do this anymore. I have to get through the divorce so I can build a new life. I love my job, but I will understand if you have to replace me," I said.

Marcy was understanding and said, "Take the time you need."

"Thank you," I said.

Marcy said, "Most people don't realize that when they get married, under the eyes of God, the two shall become one. When you get a divorce, you experience the literal ripping apart of one being, back into two."

"What a poetic description of such a horrific experience," I said.

"You do a great job, and I want you back as soon as you are able," she said. "In the meantime, we'll hire someone from a temporary agency to do your job."

"Thank you, Marcy. Again, I'm so sorry," I said.

I went home, got into bed, pulled the covers over my head, and wished I'd never wake up again. I felt lost.

*Why does he always leave me and go down to the barn every day? Am I a terrible person to be around? What's going to happen to me? Will I be left alone the rest of my life? How will I afford to live?* I thought. *He was supposed to take care of me when I was old, and I'd take care of him. He was supposed to fight for me. Why am I so dispensable? Why doesn't my husband love me? WHY DOESN'T MAX LOVE ME?*

I felt desperate. All I could do was cry, and sleep, and cry.

Max came home around 10:00 p.m., and his noise woke me up. I cried all night long, knowing my husband, the man I loved, was down the hall and no longer wanted me. It was killing me.

I heard Max get up in the morning for work. I managed to get out of bed. I thought, *If I could make myself a cup of hot tea, I'd at least get to look at him before he left. I miss him and love him more than I realized. I'm lost without him.*

I put the teakettle on and sat in a chair waiting. I was a nervous wreck and started shaking. *Oh my God, there he is.* My mind raced. *I forgot to think this through. I didn't comb my hair, or brush my teeth, or wash my face.*

*I'm so ugly!* My shaking was uncontrollable. I didn't know what to do, and I was panicking. I wished I could melt into the floor and disappear forever.

The teakettle was screaming, and I never heard it. Max went over to the stove and turned it off. My head was down, but I could see him coming over to me. "Are you okay?" he asked.

Max approached me with his hand extended, as though he were going to touch my shoulder or back. "DON'T TOUCH ME!" I screamed at him.

He stopped, lowered his arm, and just looked at me. I was still shaking and now crying. I looked like hell! I turned away from him. "DON'T LOOK AT ME!" I said with tears running down my face.

"I'm worried about you," Max said.

"Don't be," I said sobbing.

"I want to help you," he said.

"You can help me by dropping over dead. Your mother, too!" I said. "You've both ruined my life. If I stay married to you, I'll have nothing. I hate you!"

"What do you want from me?" he asked.

"All I need from you is your fucking check!" I yelled.

Max didn't know what to do for me, so he didn't do anything and went to work. I crawled back into bed. *What is happening to me? I feel crazy most of the time. The sadness and heartache have taken me over. It's more than I can bear, and I don't want to live anymore.*

A couple hours had passed. Max woke me with a phone call. "Beth, you need to make an appointment with your therapist."

"Okay," I said, still groggy from sleep.

I called Dr. Shaw but her appointment book was full for months. I called Nora and asked if she knew of a therapist I could call. I was losing my mind, and I needed help. Nora had many friends, surely one of them had been to a therapist. Within minutes, Nora called me back with a phone number. I went back to bed.

Marie called. "Beth, are you okay? Max called and sounded concerned."

"Max concerned? Please!" I said. "I'm fine, don't worry about me." I hung up from her and went back to sleep.

When I woke up later that afternoon, I called the number Nora had given me, left a voice message, and went back to bed. I slept the rest of the day and through the night. The next morning, Max knocked on my door. "WHAT?" I said.

"Can I come in?" he asked.

"The door's open," I said, then pulled the covers over my head so he couldn't see me. I felt ugly and unloved.

"Beth, I'm concerned about you," he said without emotion, as if he had to say it.

"If you were concerned, you'd stay married to me and take care of me and love me. But you don't, so I have to do all of this myself. Don't burden yourself. I've called a therapist, and when she calls me back, I'll make an appointment. So you can go to work now with a clear conscious," I said crying.

"Aren't you going to work?" Max asked.

"No, I'm getting a divorce, so I have to find a new place to live, and I have to pack up all of my things," I said with sarcasm. "And I have a nervous breakdown to go through between now and then. I can't do all that and work, too!"

**September 14, 2008**, **Therapist 2** – My new therapist, Anna, said, "Vent your anger, yell, scream, cry, and swear; do whatever you need to do to remove the toxic anger from your system."

I yelled, screamed, cried, and swore, all in the solitude of the guest room. What a waste of time and energy. This method of release was getting me nowhere.

All alone in the house, and in the safety of my room, all was dark except for the hall light that shone in from beneath my closed door. I shut my eyes and started screaming, over and over: "I HATE YOU. WHY DON'T YOU LOVE ME? I'M YOUR WIFE FOR GOD'S SAKE! YOU'RE KILLING ME! I WISH I WERE DEAD! I WISH YOU AND YOUR MOTHER WOULD DIE!" I screamed out in pain, crying.

When I opened my eyes, the lights were off outside my door. Apparently, Max had come home, heard me screaming and crying, shut off the lights, and gone to bed.

Anger was swelling up inside of me like a volcano. How dare he ignore me! I screamed out one more time, "I FUCKING HATE YOU! I thrashed around in bed out of frustration. Was it possible to feel the rage coming right through me? My nerve endings were screaming throughout my entire body. If I could unzip my skin and jump out of it, I would.

I could not imagine how I would ever get through this alive. I wanted to cut myself and exchange one pain for the other.

Why not vent my anger directly at the person who had created it? I got up and walked down the hall. I opened his bedroom door and began to scream, cry, and swear at my husband. "I HATE YOU, YOU ASSHOLE! I HATE YOU, I HATE YOU, I FUCKING HATE YOU!"

I went back to the guest room and slammed the door! Unfortunately, this didn't make me feel good at all. I felt worse than ever. The meanness that came out of me reminded me of someone who needed an exorcism. I was spewing verbal vomit! All I could do was curl up in the fetal position and pray it would all stop. I knew I was going crazy. Please, God, make it stop!

The next morning, I woke up a mess. My throat was sore, and I was shaking. I started sobbing all over again. I got up, went into the kitchen, and sat down in a chair next to the wall.

"Max," I said sobbing, "I need a check for my therapist."

Max, clearly upset by my display of insanity, said, "Beth, I don't know much about this therapist you're seeing, but I think you need to see someone with more credentials, someone with a PhD. Does she have a PhD?"

"No, I don't think so," I said.

Because Max was paying for it, I felt it only fair to take his advice.

When I called Anna to tell her my husband wanted me to see a psychologist or psychiatrist, she asked why. I explained to her that I had been trying to remove the anger from my system so that I could heal and move on. Yelling at an empty room did no good. Driving in the country and screaming at the top of my lungs only gave me a headache. When I told her I had decided to vent my anger at the person who was making me angry, she said, "You *never* have the right to vent your anger at another human being!"

I gasped and said, "What? Did you really just say that? Anna, don't you think this is something you should have mentioned to me earlier?" Anna apologized for the misunderstanding. The damage had been done, as far as I was concerned, and nothing could undo it. Worse yet, I now looked crazy in the eyes of my husband. *What must he think of me?* My depression was making a part of me unrecognizable, even to myself.

I called my neurologist to see if he could prescribe something stronger. I explained that the Excellipam I was taking worked well for a few days, and then it dissolved into nothing. He prescribed something else and told me to take half a dose of Excellipam for five days and start taking half a dose of the other. This would allow my system to smoothly transition from one medication to the other.

After speaking with my doctor, I anticipated feeling really good. Unfortunately, approximately ten days later, I felt even worse than before. I never knew there was a deeper, blacker hole of hell called depression that I would find my way into. This was like nothing I had ever experienced before. It was huge and heavy. A feeling of overwhelming sadness surrounded me, following me, hugging me so tightly I wanted to kill it and kill myself to make it all go away.

I understand why this warning accompanies all anti-depressants: "This medication can cause thoughts of suicide or dying, attempts to commit suicide, or worsening depression or anxiety, etc."

Every person's system reacts differently to medication. I was told it would take time for my first anti-depressant to build up in my system before it would work. I felt noticeably better in three days, not the two weeks explained to me. Instead of asking for a different, more powerful medication, I should have asked for a stronger dose of what had already proven to make me feel better. Because I didn't, I was now more depressed than ever. I wanted to kill Max, his mother, and myself.

I was having a really bad day. The thoughts were overtaking my brain, and I was becoming irrational. I knew I was capable of things I'd never given thought to before. *I better call Max*, I thought.

"Max, it's Beth," I cried. "Please don't come home."

"Where am I supposed to stay?" he asked angrily.

"Stay at the funeral home. You've stayed there before. I'm asking this in your best interest. I can feel the anger swelling up within me. Please stay there," I begged him and then hung up.

The next afternoon, I called him again. "Max, I want to let you know it's safe to come home. I'm feeling better today."

"Thanks for warning me yesterday," Max said.

"I was afraid of what would happen if you came home," I said. "I did it for me as well as for you."

When Max came home, he said, "I think you should see a psychiatrist."

"Could you find me a psychiatrist?" I asked. "I have no energy to do it. I'm drained. Can you make sure she's close to home and that my insurance will cover the appointments? Anytime is okay for me."

**October 15, 2008** – Within a couple days, I awoke one morning to find a note on the counter with the name and phone number of a psychologist. Her name was Dr. Shirley Curtis.

The next time I saw Max, I asked, "Did you call Dr. Curtis and make me an appointment?"

"No," he said. "Did you want me to?"

"Didn't we have this conversation already?" I asked. "This is part of the problem. You don't listen to me. I'm not a priority. Everyone's needs always come before mine."

"Beth, what do you want me to do? Do you want me to call Dr. Curtis?"

"Don't bother," I said sarcastically, with tears in my eyes. "Your mother probably has something more important for you to do. Go away. I'll take care of it myself!"

**October 21, 2008, Therapist 3** – I made and showed up to my first appointment with Dr. Curtis. "Tell me about what brings you here?" she asked.

"I'm going through a difficult divorce. I'm having problems letting go of my husband, a man I truly love. I don't think he loves me, or ever loved me. It's my belief my husband isn't capable of love," I said.

"Is Max having an affair?" Dr. Curtis asked.

"No," I said.

"Well," she said, "men only walk away from a marriage for one of two reasons: either they're having an affair, or they've become financially greedy."

"Really," I said, "I don't see either relating to Max."

"How would you describe Max to me?" Dr. Curtis asked.

"I feel my husband is disconnected. He shows no emotion, no feelings, and he doesn't really like people. He sticks to himself and spends all of his extra time in his pole barn. Max is a good provider, but a terrible husband, terrible father, and is more married to his mother than he is to me."

"Anything else?"

"Yes," I said. "Max is a liar and claims he hates confrontation; however, he had no problem confronting his mother on land she wanted to give to his sister. And he had no problem with confrontation when he dcmandcd an attorncy givc him an invoicc brcaking down all the legal documents and appointments he was being charged for. He walks away from me whenever I talk to him. He never wants to go anywhere, unless it's of his choosing, and, even then, he doesn't want to take me with him. It's like he doesn't like me.

"The very reason I'm divorcing Max is because he and his mother have gone behind my back and discussed my life, my son's life, and what financial outcome the two of them feel will sustain my life once they are gone. They've done all this without any consideration to my thoughts on the subject. It's almost like they are the married couple and I am the neglected, unwanted stepchild. It's disturbing. It's beyond disturbing!"

"What about holidays and birthdays?" she asked.

"Max doesn't know me, and he's never tried to get to know me. He doesn't know what I like, so any gift given by Max has been thoughtless and minimal. For example, several years in a row, for my birthday he gave me a bottle of liquor— Irish Crème—and a funny card. The entire collection of cards I've received from Max since we married are funny, not loving.

"Christmas, I'd purchase items, wrap them, and label them from Max. Or, I'd asked him to make me a towel rack or coat rack—something he could weld. He likes to play in his pole barn and make things. Last year, I asked that he weld me two large planter baskets to hang on the outside of the kitchen and garage window. That's what he gave me for Christmas, but now I have to leave them behind—they're attached to the house. I can't use them now anyway, I have to move."

Dr. Curtis said, "Given your description of him, Max sounds like a narcissist."

"Is this a disorder or mental illness that's curable with therapy or medication?" I asked.

"It's a personality disorder. And *no*, Max will *never* change. Tell me what life was like before you got married?" Dr. Curtis asked.

"He was really nice to be around," I said. "I had been married before, so Max seemed really immature to me, but that was something I knew would go away with age. When Max and I dated, he liked talking to me and taking me places. He used to smile and laugh. He hasn't done that in years. He was so handsome and well built. He's actually very good in bed. He was the only man who took the time to give me an orgasm. I'd been around the block a few times, so to speak, but never had the experience. I feared something was wrong with me, or I was frigid or something. Max treated it like his mission in life, and he conquered it! That was all before he proposed to me." I started to cry.

"After Max asked me to marry him, he became a different person. We didn't even spend the night together our first night of marriage. Max went back to the funeral home with his family and took a nap in his bedroom. When he got up, he didn't even call me. I was at my apartment waiting for him for over four hours. I finally called to see where he was. Max told me to come to the funeral home because his aunts and uncles were all there eating leftovers from the rehearsal dinner the night before.

"Do you still love Max?" Dr. Curtis asked.

"Yes, I love being around him, and I love how he smells. I love when he hugs me; it makes me feel small and protected, like I have nothing to worry about," I said.

"What else do you love about him?" she asked.

"I used to love it when we went out together and took short trips to Cincinnati and long trips to warm places in the winter. I miss being with him," I said.

"When?" she asked.

"Years ago. We haven't done anything in a long time," I said.

"What would Max say he loved about you?" Dr. Curtis asked.

"Probably nothing. He doesn't even like me. Max avoids me at all cost," I said crying.

Dr. Curtis sat back in her chair and looked over the top of her reading glasses. "You don't love each other, you're addicted to one another like a bad habit," she said. "What would you like to see as an outcome of your therapy?"

"I want to be free of pain and heartache. I want to be with someone who wants to be with me. Someone who wants to talk with me, who likes me, and looks forward to seeing me," I said.

"Given the information about your wedding night, I feel Max didn't really want to marry you," Dr. Curtis said. "He wasn't strong enough to back out of it, or he did it because that's what was expected of him. Our time is almost up. Do you need a prescription refill?"

"Yes," I said. "I need it for 20 mg of Excellipam."

**October 28, 2008** – Dr. Curtis sat down with pen and paper in hand. "Are you and your husband still living together?" she asked.

"Yes," I said.

"Are the two of you getting along okay, living under the samc roof during this timc?"

"It's really difficult. Whoever suggested husbands and wives should have to live together until the divorce is over should be beaten with a stick," I said. "Max did say he'd buy me out now, so I could move out. I have to tell you, it really bothered me last week when you said I didn't love my husband. That's not true. I love him so much that it's killing me knowing I'm going to lose him. I get up early in the morning sometimes, just to catch a glimpse of him."

"Does Max know you love him?"

"Yes," I said.

"Do you think you're willing to work it out with him?" she asked. "And if so, do you think he would be willing to work it out with you?"

"I would love to work it out, but I'm not sure Max wants to."

"Well, that's what you need to find out. Don't give him an ultimatum. Ask him if there is a chance it could be worked out, and, if so, is it a 50% chance, 90% chance, etc. This will give you information to help you move forward, one way or the other."

That evening, I waited for Max to come in. As usual, he was still in the pole barn at 10:00 p.m. I couldn't wait any longer. I drove down to the barn. Max was watching a DVD on a television he must have recently purchased to keep there.

"Are you avoiding me?" I asked.

"No," he said.

"Well, actions speak louder than words," I said shrugging my shoulders and making a silly gesture with my hands.

"I was about to go to bed, but I wanted to ask you something before I did. Twenty-two years is a long time. Have you thought about trying to work this out with me?"

"No," he said. "I'm comfortable with this."

"Okay," I said, "I just needed to ask. I want you to know I'm sorry for yelling the things I did at you."

I left the barn, went back up to the house, and got into bed. Then I took an imaginary pair of scissors and cut the cord from my heart to his. This was something the first therapist told me to do.

The following morning, I felt good. I was ready to move on. I spent all day packing.

**October 30, 2008** – Today is my birthday. For many years, I have given myself a special birthday (after being disappointed by my husband year after year): I take myself to a movie, buy myself a gift, and buy myself a cake. It's a party for one.

This year, I went to the movie with my friend Nora and then went for dinner with a couple of school friends, Mary and Kay. Later, I met up with my friend Lea for a drink. I got home at midnight to find that Max was not at home. He'd left a card on the counter, with a sticky note attached to it that said, "I went to Warfield Creek to spend the night at Burt's."

My heart sank. Max never goes away during the week; this was Thursday night. Dr. Curtis was right, Max was having an affair!

I was so upset, I was shaking. I opened the card. It was one of those *stupid* funny cards. The kind he *always* gives me! God forbid he should ever give me a card that says something nice, something heartfelt! I was faced with one last meaningless birthday card that said, "Happy birthday, you're just a teeny bit older," Max.

That bastard! I ripped the card into tiny pieces and threw it like confetti into the air.

"OH-MY-GOD!" I screamed in pain as loudly as I could.

I had visions of my husband now in bed with some young, perfectly built slut! I grabbed the phone and dialed his cell. Max answered.

"Why don't you just admit your seeing someone, you ASSHOLE," I said and hung up.

I stormed into my bedroom, kicked off my shoes, and threw them across the room. Three minutes later, while I was in the process of getting undressed, the phone rang. It was Max calling me back.

Now I was really pissed, roaring crazy, out-of-control insane! I imagined Max having to get out of bed with his whore, put on his pants, and tell her he'd be right back. This would take all of three minutes, right? The phone rang again. I answered it.

"WHAT? Did you leave your slut to call me?" I slammed the phone down.

The phone rang again. I picked it up. Max said, in a calm and condescending voice, as though I were a 2-year-old, "Now Beth, I'm not seeing anyone. No one is here except Burt and his wife. Do you want to speak to Burt's wife?"

"Oh, right," I said, "Burt's wife! Do you think I'm STUPID? YOU ASSHOLE!" I slammed the phone down again. I was enraged and irrational. *I'm so pissed, if he were here, I swear I'd kill him!*

The phone rang again. I didn't answer it. Instead, I pulled it off the wall, opened the front door, and threw it into the driveway. I ran around the entire house, pulling out all the phones. One by one, I yanked them from the wall, and one by one, I tossed them with great force into the driveway, each one exploding into chips and chunks of plastic and metal.

Yes, with this display of mental insanity, I found comfort. I took allergy medicine to help me sleep, and went to bed.

Max didn't come home until Sunday. He said he was spending one night, but I didn't see him for three. I was drained.

"Do you have a minute? I need to speak to you," I said.

Max glared at me and finally yelled, "I'M NOT SEEING ANYONE!"

"That's what I wanted to talk to you about. Do you have a minute?" I asked.

"NOT REALLY," he said.

"Okay, then I'll talk to you later, but I do need to talk to you," I said.

When Max came home that evening, I asked him to sit down.

I said, as I started to cry, "I want to apologize. I don't know if you've been with someone else or not, but I had no reason to act like that. No reason except that Dr. Curtis planted the seed in my head that you were having an affair. Had she not said it was a possibility, I never would have thought it. To be honest with you, if it had been any other time, I'd have looked at your note and thought to myself, *Yippy, he's gone for the night; I get the house.*"

"I understand," Max, said.

"Our lack of communication, the mental state I'm in, and the legacy I leave with you as we part ways, has left me feeling worse than I ever thought possible. Max, I am so sorry," I said weeping.

"Thank you for telling me this," he said.

"I'm going to start weaning myself off the drugs. I'm so tired all the time. And I'm still in deep depression. I should be packing, but instead I sleep, or sit in a catatonic state on the sofa all day. If not for my religious belief, I know I would be dead. I believe that God wouldn't forgive me for taking my own life. But, oddly enough, I'm convinced he'd forgive me for taking yours. I know this is crazy thinking. I need to move out, cry, feel my pain, and move on. My fear is that I'll continue the anti-depressants and become numb and unemotional like you," I said sobbing. "There is a new life out there somewhere for me, I just know it."

**November 3, 2008** – I had an appointment with Dr. Curtis at 1:15 p.m.

"How are you doing Beth? I was surprised by the urgency for the appointment today," Dr. Curtis said.

“It was my birthday a few days ago. I went out with friends and arrived home at midnight. Max wasn’t home, but he left me a note explaining he was going to his friend Burt’s for the night.”

“How did you feel about that?” Dr. Curtis asked.

“Normally, I wouldn’t have thought anything about it,” I said. “Normally, I’d just have gone to bed. But because *you* planted the seed that it was a real possibility my husband was having an affair, I blew a gasket. I called Max on his cell phone, screamed at him, and hung up. He, of course, called me back, so I screamed at him some more and hung up again. By Max’s third attempt, I was out of control. I pulled every phone out of the wall and threw them into my driveway. Then I went to bed.”

“Well, obviously your anti-depressant isn’t working. You need to be on something stronger.”

“No,” I said. “The reason I went off like some *mental* patient is because you planted the seed that my husband was cheating!”

“No, I don’t take responsibility for that,” Dr. Curtis said.

“I came to you in a fragile, emotional state of mind, putting my trust in you and your knowledge, and you gave me your psychology book explanation as to why men leave a marriage. But you’re not going to take responsibility for that? I’m here today to let you know I won’t be back. I’m firing you,” I said.

I left the appointment and called Marie. I needed to feel better, and she might have some insight as to how I could go about this. “Marie, I’m a mess. I’ve been taking anti-depressants but they aren’t working. I just fired my third therapist.”

"Beth, first tell me what just happened?" she said. I explained about Dr. Curtis and my birthday phone bashing.

"You need to find a psychiatrist. They are educated in mental illness and medication. You don't go to a psychiatrist to discuss your life issues, you tell him about how you're feeling. For example, 'I feel sad, I want to kill myself, or my husband, or the lady across the street. I feel like I want to stalk the man I work with, or steal from stores, or hoard everything because I find it all useful.' Do you understand?" Marie asked.

"Not really," I said.

"Therapists and psychologists are both professionals you tell your problems to, and they can help you by giving you tasks or assignments to help you work on your attitude or situation. This is called therapy. Psychiatrists are doctors you explain your feelings to, not your problems. They have the ability to prescribe and mix different medications to allow you to feel good again. Does any of that help?" Marie asked.

"Yes, thank you! You've given me information I need," I said with relief.

**November 6, 2008, Therapist 4** – There are not many psychiatrists to choose from when you live in a small town like Willow, Michigan. I did find one and made the appointment, asking for the first available date. Fortunately, I received an appointment that very day. The new psychiatrist, Dr. Asshole, and I spent two hours going over my problems. I gave every detail I could think of. I even explained that my mother was bi-polar and my husband believed I was, too. I told this doctor that I was willing to do whatever I had to do to get better. As I spoke, he typed, periodically peering over his monitor to look at me. The phone buzzed to let him know his next patient was there. The doctor stopped typing, looked straight at me, and said, "I don't think you have bi-polar. You're a *door mat.* I'm giving you a prescription that will work well with your Excellipam."

"What's it for?" I asked.

"It's a bi-polar medication," he said.

"What? You just said I don't have bi-polar."

"You don't, but the medication might make you feel better." He handed me the prescription, and I walked out the door.

I don't remember anything after that.

Normally, I wouldn't think much about forgetting the drive home. Sometimes my body goes on autopilot, and I get home in a blink, almost like magic, without any recollection of it. But this particular day, I was given a prescription, stopped at the pharmacy, and waited for it to be filled before driving myself home. And I don't remember anything about any of it!

This new doctor, a psychiatrist, was the fourth medical specialist I'd seen, and I had high hopes he would finally be the one to help me. Instead, he ended up being the one to push me over the edge. Don't these assholes know that people come to them in a fragile state of mind? We come to them in our most vulnerable state, looking for their expert help and advice. Don't they teach that anymore?

I was spending all day and night in bed. I wanted to disappear. I wanted to be dead. Sleeping helped me to forget the pain.

I called my friend Jane. She has been my friend since elementary school. She knows me better than anyone. "Jane, you have experienced depression, anxiety, and every other miserable thing that a human can go through. And that's why I'm calling you," I said.

"What's going on with you, Beth?" Jane asked.

"I feel miserable, like I'm drowning in a black hole of heavy nothingness. It's so heavy it weighs me down. I'm consumed with sadness," I said. "I just want to be dead."

"That's your depression talking," Jane said. "How else are you feeling?"

"Sometimes I feel so desperate, like I could be a stalker, or a drug addict in search of a fix," I said. "I feel like I don't want to lose Max. Sometimes I get so aggressively angry. He doesn't want me anymore. He doesn't care about me anymore. I feel out of control, like I could kill him and myself. I'm not *that* person," I said crying. "I would never harm him or myself like that. I don't like feeling so emotionally fucked up. I don't know who I am anymore."

“That sounds like anxiety,” Jane said, “but it could also be that you’re not on the right anti-depressant.”

“I’ve been trying different anti-depressants,” I said, “but nothing is helping. I don’t like this feeling or these thoughts. I recognize they’re wrong, but I can’t stop thinking them. Most of the time I want to kill Max and Irene! I could actually kill them! And the really crazy part is, I think God would forgive me! How messed up is that? I just want something to make it stop!”

“That’s your anxiety,” Jane said.

“But I’ve tried different anti-depressants, and they made me more depressed,” I said.

“Focus on the anxiety first,” Jane said. “Then deal with the depression. Sometimes it’s the anxiety that makes us feel depressed. Do you have any medication for anxiety?”

“I think I got some November 6th from the hospital during my breakdown, but I don’t have any now,” I said.

“Breakdown? What happened?” she asked.

“I was such a mess after I left the psychiatrist’s office. I don’t remember anything from the time I left, until the time I got home. I went to see this new doctor, the fourth doctor, a psychiatrist. Prior to that appointment, I called my sister Marie, who’s a physician’s assistant. Given her medical background, I thought she might have some insight about what I needed to do. Marie said, ‘You need to see a psychiatrist. They work with medication and can mix up a medication cocktail that will work for you. That is their area of expertise.’”

I continued, "There are few psychiatrists in my area—like two of them. And, of course, out of the two, I picked Dr. Asshole. It was the worst day of my life. I blanked out, went to the store, filled a prescription, and drove myself home, and I don't remember doing any of it."

"What do you remember?" Jane asked.

"I remember the doctor giving me the prescription and thinking, *Why is he giving me a prescription for something he says I don't have? ...I'm a door mat. I'm a doormat? I'm one of those pathetic people who allow others to walk all over them? I have no backbone? I'm pathetic. I'm weak and pathetic!* The next thing I remember was sitting in my car in my garage. The car was shut off, and Max was knocking on my window. I was sobbing uncontrollably. I felt like I'd just had the life sucked out of me. I was weak and more depressed than ever, which was beyond hell. I was consumed with death. I thought, *I'm going to kill myself because I can't take it anymore. God will understand.* Max opened my car door. The words just flew out of my mouth, 'Take me to the hospital.'

"He helped me into the passenger side of my car. When I got in, I saw the new pharmacy bag. I don't know how it got there. I pushed the new prescription to the floor. I couldn't stop sobbing. I cried all the way to the hospital. It was as though my stomach and my heart were connected, and both were being punched in slow motion, giving me more mental anguish than I'd ever experienced in my life. Every second seemed like a minute of torture. All I wanted to do was to die.

“We arrived at the emergency entrance. Max called from his cell phone to let them know we were on our way. By the time we pulled in, there were two male nurses waiting for me with a wheelchair. I was still sobbing uncontrollably. They opened the door and helped me out and into the chair. Max went to the waiting room while I went sobbing down the hall in a wheelchair.

“The nurse asked, ‘Why are you here? Do you have any allergic reactions?’

“Still crying, I explained, ‘I’m not allergic. I’m getting a divorce I don’t want.’

“He said, ‘I understand, I’ve been there,’ and raised his hand to wiggle his fingers, showing me there was no wedding band. ‘We are going to do our best to help make you feel better right now. There are all sorts of good medications here to do it. We’ll continue giving them, one by one, with time in between. This will give your body time to accept the medication and to see if it works or not. Let’s start with this one first.’ The nurse gave me a pill.

“An hour later, he returned to see how I was doing. ‘How are you feeling? Any better?’ he asked.

“‘I now have a headache,’ I said, still crying.

“‘I’ll be right back,’ he said. ‘I’ll ask the doctor for something else to give you.’

"A short time later, a young physician's assistant named Sharon came to talk to me and evaluate my mental stability. I explained, 'I'm going through a divorce, and my husband doesn't want me anymore. I was the one who filed, but I truly expected him to say: *Don't do this, please. Stop. I love you. We can work this out.* But instead, he showed no feelings, no sign of sadness, no emotion whatsoever. The rejection and lack of human compassion is killing me, mentally and physically.'

"Sharon, the P.A., said, 'Well, I can see we don't need to send you to the psychiatric ward. You're going through a life-changing, stressful time, and that's what I'm going to write in your chart.'

"'Thank you for understanding, Sharon,' I said still weeping.

"She said, 'Right now we want to help you feel better.' She left my draped cubical.

"Moments later, a female nurse came in with a syringe. She stated her name was Eileen and said, 'The shift has just changed, and I'll be your nurse for the rest of the evening. I have something for you in the form of a shot. If it works, you'll be given a prescription to have filled, and then it's important for you to follow up with your doctor.' I received the shot in my right butt cheek. Within minutes, I was asleep. Nurse Eileen woke me up about an hour later. 'Beth, how are you feeling now? Would you like to stay the night?'

"'No, I'm feeling so much better, thank you. I'd like to go home.' I was afraid if I spent the night, Max would find the wherewithal to have me committed. Nurse Eileen left the room and came back with a wheelchair. I got in, and she took me to the exit door. Max was waiting in the driver's seat of my car, and the passenger door was open.

I got in and Max drove to a 24-hour pharmacy on the way home, where we had the prescription filled. I was driven home in silence and went to bed by myself. I don't remember if Max stayed in the house that night or not.

"The next day was hazy, and I slept most of it away. When I got up to go to the bathroom, my body felt really numb, sluggish, and tired, like walking around in a fog or a dream. Sometime in the late afternoon or early evening, Max called. 'Have you taken another pill yet?'

"'No,' I replied.

"'Don't you think you should?'

"'I don't know. I can't think,' I said. 'I feel drugged. Do you think I should take another one, Max?'

"'Yes, Beth, keep taking them.' I took a pill and went back to bed. I stayed home alone and asleep for several days.

"Sometime after that, my friend Nora called and asked me how I was feeling. 'I don't want to take the medication anymore,' I said. 'It makes me so tired. But Max wants me to stay on it.'

"'What are you taking?' she asked with concern. 'And when did you start taking it?'

"'Lor-adz-a-ti-van or Act-ti-pan. It's one of those, or both, I don't know. I can't think. I'm so tired I just want to sleep. I've been taking them since Thursday, after I got home from the hospital.'

"'It sounds to me like you're overmedicated,' Nora said.

"'But Max said I should keep taking them and stay on it,' I replied.

"'I'm sure he does,' Nora said. 'You being catatonic may be in Max's best interest, but it's not the best thing for you. Try taking half of it. It might be just enough to make you feel better without putting you to sleep.'

"'What day is it? I don't think I should take any medication today. I've got to get some of this out of my system so I can think. I promise to try it tomorrow if I'm still feeling crappy.'

"'Today is Tuesday. I was hoping I could take you out to a movie to get you out of that house,' Nora said.

"The next day, I was feeling like crap, so I took half of the anxiety pill. Within thirty minutes, I felt better. Unfortunately, I ran out of pills. I needed to go to my neurologist and see if he'd prescribe more for me."

Jane said, "Beth, I wish I'd known this was happening. I wish I could have been there for you."

"You work and have your own things to deal with," I said. "I'll be okay. Thanks. You've helped me understand part of my problem. I now realize I have anxiety as well as depression. I'll call you soon."

### *Alimony*

**November 3, 2008, 9:00 a.m.** – My request was for $1,000 a week for ten years. This figure sounds high, but Max could easily afford it.

But, because my husband claimed he only makes $90,000, my alimony would only be $1,300 a month for ten years. Max decided to finally increase his salary from $65,000 to $90,000 during our divorce, knowing that no one would ever believe he made such a low amount, given his title as president of the corporation and the payroll of his other employees.

Max and I were sent to mediation to meet a third-party attorney, Mr. Gray, along with our personal attorneys. Max and his attorney were in one room, and my attorney, Mr. Jones, and I were in another.

"Max agreed to pay a lump sum cash settlement of $150,000, with no taxes to pay," Mr. Jones said. "I think we can do better." My attorney left my room and entered the room where Max, his attorney, and Mr. Gray, the mediator, were. When my attorney came back into my room, he had Mr. Gray with him. I was an emotional mess.

"I just met Max," Mr. Jones said. "He seems like a nice guy. Max is offering you $150,000, and I think you should take it."

"You just told me minutes ago that we can do better," I said, confused.

"Yes, that's what I thought, but Mr. Gray, the mediator, said this was a good settlement, given the fact that Max only makes $90,000," Mr. Jones said.

"That's bullshit! Max makes multiple times that! Look at our tax returns; it's all right there! I will kill him and go to jail the rest of my life before I accept that bullshit settlement!" I said. "Let's take him to court!"

"No, that's not a good idea," Mr. Jones said. "We could lose. Irene has stated that if we take this to court, she will testify Max will no longer get a bonus if you are to get one penny of it. She will give him money in other ways."

Mr. Gray and Mr. Jones both said this was the best I could do. The alimony could only be based on his actual yearly income, not his bonus.

"It's now very clear to me why, all these years, Max never increased his wages. His bonus kept growing, but not the yearly wage. I have to walk away with less because he lies? Max's mother claims this money is a gift? Max worked for that money. He paid taxes on that money. This isn't right! My alimony should be based on his taxable income. He has been setting me up for destruction most of our marriage, and now you want me to just sit back and take it? Let's take him to court," I said. "I think we could win!"

"But if we don't win, it could cost you more money," Mr. Jones said.

My mind froze in shock at what I was hearing. I had a gut feeling I picked the wrong man for the job, and there was nothing I could do about it now. When I met Mr. Jones, I truly thought he understood and was going to be the one person to help me through this. Now he was telling me Max seems like a nice guy? Max was not paying him, I was! What must Mr. Jones think of me? Do I appear to be someone who's asking for more than I deserve? Am I a pushover? I wanted fairness. This was not fair!

I left Mr. Gray's office feeling more vulnerable than ever before. Was my life really going in this direction? Was there still time to find a stronger attorney? One that would fight for me and get me the financial assets I legally deserve?

### *I Need Legal Help*

**October 13, 2008** – I went to see Mr. Moore, a new attorney, one who had some strength in the courtroom and would fight for me. He had a reputation of being a real ball-buster. He gave the appearance he was someone to be feared.

Years ago, while going to cosmetology school at night, I worked in a title insurance office during the day. I was the receptionist in the front lobby. Mr. Moore would come in to get title searches done for his clients. He was very intimidating. The moment he walked through the door you sensed you were about to be yelled at. He walked over to my desk and stood glaring at me, motionless and without expression. He ordered his title work from me and, like always, wanted it as soon as possible. He'd stand there glaring at me until I looked up at him. Intimidated, I'd shyly look up, hoping he wasn't going to yell at me about something.

"Well, don't you want to know my name?" he'd growl.

Like I could ever forget who he was. "No, I know who you are," I said, anticipating more anger. "You're Mr. Moore, correct?"

"Yes," he said, and turned and walked out the door.

One day, the local phone book arrived. There on the cover was a picture of Mr. Moore.

The next time he came in, we went through the same routine. "Don't you want to know my name?" he said.

I said, "I know who you are. Your face is on the cover of my phone book." To my amazement, Mr. Moore cracked a smile.

This was the man who would be a good choice for my legal battle. I typed up some information and dropped it off at his office, then made an appointment, which took a couple of weeks to get.

I was really looking forward to this appointment. I arrived ten minutes early. The receptionist was organizing some papers when I came in. I sat down. She looked at me and started to say, "What is your n—" The phone rang. She answered it and said, "Yes, someone is here. Let me find out, and I'll let you know." Again she said, "What is your name please?"

"Beth Edwards," I said.

The receptionist picked up her phone and rang Mr. Moore's office. "Beth Edwards is here for your 1:30 appointment," she said. Mr. Moore must have started scolding her. She said, "Yes, but I didn't know it was her. How could I tell you it was her, when I hadn't gotten her name yet?"

She hung up the phone and put her hand in front of it as if to say, *Stop*! Then she looked up at me and said, "Mr. Moore will be right with you."

Mr. Moore came out of his office and gave me an icy look. "Mrs. Edwards, come into my office and have a seat," he said. He didn't even shake my hand.

"Mr. Moore, thank you so much for seeing me. I know what a busy man you are."

He sat behind his desk and crossed his arms. "I've read your paperwork. Explain what your concerns are."

I said, "I apologize for the lengthy story I sent, but twenty-two years requires time to explain. There has been some manipulation and—"

Mr. Moore cut me off. "Let me tell you the basic things to focus on in your divorce," he said. "Child support, separation of assets, and alimony. My job is to take the emotion out of the situation and present only the legal facts."

"Yes, but what about what Mr. Roberts did?" I asked.

"Mr. Roberts is Irene Edwards's attorney. He can do what he likes," he said.

"But didn't he cross the line?" I asked.

"No, I don't see that he crossed any line. As Irene Edwards's attorney, he is protecting the Edwardses' assets," he said.

"I understand that," I said. "I'm not interested in what the Edwardses have. I want to make sure I get what is due to me after many years of marriage and manipulation."

"What are your concerns?" he asked again.

"My husband purchased two life insurance policies and has put them into an Irrevocable Trust. Wouldn't I be entitled to the cash value of those policies?"

"Are you sure there is a cash value, not term policies?" he asked.

"Yes, I'm pretty sure they are," I said.

"Were they paid for by your husband?" he asked.

"Yes," I said. "The money was deducted from his salary."

"That may or may not be," he said. "If the mother has been covering all areas to make sure only the family is to inherit, it's possible there have been some other things done to provide the funds for these policies. If your husband did pay for the policies, you have a right to half the cash value, but Max would have to provide that money from another area, because they are in an Irrevocable Trust, and they cannot be touched."

"Not that I want it, but the 33 acres that Irene deeded to Max's Trust—I have no right to it?" I asked.

"That's correct," he said. "Welcome to estate planning."

"How can a couple be married for twenty-two years and someone gives one of them something and the other has no right to it? This makes no sense to me. Whatever happened to 'The two shall become one'? Or anything acquired in the marriage belongs to both husband and wife? I'm experiencing the ripping apart of the flesh of this marriage, but he keeps most of the assets because his mother manipulated it that way? What is wrong with this picture? What happened to legal fairness? Who makes these rules?" I said, starting to cry.

"Why did you call me?" he asked.

"Because you are intimidating, and I believe people listen to you. You appear to be the kind of man who will fight for his client. In the beginning, I hoped my attorney, Mr. Jones, was going to look out for my best interest. Now I'm not so sure," I said.

"If you pull out now, in the middle of your divorce, and replace your attorney with another one, you will lose credibility. The attorney you have selected is well respected.

I may make a statement with my courtroom attitude, but the judges get used to the personalities of all the local attorneys, and, therefore, it doesn't mean the same to them as it does to you. The bottom line is the law," he said. "The law is the same, whether you walk into the courtroom with your current lawyer or with me."

"Do you have someone to talk to?" Mr. Moore asked.

"Are you referring to a therapist?" I asked.

"Yes," he said.

"Yes," I replied.

"I have always prided myself on being a fair and honest individual," I said with tears running down my face. "I don't steal and I don't lie. I want to leave a legacy of truth and kindness. What kind of legacy will they leave?" I got up, and gathered my papers. "Thank you for your time," I said as I walked out of the office.

When I got to my car, I burst into tears. *Mr. Moore thinks I'm a mental case. Maybe I am. But if I am, why isn't my husband trying to take care of me? Why does he want to leave me all by myself and without the money I deserve?*

I drove home, walked in the door, stripped off my clothes, crawled into the safety of my bed, and continued to cry. The depression had been coming over me in waves, and today I was drowning. I felt hopeless and homeless. How would I ever survive?

### *I'm a Mess*

**November 12, 2008** – I hadn't seen Max since he dropped me off at home from the hospital about a week ago. I had gotten little sleep last night and woken up very aggravated. Stewing over the fact that my husband doesn't care about me and might as well throw me out with the trash made me upset and angry. I wanted revenge. I pulled out some paper and started writing. I felt if I could somehow get the words out, I'd feel better; and if I could get the words out for Max to hear, maybe he'd see I was a mess without him. Maybe he'd see he needed to change his mind. Maybe he'd show feelings of remorse, sadness, or regret for what he'd done and demonstrate to me that he was at least human.

I called Max and told him there was a problem with the plumbing in the master bathroom and I needed him to look at it. There was a sewer smell coming up from the shower because it hadn't been used. All I needed to do was run water to make it go away, but today I needed Max to do it. I needed to see Max so I could read the letter aloud to him.

When Max arrived, he walked into the bathroom and said, "You just have to turn the water on every so often or the drain dries up and gives you that smell."

"Max, I have written something I want you to hear."

I started to read aloud: "I have loved you and taken care of you for twenty-two years."

Max said, "And I did the same for you."

"All I ever wanted to do is take care of you. All you ever wanted was to take care of yourself."

Max said, "That's not true."

"My thoughts or feelings were never given any consideration throughout this entire marriage. You say you never lied to me. I have six pages of lies you have told me. A man is supposed to leave his parents and cleave to his wife."

Max said, "Oh…that again?"

"In twenty-two years, that has never happened, and this marriage is a lie because of it. Your mother has always come first."

Max said, "That's not true."

"You always took your mother's side rather than mine. Your mother's opinion was always given consideration, but never mine. She was more your wife than I ever was. You called her every day, even when we were on vacation. You always spoke nicely to her and had lengthy conversations. This has not only irritated me, but also left me feeling alone and unloved by you. You were never anything but curt with me. Why should I have to compete with your mother?

"I watched as your mother worked you to the point of three breakdowns. And who was there to take care of you? Me! I called her, and I told her you wouldn't be into work until you were well. I called, not you! I did this because I loved you. You couldn't talk to her. You were afraid of her!

"You said you had no memory of your mother ever telling you she loved you. No words, no hugs. I went to her several times to get her to show you her love—to tell you the words or give you a hug. But she wouldn't do it.

At 49-years-old, you finally heard your mother tell you she loves you after showing you the letter I had written in response to hers. And you still took her side. Did I ever get any credit for that, did you ever thank me? No! You waited forty-nine years to hear what you should have heard all your life. Yet, I'm so easily discarded.

"You hit me three times in your sleep over the last two years. Even though it was done in your sleep, does that make it right? I suffered from it. You toss and turn, thrash about and punch the bed, the pillow, or me; shouldn't this be considered 'involuntary spousal abuse'? Who are you fighting with? It's not my name you're yelling—it's your mother's!

"You have ripped my heart in two. You have taken my pride and humiliated me. I went to four therapists, did what they said to do, took all the pills they told me to take. I did it because I loved you. I begged you not to go through with this divorce. I said I'd change, lose weight, go to the gym, grow my hair down to my ass, take more pills, do anything, just please, after twenty-two years, don't do this. And you smiled and said, 'No, I'm comfortable with this.'

"So now, after all the years of marriage, you are not willing to give me the alimony I deserve? You don't have a car payment—your car is provided to you from your business, along with a gas credit card. And you can't afford it? You're a spoiled brat!"

"How much are you asking?" Max said.

"I'm asking for $1,000 a week for ten years. You've forgotten all the good things I did to help make your business more successful. And you've forgotten that I've spent every year of our marriage convincing people your mother is really nice person once you get to know her.

I've never told anyone what an ice cold bitch she really is. That alone has to be worth something, for goodness sake! You took the best years of my life, and now you want to steal the rest of my years away. I don't know how to be single or live on my own."

Max rolled his eyes and started for the door.

I panicked and yelled at him, "I never want to see you again!"

He left without a response. And I never saw him again.

Filled with anguish, all I could do was go to bed and hope it would all be better in the morning.

When I awoke, I started crying all over again. I was an emotional mess and had anger issues as well as depression. I sounded like an idiot, yelling things at Max the way I did! The desperation had me spinning out of control. *How much longer do I have to feel like this? I don't want to live without Max, but why? He has never given me the attention I need. We have nothing in common. Why do I need him so much? I don't want to need him. I don't want to love him. I don't want to think about him. I don't want to live!*

In bed, I pray: *God, please take my life, I don't want it anymore. I don't want to feel like this anymore. Please, give my life to someone who is praying for the extension of their own life. I'm sorry, I don't want it. Please take it, before I'm forced to take it myself. I'm suffering.*

The thought of death, so final, sounds inviting and comforting. I know these are crazy thoughts, but I don't care. I'm miserable and I just don't care.

**November 24, 2008** – My brother David called. I told him I was getting a divorce, and I was so depressed I wanted to take my own life.

David said he was sorry to hear this, then asked if Max is gay. "I don't know. I don't think so," I said. "There are signs that make me think it's possible, but Max is such an extension of his mother—I've always thought his behavior is just that of a man who is so close to his mother that he begins to act and speak like she does. That alone can make a man appear odd—like men who never move out of their parents' house and live with their mother forever. There is something unnatural about it; it makes them strange individuals. Not to say that gay people are strange. I'm trying to understand him and explain him at the same time. Why would a mother make her son feel so obligated to her? Isn't our job as parents to teach our children to move out and become self-supporting? Let them live their own life as they choose? I see this as mental abuse, more than anything else. If we only knew how badly we could mess up our own children by things we say or do, or don't do for that matter, do you think we'd make a conscious effort to change our ways?"

"I don't know...I just don't know," he responded.

David recently went through a bad breakup, and, like me, he's in a deep state of depression. We talked about our misery and found comfort in each other's pain. We were both going through the same feelings: feeling depressed, wanting to die, understanding the finality of death and not caring. When we have healthy minds, we don't really like to think about dying, but with depression, the thought of being dead and stuck in the ground doesn't sound so bad. It's almost like a magic earth fairy that's calling our name. We are trying to resist, but the earth fairy makes death looks so attractive.

"I just want to curl up into a ball and get under the cool earth and sleep until the bugs eat me," I said. "It's like my skin is craving it. Does that make sense?"

My brother said, "I know exactly what you mean. I feel the same. Depression sucks. I'd rather be dead than feel like shit every fucking day."

Within days of my call with David, I got a call from a friend of his. He said, "David is in severe depression, and he doesn't know what to do that will help."

"Take him to the hospital," I said. "They will medicate him so he'll feel better."

"Your brother won't go to the hospital. He's afraid they'll commit him."

"As long as he doesn't tell them he wants to take his own life or kill someone, they won't keep him," I said.

David was taken to the hospital and diagnosed with depression.

* * *

Still at home on medical leave, I lie on the floor. *Please God, let me die. Let me go to bed and not wake up. Please take this miserable gut-wrenching pain away. I can't tolerate it anymore. I should be crying tears of blood. I should be dying of a broken heart. I've been ripped in half, and I don't want to go on as one half. I want my other half back! PLEASE...*

The following morning was more of the same. I woke up clenching my chest. My eyes were puffy from crying so much and stung when I touched them. I'm still alive and don't want to be, my heart is broken. The pain is killing me slowly. I can't do this anymore.

By mid-morning, I called Dr. Gerald and asked to try another anti-depressant. “I can’t take this pain anymore; I want to take my own life.” My doctor asked me to come in right now. He gave me a prescription for Excellipam, increasing it to 40 mg. He also extended my medical leave of absence until January 1, 2009.

**November 26, 2008** – I have not seen my husband since I yelled at him almost two weeks ago. It’s been nice not having him here, not having to see him and feel the pain of rejection every day. I have been very busy packing up the house. Once I pack up a room, I redecorate it with what’s left. I want the house to be put together with the items that belong, or that I have left behind for Max. I’d like Max to be able to come into his home on the day I have left for good and feel a sense of home instead of vacancy. I still love him, and it’s important to me to leave on a good note. I hope it will overshadow the yelling I did and leave him with memories of kindness instead of insanity.

My brother David talked to me about a book he wanted to get. Tired of packing, I felt the need to get out of the house. All I do is cry, pack, and sleep. I drove to Bingham’s Bookstore and located the book my brother had asked for. I also picked up a book on dying. I once heard the stages of divorce were the same as death. I wanted to know which stage of death I was currently in. As I approached the checkout, I saw a familiar face, Ray Gregory.

Ray was a classmate from high school. We’d had a science class together. Even though we didn’t know each other outside science class, over the years, when we ran into each other at the grocery store, we’d say hi and sometimes chat for a few minutes. We both lived in the same area and shopped at the same grocery store.

Many years ago, Ray had wanted to take me out. At the time, I was dating Max. I never liked the complication in my life of dating more than one person at the same time. I had tried that once in my teens, and it left me torn between two guys. I never wanted to do that again.

The week before Max and I were to be married, I ran into Ray while shopping. "So how's everything with you, Beth? You still look great," Ray had said.

"Thanks, Ray. I'm getting married next week to Max."

"Why don't you blow that off and go out with me instead," Ray said, laughing.

"I don't think so, but thanks for asking. Good to see you."

"Good to see you too, Beth. Congratulations," he said as he walked away.

That was twenty-two years ago. Ray still looked the same, just older. As I got closer, I could see Ray recognized me, too.

"Hi, Ray," I said.

"Beth, how are you? You're still so beautiful. How's Max?"

"Max and I are in the process of getting a divorce," I said.

Ray's face lit up. "I'm sorry to hear that. How are you taking it?"

"I've been better," I said.

"Do you have time for a cup of coffee?" he asked.

“Sure, let me pay for my books, and I’ll meet you over in the café,” I said.

My books were in a bag and I headed to the café. Ray was seated at a table for four. I sat down across from him. He smiled. “What can I get for you?” he asked.

“It’s a little late in the day for coffee. Would you mind getting me a bottle of water?” I asked.

“Whatever you want—if you want water, then water it is,” he said.

He came back to the table with his coffee and my water. I’d been thumbing through David’s book to see what it was about.

Ray sat down and smiled. “It’s funny that out of all of our classmates, you seem to be the one I run into the most,” he said.

“Yes, I think you’re right. Did you ever get married? I remember several years ago you introduced me to a tall blond who was your girlfriend at that time.”

“No. She and I were living together for a couple of years. She moved out because she wanted me to ask her to get married. I got a ring and proposed, but she said no. She’d fallen in love with the jeweler,” he said. “Then there was another girl I dated for about five years, but that didn’t work out either.”

Ray and I talked for a couple hours. I explained the divorce and my mental state because of it. It was the first time in a very long time that I had a man sit across from me and give me his undivided attention.

He looked at me while I spoke, without looking around or asking that I repeat what I'd last said. We were having a real conversation. I had forgotten what it was like. I missed communication with a man. It had been so long, I hadn't realized I'd missed it. I thanked Ray for my water and the conversation.

"If you ever have the need to get out again and you'd like to go for coffee, dinner, or a movie, I hope you'll give me a call," he said, giving me his number.

"Yes, I'd like that. I'm currently packing and looking for a condo, but I do love to go to the movies, and I need to get out more," I said, and gave him my phone number.

Women fall in love through the ears, and men fall in love through the eyes. Not that I had fallen in love just yet, but having a man look at me with interest and hang on my every word left me hopeful. Had this person, who'd now shown me attention and empathy, been Jack the Ripper, I'd have fallen for him, too.

I spent Thanksgiving writing. I had a box loaded with notes and wanted to put them in some kind of order. In my attempt at organization, I started writing this very book. I wrote from morning to night, filling thirty-eight pages, before packing it all away.

Saturday morning, I came across a box of pictures. I took scissors and started cutting Max's face out. By afternoon, I needed fresh air; it would be nice to get out. I'd take a quick shower and see if Ray would like to meet for coffee. I had no sooner finished the thought and my cell phone rang. It was Ray.

"Hi, Beth, I decided to call you, instead of waiting for you to call me," he said.

"Actually, I was going to call you a little later," I said.

"Did you want to meet for coffee or something quick to eat? I don't want to be gone too long because I still have so much packing to do."

"Why don't we meet at The Coffee Shop on Grand Ravine," he said. "Six o'clock?"

"Sure. I'll see you in a bit," I said.

This felt so weird to me. I have a husband I love and want to be with, yet I'm meeting a man for coffee. How did I get here? It's just coffee, I reminded myself...just coffee.

I arrived at The Coffee Shop before Ray and brought in a magazine to keep myself occupied while I waited. When he came in, his smile lit up his entire face. It was obvious he was happy to see me. *I wish Max smiled when he saw me*, I thought. But Max no longer wanted me as his wife, and I couldn't afford to stay married to him. I had to move on. Max hadn't given me much of a choice.

Ray asked, "How's your day gone so far?"

"Pretty good," I said. "I've gotten a lot done, but there's still so much left to do. I haven't found a place to move yet, so that will be my project next week."

"Are you looking for a house?" Ray asked. "There are a couple of homes for sale in my neighborhood." He told me where he lived and that he had a train layout in his basement.

"A train layout—do you mean toy trains? That run on a track?" I asked.

"Yes, it's a hobby of mine. It gives me something to do when I'm home at night," he said.

"I love tiny things," I said. "I would love to see it. Can I see it now, or is your kitchen a mess?"

"No, my kitchen isn't a mess, and yes, we can go see it now. I'll drive," he said. "Leave your car here, and I'll bring you back."

Ray lived only a few miles from The Coffee Shop. When I got into his car, it was nice and clean, and it was obvious to me he kept it this way. I could tell by the smell and the appearance of the carpet. I like a man who keeps things clean.

His house was another reflection of his cleanliness. It was also very colorless; I'd swear I was in a new home. "How long have you lived here?" I asked.

"It's been about eight years."

"Do you have someone who cleans for you?" I asked.

"No, I do it myself," he said. "A few years ago, I started throwing away stuff I wasn't using, until I got down to the things I use regularly. It keeps me from having to spend all day or all weekend moving things around to clean. Enough about my cleaning habits, let's go down and look at the train."

The train layout in Ray's basement took up at least half the room. It was like an entire city built in the small area. I walked around and could hardly take it all in. So many tiny details: shrubs, grass, window shades on the trains, and, look, there are people inside, too. Ray turned the train on for me and pulled out a map. He had several tracks that all came into the same station.

"Wow, this is impressive! I've never seen anything like it," I said.

"This is my version of Jersey Station," Ray explained. "See, there's the pier with some Navy men that just got off their ship."

"It's the most incredible, detailed thing I've ever seen. Max would love this! He has some old trains from his childhood that he brings out at Christmas. If he knew he could create something so magnificent... He's got the perfect basement to do it in. The basement of our home is the size of a bowling alley," I said. "It would be perfect. You should come over and see the house I designed before I move out."

"No, I don't think that's a good idea," he said. "Max is a good guy. He's never done anything to me. I wouldn't want to offend him by being in his home while you're going through a divorce."

"What? You won't come and look at the house I designed because you're afraid you'll offend Max? What about offending me?" I asked. "Are you taking his side? Divorce is like war—you must pick a side. There are no sidelines and no fence sitting; you can't play middleman. If you're not on my side, then you're on his, and if you're on his, then I want nothing more to do with you. That's just the way it is."

"How about we don't talk about it anymore?" Ray suggested. "I don't want to upset you or him. Are you ready to go?"

Ray took me back to The Coffee Shop, dropped me at my car, and I went home to bed. My divorce was eleven days away, and I needed to concentrate on where I was going to live. Over a year ago, I kept an eye out for a condominium for Lea, after her divorce from Craig.

There were a couple of new developments that had wonderful curb appeal; one in particular had details that I would put into a home myself.

I pulled into the driveway of the model unit and called the number on the for sale sign. “Hello, my name is Beth, and I’d like to see the model if you’re available,” I said. “You can be here in ten minutes? Great, I’ll wait.”

The model was beautiful from the outside. It had a carriage house look about it, with stonework that made it look like home. On the inside, it was even more beautiful, and was painted a muted gold. The décor was Old World, just my style, with a stone fireplace from floor to ceiling. I put an offer on it and got it. I was set to close the afternoon of my divorce, December 10, 2008.

I had something to look forward to. I was starting my new life in a new condo. I called Ray to share my news. “Hi, Ray,” I said. “I purchased a condo today!”

“Great!” he said. “Would you like to go out to dinner to celebrate?”

“Why don’t I grab pizza and a salad and bring dinner to your place tonight?” I suggested.

“Sure,” he said. “See you around six o’clock.”

I took dinner to Ray’s, as promised, and brought a movie too. He put the movie in, but we talked right through it. Ray is a wonderful artist and has several pieces of his work on the walls of his home. I told him he should continue painting and maybe one day he could make a living selling his work in a gallery. Ray explained the process of his art, and, before I knew it, the clock struck 10:00 p.m. Ray was a gentleman and never made a pass at me.

I told him that my court date was coming up soon, and if Max wanted to repair the marriage, I would stay married to him. We ate our dinner, and I went home.

In the days ahead, I suffered my depression like a death notice. It was as though I were getting ready for an execution.

I couldn't help but imagine Max in *our* bed with someone else. It was *my* bed, and he was *my* husband. I lay on our bed and cried, then turned over and started to beat on the bed with my fists.

"I curse this bed!" I said pounding my fists into the mattress. "Max will never find happiness in it." I slept in our bed that night.

When I got up in the morning, I was filled with anxiety. In my mental state, I chose to put on a pair of thong panties and clean the house in them. Many hours later, I took them off and stuffed them into the sofa, as a means of marking my territory. Before I went to sleep that last night in my home, I took Max's toothbrush out of his drawer in the bathroom and peed on it.

Tomorrow was my divorce. Everything I owned was boxed up and ready to go. I went to bed.

My attorney, Mr. Jones, met me as I arrived at court. "How are you doing today?" he asked.

"I've been better, but I'll be okay. Could you make sure I'm not asked if there is a chance my marriage could be saved? I remember being asked that when I went through my first divorce, and I can't lie."

"It's time," he said.

*Oh my God, I'm going to pass out. How did I get here? Where is Max? Oh God, help me!*

I felt numb. I walked to the podium with Mr. Jones. The judge asked several questions. I stood there in a state of shock. *This is really happening.*

The judge asked, "Has there been a breakdown of the marriage?"

Mr. Jones leaned into me and said, "Say yes."

"Yes," I said, still in shock. *I can't believe this is real. It feels like a dream.*

The judge asked, "Is there any possibility that this marriage can be saved?"

Mr. Jones leaned into me and said, "Say no."

"What?" I said. *Oh my God, I've promised to tell the truth and now...*

"No. Say no," Mr. Jones encouraged me.

"No," I said, in a state of panic. *The words just flew out of my mouth and there was no taking them back. It's all over now.* My attorney walked me out of the courtroom.

"I lied. I can't believe I just lied. I swore to tell the truth, so help me God. I just lied to God," I said, still in shock.

"Don't worry about it," Mr. Jones said. "He'll forgive you."

*What just happened? Who is this man I've hired? I thought he was a good family man, and he encouraged me to lie to God? He can't speak for God, and, at this moment, I felt like I was going straight to hell.*

Max never showed up. Apparently, he didn't have to. I hadn't seen him since I yelled at him a month ago, and now I'd never see him again. The man I love, the man I intended to spend my life with, is now my ex-husband. How could it be possible that a 22-year marriage could be dissolved in ninety days? I was devastated. I felt like someone had just stolen my life from me.

I walked to my car, got in, and cried. As I dried my eyes, I called Max.

"Hi, Max. It's over," I said. "We're divorced. I was surprised that you weren't there."

"Wow…I didn't know how I'd feel at this moment," he said. "I was told I didn't have to come. I suppose I could have, and handed them my heart."

"Oh, you have one of those?" I asked.

"Max, before I forget. Don't use your tooth brush. I peed on it last night."

Max laughed. "Thanks for letting me know."

We both said, "Goodbye."

### *Beth's Thoughts*

I would recommend a prenuptial for everyone. Marriage should be looked at like a business: you will invest your time and your life and, if you get a divorce, you may never get back what you've put into it. It does not matter if you have nothing going in. You build a life together, from a promise made to one another. Had I given Max a prenuptial that stated he would have to pay me $25,000 for every year we were married and an additional percentage of his taxable earnings upon divorce, he, most likely, wouldn't have wanted out. And Irene, most likely, would have behaved herself.

Then again, maybe not.

It seems odd how life's events affect the ones involved so differently.

Why would a person get married and spend most of the twenty-two years of marriage separating himself and his assets from his wife?

Why would a mother not tell her son she loved him and respected him as the man he had become? Why would his mother think it okay to deny me financial stability? And why would Irene think it okay to replace her husband with her son? Not in an incestual way, but in every other way. It's not right, and it's not normal. But she will have to explain to God why she did what she did and hope that He'll understand.

A valuable lesson I have learned: People don't say what they mean. Most don't stand behind what they say. The people closest to you will swear you said or did something you know you would never say or do. But because they are so adamant about it, you begin to wonder, especially when they are people who care about you. They are not an enemy. So you are forced to re-think things.

Perhaps I did say that. Maybe I did do that. I have no recollection of it, but if you say I said it, or did it, maybe I did. Maybe I don't know my own mind. Maybe my mind isn't as clear as I've always thought it was.

The really sad thing is that the people closest to you will put words in your mouth and manipulate you into believing you actually said them, or did something. In reality, it is you who are clear about what was or wasn't said or done, and they are only looking out for their own best interest.

**February 2009** - I believe myself to be mentally unstable. The recent divorce has left me devastated. I work hard every day to present myself as just another normal person.

Why would my husband think it okay to give away 33 acres, but not give me the alimony I deserved?

I have the desire to stab my ex-husband over and over—twenty-two times to be exact. It would give me pleasure. The only thing that would give me more pleasure would be to cut into my ex-mother-in-law's chest cavity and search for a heart; as I'm sure I'd find nothing there.

What a horrible thought, what a heinous act.

I used to say, "I feel like I'm losing my mind!" And now I know I have.

*God will forgive me*, I say to myself. You can't act like they have. You can't ruin lives like they have. Yes, God would forgive me. But what if I could not forgive myself? Would I end up in a state of mindlessness, a patient in a mental institute who stares blankly out the window? Or put myself out of my misery, the way my grand-pap did when I was a child?

When I told my sister Marie I was losing my mind, she responded, "If you think you're losing your mind, you're probably not. When you do crazy things you accept as normal, that's when you're crazy."

My mother attempted suicide when I was a child. We, her children, learned to say, "Mother is not well." To us it sounded better than, "She went crazy" or "She went nuts." Fortunately, thanks to modern medicine, my mother is not crazy, and she has her mental illness under control. She has become one of the sweetest people I know.

But what happens when we do lose our mind? Do we get it back? Do we lose only part of it? Do we spend the rest of our life trying to find it?

Divorce is like war. Your friends and family must pick a side. If you meet someone along the way who says they can't pick sides because they liked you both, trust me—they have picked their side, and it's not yours.

But who really cares? This is the time when your true friends will step up and make themselves known. They will continue to stop by and call often to check on you. They'll encourage you to go out, even when you can't imagine leaving the safety of your bed, the bed you haven't left in many days.

My bed became my safe haven, my cave, my private domain. It had always provided me with comfort to sleep. It helped me rest when I was sick, so I could get better. Surely this magic bed can heal my sadness. If not, it can at least provide me safety and comfort until I can find the mental strength to escape from it.

**December 27, 2010** – The truth, maybe...

Perhaps I've come to believe that my husband and his mother's behavior were possibly a reaction to my behavior.

I wanted to hate them both. What I hated was what they were doing to me, or against me, behind my back. I was given no consideration.

The truth of the matter is that I didn't know how to deal with what felt like rejection—not only from my husband, whom I truly did love, and still do love, but also his mother, who'd become my second mother.

Perhaps they should have ganged up on me, sought medical treatment for me, and looked out for my best interest instead of their own. Isn't that what you do for people you love? Or do you simply ignore what's happening, walk away, and leave them to rot in madness all on their own, with minimal income to do it?

## *A Few Words from Max*

To be fair—and I believe myself to be a fair person—I felt it important to include notes Max had written, which I found during my move from the home Max and I built together into the condominium where I now reside. He, too, was searching for answers. I can only assume that Max never read or understood the legal documents he signed. His full trust was in his mother instead of his wife.

**Max's notes:**

*How much am I supposed to take? She accused me of lying. She seems to be obsessed with money, material things, etc. I never give it a thought.*

*Questioning, who owns property, what is Irrevocable Trust, etc.*

*The disrespect (she said "fuck you" to me four times).*

*The financial problem; she liked to spend money, which I was too kind about.*

*The insults, her calling me a liar, just how much do you think I should put up with? Don't I deserve better?*

*Never have I been treated worse by anyone as I have my own wife.*

*When she asked me, every time, I gave her the honest answer.*

*I paid dearly for telling her the truth. Just because she didn't believe me, I paid the price – insults and disrespect.*

*I asked her questions; I believed what she told me. I was under the impression there was $6,000 on a credit card. She told me so. But it was actually $12,000.*

*I told her when I took $500 out of savings. She tells me nothing.*

*Credit Card Company told me she just paid $15,000.*

*She is obsessed with who owns what. I couldn't care less. It isn't important to me at all! I am too busy trying to make a living, pleasing her, and being everything to everybody.*

*I find it's better to answer my own questions, otherwise she calls me paranoid.*

*Why should I want to stay married to her? I love her and don't want a divorce. But am I supposed to continue to be disrespected, insulted, and questioned? I give all to a person who mistrusts and demeans me regularly.*

*She said she never wanted to be like her mother. Her mother said whatever she wanted, and finally her father said enough! When is my "enough"? I'm not going to be bitch slapped by her, just because she doesn't believe me. I don't have a history of being deceitful or a liar, but she treats me like I'm some kind of a zero.*

*How long should I spend my life being questioned about my motives? I never questioned her…my mistake.*

*I gave POA to my father…*

*I signed a document that cuts Zack out of everything. (Note – She is paying $1,000 monthly on Ayden's mortgage for 2 years). Did not tell me the exact details; did tell me she wanted to help, blah, blah, blah….*

*If I die, she does not know who gets what. List it out 1...2...3...*

*We had this discussion again and again, this is bullshit!*

*33 acres are mine. 1998? Change Amendment? Should have explained what a Trust is i.e., Irrevocable.*

*Re: Ayden's rent, she said she did it to help her nephew. She was being generous with money she otherwise would have spent elsewhere. She's just trying to make me look bad. After I found out she was paying the mortgage for the first two years, she offered this without my knowledge, and didn't wait for Ayden to ask for help, she just gave it.*

*She's obsessed with my mother; has manipulated this process to benefit my sister or her children? Obsessed with mother's attorney; justifies she is finding out about documents I have done behind her back.*

*My mother has been behind all of this with her attorney? What is she talking about?*

After the divorce Max wrote me a letter...

*July 14, 2010*

*Miss Beth,*

*Much of this letter was written some time ago. Feelings fluctuate daily, hourly. I probably shouldn't have sent this, but what the hell do I have to lose?*

*I've talked to Zack, and from our conversations, there have been some things I find troubling. You refer to our marriage that you thought would last forever only to find out that the person never loved you at all; thought we were worth fighting for; that you could be disposed of so easily...all these references that make implications of how you think that I felt (or feel).*

*These comments have bothered me for a long time because they are not true. I have struggled, sometimes daily, whether or not to respond to these implications. Until now, I decided not to because it is too painful and most likely not beneficial in any way. There would be nothing I could ever do to change your hateful opinion of me.*

*I have written thousands of letters in my head, but have never been able to put them on paper. Is it because the pain of communicating with you is too great?*

*Or is it because I know if I attempt to communicate with you it will just turn into you trying to show what a bad person I am and make me feel worse than I already do? (Which, by the way, is humanly impossible.)*

*Every day I grieve and am saddened over the loss of the beautiful, talented woman that you are. I am sorry about a lot of things I may have done, things that were never intentional, but "things" just the same. I do not have, nor have I ever had, a bone in my body that could purposely cause you pain. Every day I deal with the guilt of hurting you and not being able to fix everything. For this and other things, I am truly sorry. But the one thing I am particularly sorry for is this...*

*I am sorry you CHOSE to believe that I am some sort of bad person. You CHOSE to see me as a person out to screw you, cheat on you, do things behind your back, and lie to you. You CHOSE to view me with suspicion and distrust. This choice you made was never based on reality. Reality was just the opposite. I was not perfect and I did make mistakes, but I didn't deserve the bad guy label and I resent the implications.*

*I guess I can sum up my feelings like this: I had to stand at the side of a lake and watch someone I loved very much, drown. I did not try to save her because every time I threw a life preserver to her it just got thrown back. I live with this huge guilt and pain of letting you drown every day of my life.*

*Thank you for listening.*

*Mr. Max*

*P.S. Thank you for the pictures. It was very thoughtful of you. But then again, that is the type of person you are. Also, I agree with what you wrote on the envelope, that you were a "great wife." You possess many great qualities that cannot be replaced. And, like yours, my heart is broken, too.*

### *As Time Goes By*

Unbeknownst to Max, I wrote on sticky notes, scrap paper, and spiral notebooks for years. In doing this, I'd hoped to recognize my mental illness if there was one. My mother was diagnosed with bi-polar disorder, and I feared I would inherit this from her. If there were a problem, I hoped I'd be able to see it in my writing. There were days I'd be so upset by something someone said or did; I'd write it down and put it in a box kept in my closet for this very purpose. Several times a year, I'd open the box and go through my notes to discover that many times the anger was unjust.

Instead of confirming a disorder I don't have, I confirmed many things my husband refused, and still refuses, to acknowledge. What my husband and his mother did without my knowledge or input is inexcusable. They should have and could have included me in their discussions on matters that would benefit or distract from my financial support in the years to come. Had this been done to either one of *them*, I'm sure they wouldn't be very understanding.

It's been over a year now. My son called me to let me know he was taking a trip to California. Before he left for his vacation, Zack stopped at the funeral home to talk to Max. Zack said, "Max, I want you to know that even though the divorce was a terrible thing, the fact that you and I now have a relationship because of it is a good thing, and it means a lot to me. I just wanted you to know that." Zack extended his hand to Max to shake it.

Max cried and said, "Zack, I want you to know that there is not one day that goes by that I don't think about your mother. I love her and should have never let my greed get in the way, or let things get to the point that they did."

As soon as Zack got home, he called me at work. "Mom, there is something I have to tell you! Can you talk?"

"Give me a minute," I said. "I'm at work and need to take my cell phone into the supply room where I'll get a little privacy."

Zack explained he had just left Max at the funeral home and told me of their conversation. "Mom, doesn't that make you feel good?" Zack asked.

"No, it doesn't make me feel good, and it doesn't make me feel bad. It doesn't make me feel anything," I said.

"What kind of medication are you on?" Zack asked. "You don't feel anything from what I've just said? I would have thought you'd be happy to know that he still loves you."

"I don't feel anything because Max is not the man I thought he was," I said. "You don't understand what I went through. I was married for twenty-two years to a man I feel never loved me. His goal throughout my marriage was to make sure that you were left with nothing, and I was left with only my home. A home I would never be able to afford to keep. The day of the divorce, I came home and showered. I scrubbed myself so hard and for so long, I thought I would bleed. I wanted any DNA left on me from him to be completely removed. I felt as though I'd been raped. My marriage was a lie from the beginning, and it never should have taken place. Even after it did, Max should have divorced me, knowing how he felt about you and me.
Max didn't love us; we were nothing more than a burden to him. We were people he had to tolerate. Max never got to know either of us and wouldn't let us know him. I had always been there for him, but, in the end, he abandoned me.

"And you think I should feel good because he said he loves me? Those are only words used to manipulate. Max may have loved that I cooked and cleaned for him, did his laundry, always looked nice for him, listened to his complaining on a daily basis, and continued to give creative, helpful suggestions. Max loved that I never said no to him, and that I took good care of him—no matter what! But Zack, that is *not* love. Those are services Max can now pay for; and, trust me, he has plenty of money to do it. Max doesn't know love. You have to grow up with it to understand it. What Max did to you and me, you don't do to people you love.

"Enjoy your vacation, Zack. I love you, and we'll talk when you get back."

### *His Stuff*

When I recover items belonging to Max—pictures, CDs, etc.—I put them in a box, drive them to his home (my old house), and place the box on his porch.

I surprised Max one day and pulled into his driveway. We talked while he stood outside of his pole barn. I told him "I forgive you, and your mother, too. I don't hate you, I still love you."

Max did not respond with, "I love you, too," but rather, "I'm sorry. I never meant to hurt you."

Max was my husband, and Irene, in her way, was like a second mother to me. Regardless of what was done, I chose to stay until I could take it no more, and, in the end, I forgive them.

Neither Max nor his mother admit, or recognize, the destruction they caused to one human life—mine. They do not see it! Perhaps one day they'll both remove their heads from the sand. Should that day come, I pray God will be gentle on them.

I wish them no harm. In my nightly prayers, instead of sending bitterness and vengeance, I send them a reminder of all the good things I was and did, with no expectations.

Max has little to say to me. I've sent him text messages and called him a couple times to talk. I've extended myself to Max, but he extends nothing in return. From the letter he wrote to me, I took it as a sign that perhaps, one day...who knows what could be? Sadly, given the lack of response, I think I misread his letter.

### *Uncovering a Secret*

**September 2010**. I decided to re-look at Max's Irrevocable Trust, and I'm glad I did. Everything Max said about the Irrevocable Trust was true, *until his death.*

*Upon Max's death*, the Irrevocable Trust takes over everything! It becomes a vacuum and sucks everything he *and I* had into it: Property, Wills, Revocable Trusts, *for both of us*! And without my knowledge, I might add.

On the first page, it states that Max has made the Trust Department of Willow Bank & Trust the Trustee of his Irrevocable Trust.

*Understandable.*

But then it states that Max's primary concern is for the "support, education, and health" of his spouse. The term "support" means support in reasonable comfort. At least my bills would have been paid, right? But I don't think I'd be able to travel or build a homeless shelter, if that's what I wanted to do in my declining years.

After all this time, this paragraph in the Irrevocable Trust finally sheds some light:

> To merge at any time **after** Max's death, all Trust property with the property of any other Trust created by my spouse (*Beth*) or Max during life or by Will, and held by the same Trustee for the benefit of the same beneficiaries (*This must be why my Trust was almost identical to his. It appears it was all done to benefit Gladys's children*).

> And upon the same terms and conditions, the Trustee (*Willow Bank & Trust*) must merge (*put together*) **assets as a single Trust** and terminate (*cancel out*) the other Trust (*my Trust*) as a separate entity.

I would not have had the freedom to sell my own home, as it was now part of Max's Irrevocable Trust.

*Why did Max find it so important to keep me from information I should have been privy to? What were all the documents I signed? Props? And what gave Max the right to choose, to whom everything went?*

Zack had been cut out of everything. Max can give away 33 acres to a bunch of deer, but not one penny to the boy he gave his last name to?

My signature was gained by manipulation. I would have NEVER agreed to such things, and they all knew it. Better to make me crazy than cough up the truth. And as for Mr. Roberts, the Edwardses' lawyer, to have aided in the destruction of my mind, marriage, and my life is inhumane and should be considered illegal, as far as I'm concerned!

Had I stayed in the marriage, I would have become like Mrs. Perkins, the lady I waited behind in line at the bank. All of the assets were to go into Max's Irrevocable Trust, leaving the bank as the Trustee. The Trustee would have the right to deny any withdrawal request they felt was asked for unnecessarily.

### *My Brother and I*

**October 1, 2010** – My brother David and I have become closer because of our history with depression. In our last conversation on this subject, we talked about the phrase "losing one's mind."

We discussed hearing people say, "She's lost her mind" or "He's lost his mind." The words had been meaningless to us then. Today, they are the reality of what can result from a life, or a moment of devastation.

We agree, my brother and I, that there is a part of us that's gone forever. We can't put our finger on it, or explain exactly what it is, but we grieve the loss of it just the same. It's gone and it's never coming back.

But it's all going to be okay.

**THE END**

## *Please Note*

This book was written in honesty. All events are accurate and taken from my notes or memory. This book was not intended to hurt anyone. It was written to educate others as to what can happen. It was my life, as seen through my eyes. Everyone views things differently; everyone has their own perspective. This was mine.

All names, medications, and locations have been changed.

**Linda Tadajewski**
27127 Antonio Dr.
Roseville, MI 48066-7905

12917402R00182

Made in the USA
Lexington, KY
04 January 2012